Russian Foreign Policy in Eurasia

How has Russia increased its strength and power over the last 15 years? By what means did the Kremlin bring Armenia back into its orbit? Why did Azerbaijan and Georgia try to avoid antagonizing Moscow? Can we conclude that Russia has restored its sphere of influence in Eurasia?

Employing a case-centric research design this book answers these questions by analyzing Russia's foreign affairs in the South Caucasus after the end of the Cold War. Exploring the relevance for those affairs of the creation of the Eurasian Economic Union it uses neoclassical realism and regime theories as frameworks. Arguing that Russia's material power capabilities guide Moscow's foreign policies in all three South Caucasian states, the author points out that Russia responds to the uncertainties of international anarchy by seeking to control its former territory and shape its external environment according to its own preferences.

This book will be of interest to academics and postgraduate students in International Relations, International Political Economy, Comparative Politics, and Foreign Policy as well as Eurasian Studies and Post-Soviet Studies.

Lilia A. Arakelyan holds a PhD in International Studies from the University of Miami. She has worked on numerous academic and policy-oriented projects, and taught International Studies courses at the University of Miami. Her articles and books focus on Russian foreign policy in the post-Soviet space, different aspects of nationalism, ethno-national conflicts in the South Caucasus, and on international security more broadly.

Post-Soviet Politics
Series Editor—Neil Robinson

The last decade has seen rapid and fundamental change in the countries of the former Soviet Union. Although there has been considerable academic comment on these changes over the years, detailed empirical and theoretical research on the transformation of the post-Soviet space is only just beginning to appear as new paradigms are developed to explain change.

Post-Soviet Politics is a series focusing on the politics of change in the states of the former USSR. The series publishes original work that blends theoretical development with empirical research on post-Soviet politics. The series includes work that progresses comparative analysis of post-Soviet politics, as well as case study research on political change in individual post-Soviet states. The series features original research monographs, thematically strong edited collections and specialized texts.

Uniquely, this series brings together the complete spectrum of work on post-Soviet politics, providing a voice for academics world wide.

Most recently published titles

Systemic and Non-Systemic Opposition in the Russian Federation
Civil Society Awakens?
Edited by Cameron Ross

Autocratic and Democratic External Influences in Post-Soviet Eurasia
Edited by Anastassia Obydenkova and Alexander Libman

Religion, Politics and Nation-Building in Post-Communist Countries
Edited by Greg Simons and David Westerlund

Vocabularies of International Relations after the Crisis in Ukraine
Edited by Andrey Makarychev and Alexandra Yatsyk

Neighbourhood Perceptions of the Ukraine Crisis
From the Soviet Union into Eurasia?
Edited by Gerhard Besier and Katarzyna Stokłosa

Russia-EU Relations and the Common Neighbourhood
Coercion vs. Authority
Irina Busygina

Russian Foreign Policy in Eurasia

National Interests and Regional Integration

Lilia A. Arakelyan

Routledge
Taylor & Francis Group
LONDON AND NEW YORK

First published 2018
by Routledge
2 Park Square, Milton Park, Abingdon, Oxon OX14 4RN

and by Routledge
711 Third Avenue, New York, NY 10017

Routledge is an imprint of the Taylor & Francis Group, an informa business

British Library Cataloguing in Publication Data
A catalogue record for this book is available from the British Library

Library of Congress Cataloging in Publication Data
Names: Arakelyan, Lilia A., author.
Title: Russian foreign policy in Eurasia : national interests and regional integration / Lilia A. Arakelyan.
Description: Abingdon, Oxon ; New York, NY : Routledge, 2018. |
Series: Post-Soviet politics | Includes bibliographical references and index.
Identifiers: LCCN 2017002804| ISBN 9781138204515 (hardback) |
ISBN 9781315468372 (e-book)
Subjects: LCSH: Russia (Federation)—Foreign relations. |
Russia (Federation)—Foreign relations—Caucasus, South. |
Caucasus, South—Foreign relations—Russia (Federation) |
Eurasian Union. | Regionalism—Eurasia.
Classification: LCC DK510.764.A73 2018 | DDC 327.470475—dc23
LC record available at https://lccn.loc.gov/2017002804

ISBN: 978-1-138-20451-5 (hbk)
ISBN: 978-1-315-46837-2 (ebk)

Typeset in Times New Roman
by Florence Production Ltd, Stoodleigh, Devon, UK

This book is dedicated to the memory of my father, Albert Arakelov, and to my mother, Lyudmila Arakelova. All I have and will accomplish are only possible due to their love and sacrifices. Thank you for everything.

'President Putin and the Russian leadership are engaged in a massive building project of reassembling "Greater Russia". Drawing mainly on the examples of the Caucasian states, *Russian Foreign Policy in Eurasia* relates Russia's current efforts to establish a Moscow-centered Eurasian Union to the long history of Russian imperial domination under both the tsars and the communists. Arakelyan demonstrates most clearly how Moscow draws upon those historical linkages, in combination with current economic and security dependencies, to tie some neighboring states to a new Moscow-centered regional economic and political order, but also the factors that have enabled some states to resist Russian entreaties.'

Roger E. Kanet,
University of Miami

'Lilia Arakelyan's book is one of few theoretically-informed studies of Russian foreign policy in the Southern Caucasus. Following a neoclassical realist approach, she argues that Russia is motivated by considerations of regional hegemony and global status. Liberals and constructivists may disagree, but should read the book and seriously consider its arguments.'

Andrei P. Tsygankov, International Relations & Political Science,
San Francisco State University

Contents

Figures

Tables

Acknowledgements

My intellectual debts are too many to be fully acknowledged, but I am particularly grateful to my former advisor, colleague, and friend, Roger E. Kanet, for reviewing the many drafts of this manuscript and for all of his ideas, comments, and good humor that made the writing process easier. None of this would have been accomplished without his expert guidance. I am also grateful to Joaquin Roy for the role he had played in this process, helping me "to bring Europe back" into my research. I also owe thanks to Mohiaddin Mesbahi for his guidance and insight, and for helping me to find an analytical framework for this project. Your continued support has been sincerely appreciated.

On a more personal note, I thank my mother Lyudmila for her constant, endearing support and encouragement in all that I do. To Tigran, Christina, Maria and Nellie, thank you for your understanding, support, and for your patience throughout my lengthy working sessions over the last nine years. You are my strength and inspiration. To my friends from Yerevan to Miami, who have offered me unlimited encouragement and support, thanks is all yours.

Chapter 2 incorporates some material from my "EU-Russia Security Relations: Another Kind of Europe," in Roger E. Kanet (Ed.) *The Russian Challenge to the European Security Environment*. Houndmills, UK: Palgrave Macmillan, 2017, reproduced with permission of Palgrave Macmillan.

Chapter 4 incorporates some material from my "Quo Vadis Armenia? The South Caucasus and Great Power Politics" in Roger E. Kanet and Matthew Sussex, (Eds.) *Russia, Eurasia, and the New Geopolitics of Energy*. Houndmills, UK: Palgrave Macmillan, 2015, reproduced with permission of Palgrave Macmillan.

Glossary

Agreement on the Customs Union was signed in the beginning of 1995 by Belarus, Kazakhstan and Russia and aimed to remove the barriers in the way of free business cooperation between the economic entities of the three countries, and ensuring the free exchange of goods and fair competition. The Agreement by a "triad" defined the integration core, which is a present-day driver of the integration processes in Eurasia.

Common Economic Space is to ensure so-called "four freedoms": movement of goods, capital, services and labor on the territory of the Customs Union and Common Economic Space. On December 19, 2010 an Action Plan to create a Common Economic Space of Belarus, Kazakhstan and Russia was adopted and pursuant to it a package of relevant international treaties was signed. In 2012, by Decision of the Supreme Eurasian Economic Council, 17 basic international agreements establishing the Common Economic Space were commenced as of January 1, 2012. One more agreement was signed in 2013.

Commonwealth of Independent States was created in December 1991 after the disintegration of the Soviet Union. The 11 present member states of the CIS—Armenia, Azerbaijan, Belarus, Kazakhstan, Kyrgyzstan, Moldova, Russia, Tajikistan, Turkmenistan, Ukraine, and Uzbekistan—have signed only a small percentage of the agreements since its foundation.

Customs Union—the Customs Union of Belarus, Kazakhstan and Russia was formed in January of 2010 as a first step towards forming a broader European Union-style economic alliance of former Soviet Union states. The Customs Union expanded into a Common Economic Space.

Declaration of Eurasian Economic Integration was signed on November 8, 2011 by the presidents of Belarus, Kazakhstan and Russia. By this document, the leaders of the Republic of Belarus, the Republic of Kazakhstan and the Russian Federation acknowledged the Customs Union to be a success and expressed their enthusiasm in further integration. The Declaration stated the move towards the next stage of the integrative construction—a Common Economic Space (CES).

Eurasian Economic Commission—a permanent regulatory body of the Eurasian Economic Union. It started functioning on February 2, 2012.

Eurasian Economic Community is an international organization that ensures multilateral economic cooperation among its member states. The EurAsEC was founded according to the Treaty on the Establishment of the Eurasian Economic Community, signed by the presidents of the Republic of Belarus, the Republic of Kazakhstan, the Kyrgyz Republic, the Russian Federation and the Republic of Tajikistan on October 10, 2000.

Eurasian Economic Union is summoned to protect the economic interests of the association in general and all its members in particular. At the session of the Supreme Eurasian Economic Council held on May 29, 2014 in Astana, a Treaty on the Eurasian Economic Union (EAEU) that started its operation on January 1, 2015 was signed. The Treaty within the framework of its capacities ensures free movement of goods, services, capital and labor, as well as coordinated, coherent and unified policies in the economic sectors as specified therein and in international agreements within the Union. The Eurasian Economic Union currently comprised of Armenia, Belarus, Kazakhstan, Kyrgyzstan, and Russia.

Formal International Organization refers to material entities (bureaucracies) like the organizations and specialized agencies that make up the United Nations system, which possess offices, personnel, budget, and, often, legal personality.

International Institutions set the rules of the game or codes of conduct to define social practices, assign roles to the participants in these practices, and guide the interactions among the occupants of these roles.

Legal Framework of CES was formed by January 1, 2012 as a market with 170 million consumers, the unified legislation, free movement of goods, services, capital and labor. The CES is founded on the agreed actions in the key sectors of economic regulation: in macroeconomics, in a competitive sphere, in a field of subsidies for industry and agriculture, transport, power engineering, tariffs of the natural monopolies.

Regional Integration can be defined along three dimensions: 1) geographic scope illustrating the number of countries involved in an arrangement; 2) the substantive coverage or width that is the sector or activity coverage (trade, labor mobility, macro policies; and 3) the depth of integration to measure the degree of sovereignty a country is ready to surrender that ranges from simple cooperation to deep integration.

Treaty on Expanding the Integration in Economic and Humanitarian Fields was signed in 1996. At the same time the provisions of the Treaty were set to look forward—Kazakhstan, Belarus, Kyrgyzstan and Russia committed on joint future economic development. In 1998, the Republic of Tajikistan joined the Treaty.

Treaty on Establishing the Common Customs Territory and Forming the Customs Union was signed in October 2007. The Customs Union of the Republic of Belarus, the Republic of Kazakhstan and the Russian Federation began its work since January 2010 and since July 2011 started to operate at its full capacity: the customs territories of the Belarus, Kazakhstan and Russia were merged into a common customs territory.

Abbreviations

AA	Association Agreements
CIS	Commonwealth of Independent States
CSTO	Collective Security Treaty Organization
CU	Customs Union
DCFTA	Deep and Comprehensive Free Trade Area
EaP	Eastern Partnership
EEU	Eurasian Economic Union
ENP	European Neighborhood Policy
EU	European Union
FPA	Foreign Policy Analysis
FSU	Former Soviet Union
FTA	Free Trade Agreement
NATO	The North Atlantic Treat Organization
Roscosmos	The Russian Federal Space Agency
USSR	United Soviet Socialist Republics

Introduction

Russia is on everybody's mind now amidst Moscow's standoff with the West, which started with the Ukraine crisis and culminated in the use of military force in Syria to support the friendly Assad regime, followed by a cyberespionage and information warfare campaign that disrupted the 2016 US presidential election. But what seemed a sudden change in the behavior of the Kremlin in the global arena, was just a next step of a centralized Russian state that became strong enough to influence not only the former Soviet Union states (the FSU states) but also to challenge the United States and European Union in the world politics. After the end of the Cold War, the West tried to influence the countries of Eastern Europe and South Caucasus to follow the liberal–democratic path using economic and political means. However, as it has been pointed out before, institutions promoting economic interdependence cannot quickly be leveraged to build greater trust and reciprocity in the region since actors both within the shared neighborhood and outside it continue to use trade strategically (Sussex 2012, p. 35). As a result, the Western efforts to promote new regional dynamics in the post-Soviet space have fallen prey to Moscow's attempts to restore and sustain hegemonic pre-eminence in Eurasia. As I argue in this book, the Cold War mentality was one of the reasons that Russia's relations with the West were doomed to failure since the start in 1991. Western Europe and the United States feared the Soviet Union for such a long time that when Russia headed towards democratic reforms and market liberalization in the 1990s, Western policymakers were more concern with making sure that Moscow was not playing a leading role in the world politics than with the reforms themselves. Well, it did not take long to let the Jinn, that the West was still afraid of, out of the bottle.

One would wonder whether the FSU states can withstand Russia's dominance in the region, if the global players are feeling somewhat powerless to counter Moscow's actions. This book employs a case-centric research design with the ambition to build a plausible explanation of Russia's foreign policies in Armenia, Azerbaijan, and Georgia, using theories (neoclassical realism and two variants of regimes theories) as heuristic tools that act as frameworks for this analysis. It argues that Russia's material power capabilities (an independent variable) guide Moscow's foreign policies (dependent variables in this study) in all three South Caucasian states. Next, it points out that the differentiation of the independent variable helps to develop a more discriminating analysis of the effectiveness of Russia's material power capabilities and to identify specific factors that favors or hinders the success of each variant. I also bring forward normative concerns about the creation and maintenance of the Eurasian Economic Union.

What explains Russia's foreign policy in the South Caucasus and the relevance for that policy in the creation of the Eurasian Union? What laws, rules, norms, and beliefs guide the new economic bloc in the post-Soviet space? Under what circumstances does Russia create new political and economic institutions to offset the perceived advantages of rival states? Is Eurasian integration primarily a form of continental economic integration? Will Russia's foreign policies towards the South Caucasian states change after the launch of the Eurasian Economic Union in 2015?

These questions are integral for selecting the cases (the three South Caucasian states) for this study as well as designing and implementing research for these cases. This book, using theory-testing cases, argues that Moscow's foreign policy in Transcaucasia was, and still is, driven by its place in the international arena and specifically by its relative material power capabilities. I consider Russia's external relations with the South Caucasian states as a case of the Kremlin's neo-imperialist policy in the near abroad. Thus, defining the creation of the Eurasian Economic Union as a neo-imperialist concept is my main contribution to a neoclassical realism theory and the Eurasian integration study. Putin's regime used

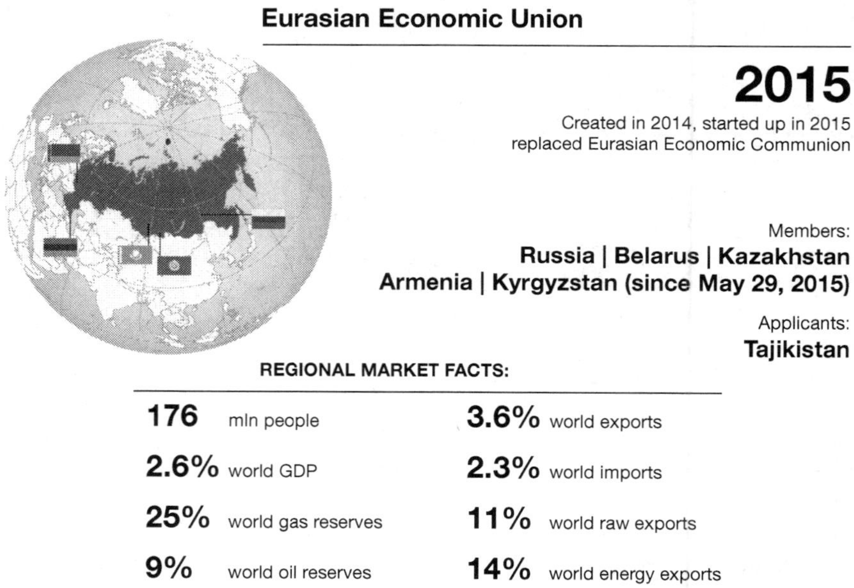

Eurasian Economic Union

2015

Created in 2014, started up in 2015
replaced Eurasian Economic Communion

Members:
Russia | Belarus | Kazakhstan
Armenia | Kyrgyzstan (since May 29, 2015)

Applicants:
Tajikistan

REGIONAL MARKET FACTS:

176	mln people	**3.6%**	world exports
2.6%	world GDP	**2.3%**	world imports
25%	world gas reserves	**11%**	world raw exports
9%	world oil reserves	**14%**	world energy exports

Figure 0.1 Eurasian Economic Union

Source: www.slideshare.net/rustradeESP/russia-for-investors

the new economic bloc for its expansionist plans in the near abroad, in order to avoid the creation of a free trade area encompassing the countries in the region (Armenia, Azerbaijan, Georgia, Belarus, Moldova, and Ukraine) and the European Union.

Organization of the book

The first chapter presents a comprehensive overview of Russia's relations with the West and how it provoked or influenced Moscow's current state of affairs with the former Soviet countries. This section also briefly discusses the main theories used in this work and the possibility of their application in the study of a Russian-led Eurasian integration process.

The second chapter outlines the research strategy and methodological approach employed in this book. First, it analyzes a case-centric research design utilized in this study with the ambition to build a plausible explanation of Russia's foreign policies in the South Caucasus. This chapter concludes that in periods where Russia's material power is very strong (during the Putin's presidency), the Moscow's foreign policy goals inclines towards imperialism. While in periods where Russia's material power is weak (during the Yeltsin presidency), Moscow's foreign policy is generally low key and conciliatory towards the West. Finally, the chapter operationalizes Russia's foreign policies interests and goals in the South Caucasus as the degree to which they are status quo (during the Yeltsin presidency) or revisionist (under Putin's rule).

The third chapter synthesizes two streams of scholarship related to foreign policy analysis and regional integration processes. The literature is immense and the review cannot be exhaustive. Therefore, this chapter is divided into two parts. The first part reviews the neoclassical realist theory, one of the four major theories of foreign policy that distinguishes between relative power, referring to the resources with which states can influence each other, and country's foreign policy interests that guide the state's external behavior. This school of thought maintains that states are likely to want more, rather than less, external influence, and continue such influence to the extent that they are able to do so. The second part reviews the regime theories. These theories sparked major debates, focusing on the various designs, motives and modalities of participation and different rates of integration. Nevertheless, processes in Eurasia were not fully embraced by the existing literature on regionalism and new regionalism. This chapter utilizes neoclassical realism and the regime theories in order to outline and explain Russia's foreign policy in the South Caucasus and the creation of the Eurasian Union.

The fourth chapter transforms a rich and detailed historical explanation of Russia's foreign policy in the South Caucasus into a more abstract and selective one framed in theoretical concepts in order to develop explanations for the outcome of each case (external policies of Moscow in Armenia, Azerbaijan and Georgia) that will reflect the theoretical framework of this study. This chapter concludes that Russia's conquest of the Caucasus fits the neoclassical realist model, since the government responded to the uncertainties of international system by seeking to control and shape its external environment. This chapter regards the case studies (Russia's foreign policies in Armenia, Azerbaijan, and Georgia) as crucial cases since they also closely correspond with a neoclassical realist theory's main assumption that the relative material power capabilities and the place in the international system define the scope and ambitions of a state's foreign policy.

The fifth chapter examines power-based and interest-based variants of international regime theory and comes to the conclusion that the explanations of both variants of regime theory in the case of Russia's relations with the South Caucasian states proved inaccurate. It shows that the Eurasian economic integration, the main pillar of Russia's foreign policy in the near abroad, is far from the complex interdependence or stabilized economy under the Moscow's hegemonic power. This chapter shows that the Kremlin is not in the position to act as an economic or political power with the capacity to supply and support the infrastructure that will permit smooth and mutually beneficial international exchange to take place in Eurasia. On the other hand, there is no feasible cooperation in the region since all the member states of the Eurasian Union as well as Georgia and Azerbaijan are involved in economic, humanitarian, judicial, and even political collaborations either with the EU, the United States, China, Turkey or Iran.

The concluding chapter reviews the findings of this book in terms of the principal position that the unipolar international system of the early 1990s and late 2000s, the European Union Eastern Partnership program, NATO's expansion plans, and American's plan to build missile defensive systems in Eastern Europe, facilitated Vladimir Putin's expansionist grand strategy in the near abroad. This chapter also points to the fact that Armenia's last minute decision to join the Customs Union at the expense of much closer ties with the European Union already aggravated the security dilemma further in the South Caucasus (Azerbaijan, Georgia, Turkey and Iran consider Armenia's last minute "u-turn" towards Russia as an undermining factor for each country's external interests in the region), increasing tensions not only among the three Transcaucasian states but also among the key players in the region—Russia, Turkey, Iran, the European Union and the United States.

Bibliography

Sussex, Matthew, Ed. (2012) *Conflict in the Former USSR*. New York, NY: Cambridge University Press.

1 After the collapse

With the disintegration of the USSR in 1991, the West expected a smooth integration of Russia and the fourteen other former Soviet republics (FSU) into the global community (Kanet 2010). While some of the FSU countries (the Baltic States and Georgia) took a big step towards Westernization, others (Azerbaijan, Belarus, Kazakhstan, Russia and Turkmenistan) emerged as new authoritarian states with capitalist economies that are heavily integrated into the global economy. Ambrosio claims that, while Georgia in 2003, Ukraine in 2004–2005 and Kyrgyzstan in 2005 experienced what he calls the "fourth wave" of democratization, when autocratic leaders were brought down by the opposition, there was a clear authoritarian backlash against democracy promotion in Russia and Belarus. These authoritarian regimes (Russia, Belarus, and Kazakhstan) support each other in resisting Western-style democratization and globalization (Ambrosio 2009).

These types of regimes, so-called "competitive authoritarianism," must be distinguished from democracy, since their leaders use formal democratic institutions as the principal means of obtaining and exercising political power, while officials in democratic regimes do not alter the playing field between government and opposition. On the other hand, competitive authoritarian regimes fall short of full-scale authoritarianism as well, since they are unable to eliminate formal democratic rules (Levitsky and Way 2002). Instead, they use more subtle forms of persecution (tax authorities, compliant judiciaries and other state agencies) to oppress the opposition. Examples of competitive authoritarian regimes include Ukraine under Leonid Kravchuk and Leonid Kuchma, Russia under Vladimir Putin, Croatia under Franjo Tudjman, as well as Albania, Armenia, Ghana, Kenya, Malaysia, Mexico and Zambia through much of the 1990s (Levitsky and Way 2002, p. 3).

Russia had made slow and limited progress towards democracy after the collapse of the Soviet Union, but this process was reversed after Vladimir Putin came to power in 1999–2000, when the government took control over the national media and core industries, including the energy sector (Nichol 2011). Since he came into office in 1999, Putin has made it clear that he wants the world to recognize Russia as one of the world's three superpowers along with the U.S. and China, not a second-tier country that would simply follow Western orders (Lo 2012). Moreover, in 2005, Putin described the collapse of the Soviet Union as "the greatest geopolitical catastrophe of the past century," the statement that was considered as alarming by many Western and former Soviet scholars and politicians (Kuzio 2006; Salukvadze 2006; Lukyanov 2012). Russia's defense minister, Sergei Ivanov, then added fuel to the fire by condemning the so-called color revolutions in Georgia (2003), Ukraine (2004), and Kyrgyzstan (2005), and claiming that they are "a violent assault on the constitutional order of some post-Soviet states," and posed a serious threat to Russia's internal and external security (Ivanov 2006). It is clear that at the time Washington and Brussels did not fully understand Moscow's eagerness to use all the means to defend its interests in the near abroad. Nothing could illustrate more forcibly the political blindness of Western powers than their reluctance to accept Russia as a key player on a global scale and in the post-Soviet space in particular following the end of the Cold War. After 9/11, Washington redirected its attention to the Middle East and the Persian Gulf that led to a greater strategic importance of the Caspian region for the U.S. government since it became indispensable in the prosecution of the Global War on Terror. Particularly, Azerbaijan in the South Caucasus and the Central Asian countries had become critical to U.S. strategic interests during the Afghanistan War since the countries allowed American aircraft to use their airspace and allowed troops and supplies to travel to Afghanistan through their territories. In addition, historically, energy resources in the Caspian Sea area attracted the attention of Western countries and oil companies. In the beginning of the twenty-first century, Central Asian states and the Caucasus once again have become sites for rivalry between Moscow, Washington, Brussels, and Beijing since the FSU countries are considered as potential allies who could facilitate access to bases in Eurasia (Sussex 2012). More than two decades after the fall of the Soviet Union, a threat of Russian revanchism that surfaced in the early 2000s as a response to increased Western involvement in the post-Soviet space, has now become a political reality in the post-Soviet space. Moscow maintained a hostile stance against the West, painted Russia as a defender of traditional values in Eurasia and Eastern Europe, in contrast to "decadent" capitalist culture in the United States and Western Europe.

As a result, some scholars and analysts in the West and in the East have viewed Russia as a revisionist power, and Russia's policy in the former Soviet space as a policy of neo-imperialism (Salukvadze 2006; Markedonov 2010; Lucas 2014). The reassertion of a self-confident Russian foreign policy under President Vladimir Putin was evident with respect to the former Soviet countries (for example, Russia's relations with the Georgians and Chechens, the gas wars with Ukraine) (Nygren 2011). Moreover, the Russian Federation in the 1990s during the Yeltsin presidency was considered to be more democratic than most of the other post-communist states of Eastern Europe and Eurasia, while the Russian polity became significantly less democratic under Vladimir Putin's leadership since 1999 (Rivera and Rivera 2009).

It is important to note that Yeltsin inherited the Soviet system in mid-collapse and was unable to establish Russia's hegemonic position not only in the international system but also in the "near abroad." After assuming political power, the

Putin administration benefited from the rise in oil prices, and Russia became stronger, not only economically but also politically. Putin was able, first, to deliver the basics of effective governance in terms of improving the health care and welfare policies, and providing the family support to prevent the demographic crisis in the Russian Federation. Second, using Russia's material power capabilities, he established Russia's position vis-à-vis the former Soviet states, including the South Caucasus.

Concomitantly, systemic pressure and incentives (the West and China's greater involvement in the region, the Nagorno-Karabakh conflict and disputes over Abkhazia and Ossetia, and Russia's energy resources that led to reestablishing its position as a regional hegemon) shaped Russia's foreign policy across former Soviet space, including the South Caucasus. Moreover, some analysts, referring to the claims of then President Medvedev about Russia's privilege interest, believe that Russia has a sphere of privileged interest in the former Soviet space. In this regard, Skak notes that it was not until after the Russia–Georgia war that this claim was "codified" in President Medvedev's five principles of Russian foreign policy: the superiority of the fundamental principles of international law; multipolarity of international system; non-confrontation with any other country; protection of the lives of ethnic Russians in the near abroad, and the development of ties with the former Soviet countries (Medvedev 2008; Skak 2011).

Despite the fact that Medvedev adopted a more liberal approach of Russia's foreign policy during his tenure, the Western policymakers still believed that then Prime Minister Vladimir Putin remained omnipresent behind the scenes (Kozhanov 2012). Mr. Putin's return to the presidency in 2012 only made it clear that Medvedev's tenure was nothing else but just the gambit (*rakirovka*) needed to manipulate the law to serve Putin's authoritarian agenda (Remington 2014, p. 1). In fact, Russian authorities have tightened control over the media and the opposition, solidified the hold of Eurasianism, and undertook an anti-Western stance. At the time, Mr. Putin's doctrine rested on three geostrategic imperatives: Russia must remain a nuclear superpower; a great power in all assets of international activity; and the political, military, and economic leader of its region (Aron 2013).

It seems that the creation of the Eurasian Union in 2015 helped to implement all three of Putin's geostrategic imperatives. Hence, despite the Russian president's public statements that the Eurasian Union would be built on the experience of the European Union,[1] while changing the geopolitical and geoeconomic configuration of Eurasia and would contribute a global effect, it is obvious that Moscow's rationale behind the Eurasian integration was to constitute a counterweight to NATO and to EU enlargement and outreach in Eastern Europe. Moreover, a new Eurasian bloc balances the EU in the west, China in the east, and creates a buffer zone to undermine a NATO-centered European security system in the former Soviet-bloc countries (Greene 2012). As I argue in Chapter 3, we cannot draw a parallel between the European Union and the Eurasian Union due to the different principles and objectives that these two supranational organizations pursue, as well as the logic conditionality for the member states accession.

In this regard, Putin's idea of a Eurasian Union has sparked strong debates, not only in the West but also in the post-Soviet space. For instance, Mikhail Saakashvili, then president of Georgia, called on Azerbaijan and other former Soviet states to unite their efforts against Moscow's imperial ambitions (Kiguradze 2013). The Ukrainian crisis once again proved that the new bloc had political rather than economic logic for Mr. Putin. First of all, the logical progression of economic integration should have established the free movement of products within the Customs Union prior to moving to the Single Economic space to ensure an unrestricted provisions of services, and only then process to an economic union with the free circulation of goods and services, finance and labor. On the contrary, the Customs Union is leading to economic integration without even considering the trade issues. Furthermore, the main source of Russia's material power—energy—was not even included in the single market. Thus, the member states will continue paying duties to Moscow on its exports of oil products based on oil imported from Russia, which means that the Kremlin will still use energy as its carrot-and-stick method to punish or reward the former Soviet Union, depending on their behaviour towards the big brother (Panin 2014). In this regard, Mr. Putin's claims that the Eurasian Union would follow the examples of the EU and other regional integration, and that "the Customs Union, and later the Eurasian Union will join the dialogue with the EU, and the accession to the Eurasian Union will also help countries integrate into Europe sooner and from a stronger position" cannot be taken seriously taking into account the Armenian and Ukrainian examples that will be covered in details in this book (Putin 2011).

Meanwhile, increased Russian capabilities during Putin's presidency helped to drive policymakers' perceptions of external threats, interests and opportunities in the South Caucasus. Russia used energy and the dispute over the Nagorno-Karabakh conflict to bully Armenia into the Eurasian Economic Union. For instance, as soon as Armenia headed towards initialing the Association Agreement with the EU, Moscow delivered up to $1 billion worth of military equipment to Baku. Arguably, fearing an outbreak of a new war, Armenia signed a treaty to join the Eurasian Union in 2015.

According to Stepan Grigoryan, head of the Globalization and Regional Cooperation think tank center, Russia, in this regard, acted upon its interests and was unwilling to let Armenia and the Ukraine sign the Association Agreement with the EU (Mkrtchyan 2013). Rikard Jozwiak considers an Association Agreement, which comprises four general chapters: Common Foreign and Security Policy; Justice and Home Affairs; the Deep and Comprehensive Free Trade Area (DCFTA); and the last chapter covering a range of issues, including environment, science, transportation and education, as the EU's main instrument to bring the countries in the Eastern Partnership (EaP)[2] closer to EU standards and norms (Jozwiak 2013). Consequently, the civil society representatives in Armenia believe that the country's decision to join the Eurasian Union was made in order to retain certain advantages for the government's officials—monopolization, corruption, violation of human rights. While many believed that Kremlin used Yerevan's heavy dependence on Russia's economy as well as the security concerns over the

Nagorno-Karabakh conflict to bring Armenia into the new union, this book also suggests that Armenia's political regime, dominated mainly by oligarchic groups, was reluctant to undertake the political changes that would have been required had they initialled the Association Agreement with the EU. For instance, Daron Acemoglu and James Robinson argue that in order to build a healthy economic and social system, a country needs to establish "inclusive economic institutions that enforce property rights, create a level playing field, and encourage investments in new technologies and skills" rather than "extractive economic institutions that are structured to extract resources from the many by the few" (Acemoglu and Robinson 2012). Since the mid-1990s, Armenia has been ruled by a privileged elite, oligarchs, a group numbering around 40, who dominate industries ranging from banking to mining, and who also hold an unprecedented political power in the country. As in Russia and Ukraine, Armenian oligarchs have parlayed their wealth into the public office, and many political parties in the country are closely associated with leading tycoons who also enjoy parliamentary immunity (Aghajanian 2012). It is also a tradition for Armenian oligarchs based in Russia to come back to their motherland on a "business mission," Ara Abramanyan (the current president of the Union of Armenians in Russia), Samvel Karapetyan (the owner of the Tashir group, whose brother Karen Karapetyan was appointed as a new prime minister of Armenia in September 2016), Ruben Vardanyan (former CEO and controlling shareholder of investment bank Troika Dialog), just to name a few Armenian–Russian tycoons who are actively involved in Armenian politics, and make sure that the country is not changing its pro-Russian course (Gabrielyan 2015). In this regard, the Armenian opposition insists that Serzh Sargsyan's single-handed decision to join the trading block with Russia, Belarus and Kazakhstan retarded the country's democratic growth, and threw the country back 25 years.

Another factor to be considered is that Georgia had initialled the Association Agreement[3] with the EU, and signed the Deep and Comprehensive Free Trade Area (DCFTA) in 2014. This means that Armenia, which borders Georgia, has taken a completely different economic course than its neighbor and will have a change of border status, which will affect not only the commodity turnover but also the movement of people (Mkrtchyan 2013). In addition, Armenia has also accepted Vladimir Putin's "Eurasian Union without Karabakh bill," which means that a customs checkpoint must be installed on the border between Armenia and Nagorno-Karabakh (the latter is not a recognized state by Russia or Armenia). As we can see, the Eurasian Union creates additional dividing lines in the South Caucasus that has already been sank in the mire of regional rivalry.

Georgia, on the other hand, is also an easy target for Putin's grand strategy[4] in the near abroad, when its two breakaway regions, Abkhazia and South Ossetia, announced their readiness to join the Eurasian Economic Union.[5] Besides, NATO's unwillingness to accept Georgia as a new member in order to avoid confronting Russia can explain why Tbilisi is moving away from a fervid anti-Kremlin stance towards balancing its relations with Moscow.

Finally, Baku is willing to team up with the friendly authoritarian Putin's regime rather than to put up with the Western criticism for violating human rights and maintaining a political system that is even less representative than Russia's. Some analysts consider the geopolitical shift towards Russia as Baku's payback for the Western intervention in its domestic issues (Hill, Kirisci, and Moffatt 2015). In turn, Russia uses the Nagorno-Karabakh conflict as a bargaining chip to maintain control over Armenia and Azerbaijan. In fact, despite the strategic alliance between Moscow and Yerevan, Russia pursues political–military cooperation with Azerbaijan, which means that the Kremlin will be hesitant to defend Armenia in case of war with its neighbour. There is speculation that Putin offered to return some part of Karabakh to Azerbaijan if the country joins the Eurasian Union (Jarosiewicz 2014). The recent escalation of the conflict between Yerevan and Baku is beneficial for Moscow since it will definitely impede the current cooperation between the West and Azerbaijan in the energy sector and will highlight Russia's role as a peacemaker and a guarantor of the stability in the South Caucasus.

It seems clear that the new integration project is nothing other than Russia's attempt to form a new alliance to counterbalance the U.S., EU, and China's rising influence in the former Soviet region. However, Moscow's reluctance to treat former Soviet states as partners rather than objects of its ambitions and executors of its orders also poses significant challenges to the decision-making process in the Eurasian Union.

On the other hand, Richard Sakwa (2013) and Andrei Tsygankov (2013), argue that neither of these views has done justice to the complex reality of Russia's foreign policy. Sakwa claims that Putin's regime was able to deliver the basics of effective governance in terms of improving the health care and welfare policies, and providing the family support to prevent the demographic crisis in the country. Therefore, the creation of the Eurasian Union by 2015 seems like a viable integration project in Eurasia. Nevertheless, Sakwa concludes that Putin's regime has become locked in a stalemate, which can be transcended by a broadening of the political options available to the government (Sakwa 2013, p. 4). For his part, Tsygankov considers Russia's foreign policy nothing other than a new civilizational discourse in order to shape Russia's domestic and international priorities and position itself as a power capable of synthesizing the Western and Islamic influences (Tsygankov 2013, p. 5).

Theories talk

Since the end of the Cold War, there has been a general decline in Russian and Eurasian Studies in the United States, which made it challenging to conduct a foreign policy analysis of Russia and the FSU states, particularly from a broader historical perspective. This book develops a framework for interpreting Russian foreign policy in the post-Soviet space by using the case study approach in order to test historical explanation, the creation of the Eurasian Union, by engaging two theoretical approaches: neoclassical realism and regime theory, which helped me to outline and to explain, to some extent, Mr. Putin's grand strategy in the near abroad over the last 15 years.

Neoclassical realism

Foreign policy analysis, according to Hudson, is characterized by an actor-specific focus based upon the argument that all that takes place between the states and beyond is grounded in human decision makers acting individually or in group (Hudson 2005). An emphasis on an actor specific approach, for Hudson, allows IR more fully to grasp human agency with its change, creativity, accountability, and meaning. It is important to note that foreign policy analysis views the explanation of foreign policy decision making as multifactorial with the intention of examining variables from various perspectives (Hudson 2005).

Rose (1998) identifies several broad schools of foreign policy analysis: 1) *Innenpolitik* theories that emphasize the influence of domestic factors on foreign policy; 2) offensive realism, which stresses the systemic factors; 3) defensive realism that considers that systemic factors drive some kinds of state behavior, but not others; and 4) neoclassical realism that incorporates both external and internal variables and maintains that the scope and ambition of a country's foreign policy is driven by its place in the international system and specifically by its relative material power capabilities (Rose 1998, p. 146).

Furthermore, the neoclassical realists argue that the impact of such power capabilities on foreign policy is indirect and complex and the systemic pressure must be analyzed through intervening variables at the unit level (Rose 1998, p. 146). It is important to note that, since the relative material power constitutes the basic parameters of a country's foreign policy, which can be summed up as "the strong do what they can and the weak suffer what they must" (Thucydides 2010). According to neoclassical realists, foreign policy choices are made by actual political leaders and elites; thus, it is their perceptions of relative power that matter (Rose 1998, p. 147). In this regard, after the collapse of the Soviet Union in 1991, Russia saw itself as an equal of the United States, but as soon as the West started challenging Russian influence in Central and Eastern Europe,[6] it became clear that Moscow was not on an equal footing with the Western powers (Orban 2008). Shevtsova (2005) argues that Yeltsin weakened the Russian system[7] by opening society to the West and abandoning some of the great-power complexes. Moreover, the Russian state eroded and lost its ability to perform elementary functions of the government under the Yeltsin's presidency. In fact, Yeltsin created a regime of elected monarchy, which she characterizes as a mixture of continuity of governance "*à la* Old Russia" and change with elements of liberal democracy (Shevstova 2005, pp. 8–16). In the same vein, Nichol argues that Russia had made slow and limited progress towards democracy after the collapse of the Soviet Union, but this process was reversed after Vladimir Putin came to power in 1999–2000, when the government took control over major media and core industries, including the energy sector. At the time, Kremlin embraced a pragmatic foreign policy that posed significant challenges to the nation-building aspirations of countries of

Central Asia and the Caucasus (Torbakov 2000). The new foreign policy doctrine that was developed under Evgeniy Primakov in his role as both foreign minister and then premier (the so-called Primakov doctrine) departed from the previous Kozyrev doctrine[8] and contained the following principles: 1) integrating Russia into the world economy; 2) establishing a multipolar world; and 3) opposing U.S. initiatives on principal issues, including NATO enlargement, the Iraqi economic embargo and military intervention in Kosovo.

Another focal point of neoclassical realist analysis that can be applied to the study of Russian foreign policy in the South Caucasus is the view that power analysis must also examine the strength and structure of states relative to their societies, since these factors impact the proportion of national resources that can be allocated to foreign policy. For instance, Yeltsin inherited the Soviet system in mid-collapse and was unable to maintain Russia's dominant position not only in the international system, but also in the near abroad. After assuming political power, the Putin administration benefitted from the rise in oil prices, and Russia became stronger not only economically but also politically. With regard to Russian foreign policy, the Putin doctrine inherited some important ideas from Primakov's policy, resisting the unilateral actions of the West and encouraging the formation of the multipolar system of international relations (Torbakov 2000). In order to advance his foreign policy, Putin tried to resolve domestic challenges. He was able, first, to deliver the basics of effective governance in terms of improving the health care and welfare policies, and providing the family support to prevent the demographic crisis in the Russian Federation. Second, using Russia's material power capabilities, he established Russia's position vis-à-vis the former Soviet states, including the South Caucasus. Finally, systemic pressure and incentives (the West and China's greater involvement in the region, the Nagorno-Karabakh conflict and disputes over Abkhazia and Ossetia, and Russia's energy resources that led to reestablishing its position as a regional hegemon) shaped Russia's foreign policy in the South Caucasus.

International regime theories

During the last two decades several attempts have been made to define the concept of international regime, which Susan Strange and other scholars considered as a failure due to the "woolliness" of the concept (Hasenclever, Mayer and Rittberger 1997, p. 8). Kratochwil and Ruggie (1986) hold that the concept of regime shares the same "imprecise" fate with many other social science concepts, including the concepts of "power" and "state." Nevertheless, the consensus definition of "international regime" was elaborated by Krasner as: "implicit or explicit principles, norms, rules and decision-making procedures around which actors' expectations converge in a given area of international relations" (Krasner 1983, p. 2). Although Krasner's definition was later challenged by some scholars, it holds two important implications: 1) international regimes are international institutions and should be studied as such; and 2) "international regime" and "international organization" are neither synonymous nor co-extensional, despite the fact that in many cases regimes will be accompanied by organizations employed to support them in different ways (Hasenclever, Mayer and Rittberger 1997, pp. 11–12). According to Keohane, the critical difference between regimes and organizations lies in the fact that regimes do not have the capacity to act, while organizations can respond to events (Keohane 1988, p. 384). It is important to note that some of the functions ascribed to regimes cannot be performed without the aid of some organizational structure embedded in the regime. Krasner's definition provided scholars of regime analysis with a valuable analytical tool for furthering the regime theory.

Some analysts believe that the interest in international regimes emerged from a dissatisfaction with dominant conceptions of international order, authority, and organization. The increasing tensions in the international economy, and the U.S. return to a new form of protectionism turned some scholars (Keohane 1984; Krasner 1983) to regimes and institutions, in order to explain the new world order (Lake 2006, p. 762). In the meantime, the collapse of the Bretton Woods system, the OPEC Oil Embargo, and the U.S. support for the Vietnam War in 1969–1973 pushed liberal IPE towards interdependence (Crane and Amawi 1997, p. 18).

Regime theory is an important analytical tool for this study, since many of its variations were formulated to explain the creation of various regimes in the West, but traditional accounts of this theory are somewhat marginal when applied to Russian-led regional projects that emerged in the former USSR. I want to challenge those theories, showing that Eurasian integration is different from EU-style integration[9] because of Russia's inability to deliver rule-based economic integration due to the absence of the rule of law within the state, and in the neighboring countries. Moreover, I want to prove in this book that geopolitical and strategic interests rather than economic and ideological dividends are the driving forces behind Russia's expansion into the South Caucasus over the course of the last four centuries, except the time when Armenia, Azerbaijan, and Georgia were the part of the USSR.

The success or failure of Russia's grand strategy in the South Caucasus depends on the state power. For instance, when Armenia was on its way to sign the Association Agreement with the EU in November 2013, Moscow pressured Yerevan to undertake a 180-degree turn around on economic integration and join the Eurasian Economic Union instead. Russia was able to change Armenia's external course using its relative power, which, following the neorealists, I have defined as "the capabilities or resources with which states can influence each other" (Wohlforth 1993, p. 4). However, as Keohane (1993) suggested, international regimes have problematic relationships to state power in the sense that they fail to explain whether regimes must rely on the support of a single dominant power or whether the rules of the regimes have significant effects apart from the influence exerted by their supporters (Keohane 1993, p. 778). In the long run the relative power of actors may change, while the rules remain the same, which suggests that the expected outcomes of the regimes based on power alone frequently contrast with those discerned within the framework of international regimes (Keohane 1993, p. 778).

According to Hasenclever, Mayer and Ritberger, there are three schools of thought within the study of international regimes: power-based (the realist approach with the main focus on power relationships), interest-based (the neo-liberal approach depends on the interest constellation) and knowledge-based approaches (the cognitivist approach emphasizes knowledge dynamics, communication and identities). The differences among these three approaches are found in their interest in the role of institutions and regimes in the international system. Hasenclever et al., taking into account the main points of all three approaches of regime theories (power, interest, and knowledge), offer two measures for institutions: 1) effectiveness, which holds that a regime is effective to the extent that its members abide by its norms and rules, and it achieves certain objectives; and 2) robustness, which assumes that a regime has "staying power" in the face of challenges to the extent that prior institutional choices constrain collective decisions and behavior in later periods.

Richard Little, on the other hand, located regime theorists within two broad schools of thought: liberalism and realism (Little 2006, p. 370). Little argues that realists are often skeptical of international law, while liberal institutionalists have accepted key assumptions made by neo-realists. Nonetheless, liberal institutionalists and realists hold very different assessments of regimes. The former focus on the way that regimes allow states to collaborate despite the uncertainty of the anarchical international system, the latter look into the state's possibility to coordinate the nature of regimes and the underlying principles and norms of regimes. Thus, liberal institutionalists hold that regimes can promote the common good, globalization and a liberal world order, which can be provided by a benign hegemon. On the contrary, realists argue that regimes generate different benefits for states, and, thus, power is the focal point of regime formation and survival. It is also worth mentioning that both approaches see states as rational and unitary actors, which are responsible for establishing regimes in order to promote international order.

The various regimes that were created in the former Soviet space after the fall of the Iron Curtain were neither effective nor robust. There have been various regional agreements maintaining economic activity and trade after the collapse of the Soviet Union in 1991, with Moscow serving as the "lender of last resort." Nevertheless, their weak institutional framework contributed to their failure in binding the domestic actors and institutions in these regional agreements (Dragneva and Wolczuk 2012).[10] Moreover, Dragneva, while examining the legal and institutional framework of the Customs Union (which evolved into a Eurasian Economic Union), came to the conclusion that this process was fraught with fragmentation, incremental development, and often changing legal and institutional regime (Dragneva and Wolczuk 2013, p. 58).

The Eurasian Union has been described as a potential extension of the Eurasian Customs Union (ECU) formed by Russia, Belarus and Kazakhstan in 2010, which imposed Russian tariffs as the common external tariffs of the union and aims at reducing non-tariff barriers, facilitating trade, and allowing the free movement of goods, services and capital across a single market of 165 million people (Tarr 2012). It is important to note that the idea of the Eurasian Union is not new and was first expressed by Kazakhstan's president Nursultan Nazarbayev in 1994, when he proposed establishing "the supranational bodies of the Eurasian Union based on principles of equality of integration partners, non-interference with each other domestic affairs, regard for sovereignty and inviolability of national borders" (Akimbekov 2011). Nazarbayev's proposal for the union became even more utopian after the various former republics cut their ties with Moscow (Akimbekov 2011; Cutler 2011). It did not take long for Vladimir Putin to realize that the idea of a Eurasian Union could be used as an additional instrument for Russia's influence in former Soviet space. While Dragneva and Wolczuk consider the ECU as an important change in integration patterns of Eurasia in terms of both design and implementation,[11] the authors note that the formation of the Russian-led regional economic bloc that already proved its viability "means that the EU is no longer the only source of effective governance in the region."

This book will consider the realist and liberal institutionalist versions of international regimes theories along with the neoclassical realist approach in order to conclude which theory provides a better explanation of Russia's foreign policy in the South Caucasus after the end of the Cold War and the creation of the Eurasian Union in 2015.

Russia's foreign policy in the South Caucasus since 1991

One of the most important features of the post-Cold War order has been the rising geopolitical significance of the South Caucasus, which includes Armenia, Azerbaijan and Georgia. This region, surrounded by Russia to the north, Turkey to the southwest, the Caspian Sea to the east, and Iran to the southeast, has become a region of strategic interest for the West and the East with the development of energy resources in Azerbaijan and in the Caspian Sea that are carried through pipelines to markets in the West. The security deficit remains of great concern for key international and regional actors in the South Caucasus: Russia, Turkey, Iran, the EU and the United States. However, some of these key players pursue their self-interest at the expense of South Caucasian states, which makes cooperation potentially problematic. While Russia is interested in advancing its influence in the South Caucasian republics (mostly in Armenia and Azerbaijan), the West is looking to minimize Russian economic and political influence in the region. In the meantime, both Turkey and Iran are trying to increase their influence in the Caspian Sea region, while promoting their national interests in the global arena. Turkey, for example, is a strategically important partner for the United States and the EU since it acts as a natural bridge to markets in the Caucasus, Central Asia, the Balkans and Gulf region as well as a gateway to energy resources such as natural gas and oil pipelines in the region (Balla 2013, p. 1). However, Turkey pursues a foreign policy that differs from Western interests and goals in the South Caucasus. For instance, despite the fact that, after the disintegration of the Soviet Union in the 1990s, Ankara declared a policy of rapprochement with the three Transcaucasian states, Turkey closed its borders with Armenia in 1993 and its position has been clearly pro-Azerbaijani concerning the Nagorno-Karabakh conflict. Moreover, Turkey established close relations with Azerbaijan and Georgia (and some limited contacts with Armenia)[12] in order to limit Russian and Iranian influence in the region (Nichol 2014, p. 17). In this regard, a number of energy and communications projects tie Azerbaijan and Georgia to Turkey: the Baku–Tbilisi–Ceyhan (BTC) crude oil pipeline, the Baku–Tbilisi–Erzurum natural gas pipeline, and the Baku–Tbilisi–Kars railway (Starr and Cornell 2005). Azerbaijan considers Turkey an ally against Iranian influence in the South Caucasus and as a balance to Armenia's strategic relations with Russia (Nichol 2014, p. 14). Moreover, Turkey is one of Georgia's main trade partners and all three countries (Azerbaijan, Georgia and Turkey) agreed to cooperate in the defense industry, according to Georgia's Defense Minister, Irakli Alasania (Global Research News 2013).

On the other hand, Armenia is one of the former Soviet states that never attempted to eject Russian forces, and, as a result, Russian influence over Armenian security policy never waned after the collapsed of the Soviet Union (Goodrich and Zeihan 2011, p. 76). Consequently, Armenian president, Serzh Sargsyan, could not resist "the offer" of Russian president, Vladmir Putin, to join the Russian-led Customs Union instead of initialing an Association Agreement with the European Union. As Tomas de Waal states in an article for Carnegie Moscow Center, "both the administration of Robert Kocharyan and Serzh Sargsyan embraced a Russian take-over of the economy, which left them political control and did not expose them to European-style competition" (de Waal 2013). Armenia also has developed close political and economic ties with Iran, in order to counterbalance Turkish strategic cooperation with Azerbaijan and Georgia. Iran views Armenia as a key country that will help Tehran to reinforce its political stance in the South Caucasus (Balla 2013, p. 3). As a result, the two countries secured a number of infrastructural and energy projects.[13] Georgia has the least developed relationships with Iran among the all three Transcaucasian states, while Baku and Tehran experience a couple of tensions, including conflicting claims on maritime and seabed boundaries in the Caspian Sea, Azerbaijani support of separatist movements among ethnic Azeris in Iran (which constitute 16 percent of the population), and Iran's pro-Armenian position in the Nagorno-Karabakh conflict (Balla 2013, p. 3).

The neorealist theoretical framework helps me to assess and identify causal connections between Russia's material power capabilities (my independent variable) and its foreign policies (dependent variables) in the South Caucasus. I expect to see that in periods where Russia's material power is very strong, the Moscow's foreign policy goals will tend towards imperialism. A key insight that emerges from this work is that the success of Russia's hegemonic tendencies and expansionist agendas in the South Caucasus varies across the three nations and time periods. Thus, I also focus upon state-level factors (the Russian state structure in the 1990s and 2000s, and Yeltsin's and Putin's perceptions of relative power) as crucial intervening variables between systemic forces and the foreign policy goals of the Kremlin in Armenia, Azerbaijan, and Georgia after the demise of the Soviet Union. In Chapters 4 and 5, I will further detail the analytical framework and two theories that were applied to my case studies.

Central arguments

I argue that over the long term the relative amount of material power resources that Russia possesses will shape the magnitude and ambition of its foreign policy. As a result, the Eurasian Economic Union will help Russia to increase its relative material power, and will help to make it possible for the Kremlin to control much of the post-Soviet space, including the South Caucasus, as well as shape its external environment according to its own preferences. With the rise of Moscow's relative power, Russia becoming more wealthy and a more powerful state once again, will be able to challenge the influence of other global players in Transcaucasia—the United States, the European Union, Turkey, Iran and China.

My study emphasizes that Russia's foreign policy in the South Caucasus is driven first and foremost by its place in the international system and, specifically, by its relative material power capabilities. I argue that Russia responds to the uncertainties of international anarchy by seeking to control its former territory and shape its external environment according to its own preferences. As a result, Putin's integration plan in Eurasia is meant to strengthen the relative amount of material power resources of Russia, and as its relative power rises, the country will seek more influence abroad. This development will create the possible normative challenges to the interests of global players in the South Caucasian region—Turkey, Iran, the United States, the European Union and China. In the meantime, while many Russian scholars (Vinokurov and Libman 2012; Lomagin 2014; Tsygankov 2014) have pointed out that Putin does not seek to restore the Soviet Union by using the idea of regional integration in the post-Soviet space, and that Eurasian integration is primarily a continental economic integration that has developed from the bottom-up, I will suggest that Russia's current foreign policy in the South Caucasus is nothing else than Putin's attempt to centralize power within Russia and the near abroad using the territorial expansion (the creation of the Eurasian Union in 2015) in order to enhance the country's material power. I argue that the unipolar international system of the 1990s and early 2000s, as well as the distribution of revisionist and status quo interests among Russia, the United States and the European Union, facilitated Vladimir Putin's expansionist grand strategy in the near abroad. Thus, this book should deepen our understanding of Russia's foreign policy in the South Caucasus after the end of the Cold War, as well as the relevance for that policy of the creation of the Eurasian Union. This work will also address the implications of my argument for the Eurasian integration literature and for the operation of the balance of power in the twenty-first century.

Notes

1 According to Velina Tchakarova, the Eurasian integration approach stems from the theoretical framework of the European economic process, which arose from the growing international interdependence of state and non-state actors after World War II to ensure peace in Western Europe (Tchakarova 2014).

2 The Eastern Partnership (EaP) is an open cooperation between the EU and six countries: Armenia, Azerbaijan, Belarus, Georgia, Moldova and Ukraine with the core objectives

to form a political association, establish and develop a free trade area, and remove a visa regime. The EaP was launched on May 7, 2009 as a tool to enhance cooperation and to support reforms in the Eastern Neighborhood of the EU as well as to control a south energy corridor from the Caspian region to Europe bypassing Russia (Arakelyan 2014).

3 Association Agreements are international agreements that the European Community/ European Union has concluded with third countries with the aim of setting up an all-embracing framework to conduct bilateral relations (European Union External Action 2015).

4 I argue in this study that Putin's grand strategy is to restore Russia's status as a key player in the international arena as well as in the near abroad.

5 The Eurasian Economic Union (EEU) that has been described as a potential extension of the Customs Union formed by Russia, Kazakhstan and Belarus in 2010 is a free trade zone within the framework of Eurasian integration that will become effective as of January 1, 2015. On October 10, 2014, leaders of Russia, Kazakhstan, Belarus and Armenia have signed a treaty that will make Yerevan a new member of the EEU along with Moscow, Astana and Minsk.

6 Central Europe for Russians was the playing field in a zero-sum game, Moscow intended to keep the region a neutral zone between the East and the West (Orban 2008, p. 24).

7 According to Shevtsova (2005) the Russian system is a specific type of governance structure with the following characteristics: paternalism, the state domineering over the individual, isolation from the outside world, and ambitions to be a great power. The leader in the Russian system is above the law and concentrates in its hand all powers, without a balancing accountability.

8 The Kozyrev doctrine (named after the former Russian Foreign Minister, Andrei Kozyrev) was adopted in 1993 and emphasized the equal, mutually beneficial, and partner-like relations between Russia and the outside world.

9 The European Union has long been the most developed model of regional integration based on the supranational "community method" rather than the traditional balance-of-power model. Moreover, the political will to share sovereignty and construct strong, legally based, common institutions to oversee the integration project. Finally, the EU integration entails a consensus approach combined with solidarity and tolerance in order not to isolate any member state if they have any major problem (for instance, as it was in the case of Greece), hesitance to move forward with policies until the majority of member states are ready, and a financial assistance to the poorer states in order to catch up with a norm (Cameron 2010). An Association Agreement is also the EU's main instrument to bring the countries in the Eastern Partnership close to EU norms and standards. It compromises four general chapters: Common Foreign and Security Policy; Justice and Home Affairs; The Deep and Comprehensive Free Trade Area (DCFTA); and a fourth chapter covering a range of issues, including the environment, science, transportation, and education.

10 Cutler 2011 and Dragneva and Wolczuk 2013 consider the creation of the Commonwealth of Independent States in 1991 as a weak approach to resolve the complex problems associated with the disintegration of the Soviet Union. The eleven present member states of the CIS—Armenia, Azerbaijan, Belarus, Kazakhstan, Kyrgyzstan, Moldova, Russia, Tajikistan, Turkmenistan, Ukraine, and Uzbekistan—have signed only a small percentage of the agreements since its foundation. In the meantime, the Eurasian Economic Community (includes Belarus, Kazakhstan, Kyrgyzstan, Russian, Tajikistan and Uzbekistan) that was launched in 2000, and the Collective Security Treaty Organisation established in 2003 (Armenia, Belarus, Kazakhstan, Kyrgyzstan, Russian, Tajikistan and Uzbekistan as the member states) have been more effective in promoting specific interests.

11 According to Dragneva and Wolczuk (2012), the ECU operates in the context of Russia's accession to the WTO, and, while two other members of the ECU: Belarus and Kazakhstan remained outside it, Russia's accession protocol is meant to be in integral part of the legal framework of the ESU. Thus, according to authors, the ECU represents a modernized economic regime, which is different from previous integration projects within the post-Soviet space.

12 Turkish Foreign Minister, Ahmet Davitoglu and Armenian Foreign Minister, Edvard Nalbandyan signed two protocols on "Establishing Diplomatic Relations", which called for the two sides to establish embassies in each other's capitals and on "Development Bilateral Relations" on October 10, 2005. Nevertheless, the parliaments in both countries failed to ratify the protocols because of Turkey's denial of the Armenian Genocide of 1915 and Azerbaijan's objections, the later threatened to retaliate against its "big brother" by taking a number of steps, including cutting off oil supplies (Sassounian 2009; Tastekin 2013).

13 Yerevan and Tehran signed numerous bilateral agreements (one of them is a gas pipeline, which was inaugurated in 2007 that runs from Tabriz in Iran to Sardarian in Armenia) mostly for commercial and political purposes, including developing geo-economic relations with the European Union. Although, after Armenia's decision to join the Customs Union, Iran is concerned that Russia, which already controls Armenian political, economic, and security spheres, will limit prospects of Iranian relations with Europe.

Bibliography

Acemoglu, Daron and James A. Robinson (2012) *Why Nations Fail: The Origins of Power, Prosperity, and Poverty*. New York, NY: Crown Publishing.

Aghajanian, Liana (2012) "Breaking the Grip of Oligarchs: How a tragic twist of fate is fueling a revolt against Armenia's overweening tycoons," *Foreign Policy*. November 5.

Akimbekov, Sultan (2011) "The Eurasian Response," *Tsentr Azii*, No. 19 (56). January.

Ambrosio, Thomas (2009) *Authoritarian Backlash: Russian Resistance to Democratization in the Former Soviet Union*. Burlington, VA: Ashgate.

Arakelyan, Lilia A. (2014) "The Soviet Union is Dead: Long Live the Eurasian Union," in Roger E. Kanet and Remi Piet (Eds.) *Shifting Priorities in Russia's Foreign and Security Policy*. Aldershot, UK: Ashgate.

Aron, Leon (2013) "The Putin Doctrine: Russia's Quest to Rebuild the Soviet State," *Foreign Affairs*. March 11.

Balla, Evanthia (2013) "Turkish and Iranian Interests and Policies in the South Caucasus," *NOREF Policy Brief*. April.

Cameron, Fraser (2010) "The European Union as a Model for Regional Integration," *Council on Foreign Relations Press*. September.

Crane, George T. and Amawi Abla (1997) *The Theoretical Evolution of International Political Economy: A Reader*. Oxford, UK: Oxford University Press.

Cutler, Robert M. (2011) "Putin Declares 'Eurasian Union' Goal of Russian Foreign Policy," *Analyst, The Central Asia-Caucasus Institute*. October 19.

de Waal, Thomas (2013) "An Offer Sargsian Could Not Resist," *Carnegie Moscow Center*. April 9. http://carnegie.ru/commentary/?fa=52841 (accessed May 18, 2015).

Dragneva, Rilka and Katarina Wolczuk (2012) "Russian, the Eurasian Customs Union and the EU: Cooperation, Stagnation or Rivalry," *Chatham House, a briefing paper*. January.

Dragneva, Rilka and Katarina Wolczuk (2013) *Eurasian Economic Integration: Law, Policy and Politics*. Cheltenham, UK: Edward Elgar.

European Union External Action (2015) "EU Association Agreements," October 10. https://eeas.europa.eu/headquarters/headquarters-homepage/3763/eu-association-agreements_en (accessed February 10, 2016).

Gabrielyan, Emma (2015) "Why Does Russia Send Oligarchs to Armenia on a Business Mission?" *Aravot*. October 22. http://en.aravot.am/2015/10/22/172588/ (accessed August 28, 2016).

Global Research News "Azerbaijan-Georgia-Turkey Military Cooperation to "Protect Pipeline," August 5, 2013.

Goodrich, Lauren and Peter Zeihan (2011) *A Crucible Nations: The Geopolitics of the Caucasus*. Austin, TX: Stratfor Global Intelligence.

Greene, James (2012) "Russian Responses to NATO and EU Enlargement and Outreach," *Chatham House, a briefing paper*. June.

Hasenclever, Andreas, Peter Mayer and Volker Rittberger (1997) *Theories of International Regimes*. Cambridge, UK: Cambridge University Press.

Hill, Fiona, Kemal Kirisci and Andrew Moffatt (2015) "Retracing the Caucasian Circle: Considerations, and Constraints for U.S., EU, and Turkish Engagement in the South Caucasus," Turkish Project Policy Paper. *Center on the United States and Europe at Brookings*. No. 6, July 15.

Hudson, Valerie M. (2005) "Foreign Policy Analysis: Actor-Specific Theory and the Ground of International Relations," *Foreign Policy Analysis*. February 4.

Ivanov, Sergey (2006) "The New Russian Doctrine," *Wall Street Journal* (Europe). January 11.

Jarosiewicz, Aleksandra (2014) "Azerbaijan—a Growing Problem for the West," *Ośrodek Studiów Wschodnich*. September 15. www.osw.waw.pl/en/publikacje/osw-commentary/2014-09-15/azerbaijan-a-growing-problem-west (accessed January 3, 2015).

Jozwiak, Rikard (2013) "Explainer: What Exactly Is An EU Association Agreement," *Radio Free Europe Radio Liberty*. November 20. www.rferl.org/content/eu-association-agreement-explained/25174247.html (accessed April 7, 2014).

Kanet, Roger E. (2010) "From Cooperation to Confrontation: Russia and the United States since 9/11," in Bertil Nygren, Bo Huldt, Patrik Ahlgren, Pekka Sivonen and Susanna Huldt (Eds.) *Russia on Our Minds: Russian Security Policy and Northern Europe*. Stockholm, Sweden: National Defense University.

Keohane, Robert O. (1984) *After Hegemony: Cooperation and Discord in the World Political Economy*. Princeton, NJ: Princeton University Press.

Keohane, Robert O. (1986) *Neorealism and Its Critics*. New York, NY: Columbia University Press.

Keohane, Robert O. (1988) "International Institutions: Two approaches," *International Studies Quarterly*, Vol. 32, No. 4, pp. 379–396.

Keohane, Robert O. (1993) "Regime," in Joel Krieger (Ed.) *Oxford Companion to Politics of the World*. New York, NY: Oxford University Press.

Keohane, Robert O. (2003) "The Theory of Hegemonic Stability and Changes in International Economic Regimes, 1967–1977," in Roe C. Goddard, Patrick Cronin and Kishore C. Dash (Eds.) *International Political Economy: State Market Relations in a Changing Global Order*. Boulder, CO: Lynne Rienner.

Keohane, Robert O. (2005) *After Hegemony: Cooperation and Discord in the World Political Economy*. Princeton, NJ: Princeton University Press.

Keohane, Robert O. and Joseph S. Nye, Jr. (1977) *Power and Interdependence: World Politics in Transition*. Boston, MA: Little, Brown.

Kiguradze, Temur (2013) "Posledniaia Rech' Saakshvili v OON Ponravilas' Gruzinam," *BBC Russia*. September 26.

Kononenko, Vadim and Arkady Moshes (2011) *Russia as a Network State: What Works in Russia When State Institutions Do Not?* London, UK: Palgrave.

Kozhanov, Nikolay (2012) "Russian Foreign Policy after Putin's Return," *The Washington Institute*. May 12.

Krasner, Stephen D. (1976) "State Power and the Structure of International Trade," *World Politics*, Vol. 28, pp. 317–347.

Krasner, Stephen D. (1983) *International Regimes*. Ithaca, NY: Cornell University Press.

Kratochwil, Friedrich and John Gerald Ruggie (1986) "International Organization: A State of the Art on an Art of the State," *International Organization,* Vol. 40, No. 4, Autumn, pp. 753–775.

Kuzio, Taras (2006) "Ukraine is Not Russia: Comparing Youth Political Activism," *SAIS Review*, Vol. XXVI, No. 2, Summer–Fall.

Lake, David A. (2006) "International political economy: A Maturing Interdiscipline," in Barry R. Weingast and Donald A. Wittman (Eds.) *The Oxford Handbook of Political Economy*. New York, NY: Oxford University Press.

Levistky, Steven and Lucan A. Way (2002) "Elections without Democracy: The Rise of Competitive Authoritarianism," *Journal of Democracy*, Vol. 13, No. 2, April.

Little, Richard (2006) "International Regimes," in John Baylis and Steve Smith (Eds.) *The Globalization of World Politics: An Introduction to International Relations*. New York, NY: Oxford University Press.

Lo, Bobo (2012) "10 Key Questions of Russian Foreign Policy," *Meeting Summary: Russia and Eurasian Programme, Chatham House*. March 26.

Lobell, Steven E., Norrin M. Ripsman and Jeffrey W. Taliaferro (2009) *Neoclassical Realism, The State, and Foreign Policy*. Cambridge, UK: Cambridge University Press.

Lomagin, Nikita (2014) "Russia's CIS Policy and Economic and Political Transformations in Eurasia," in Roger E. Kanet and Remi Piet (Eds.) *Shifting Priorities in Russia's Foreign and Security Policy*. Aldershot, UK: Ashgate.

Lukas, Edward (2014) "Edwards Lukas: Russia is a Revisionist Power; Greater Danger Lie Ahead." *KyivPost*. September 2. www.kyivpost.com/article/opinion/op-ed/edward-lucas-russia-a-revisionist-power-greater-dangers-lie-ahead-363081.html (accessed June 20, 2017).

Lukyanov, Fyodor (2012) "The Form and the Essence of the Eurasian Union? Russia in Global Affairs," No. 3, July/September.

Markedonov, Sergey (2010) "Radical Islam in the North Caucasus: Evolving Threats, Challenges, and Prospect," *Center for Strategic and International Studies*. November.

Medvedev, Dmitry (2008) "Interview Given by Dmitry Medvedev to Television Channels Channel One, Rossia, NTV," *The Presidential website of Russia*. August 31. http://archive.kremlin.ru/eng/articles/about_siteEng01.shtml (accessed September 19, 2013).

Mkrtchyan, Gayane (2013) "Civil Society reacts to CU Agreement: Joining Customs Union will 'throw Armenia back 25 years'," *ArmeniaNow.Com*. December 17.

Nichol, Jim (2011) "Armenia, Azerbaijan and Georgia: Political Developments and Implications for U.S. Interests," *Congressional Research Service Report for Congress*. Available at www.crs.gov.

Nichol, Jim (2012) "Russian Political, Economic, and Security Issues and U.S. Interests," *Congressional Research Service Report*. February 10. www.nam.org/Issues/Trade/Russia-PNTR/CRS-Report--Russian-Political--Economic--and-Security-Issues-and-U_S_-Interests/ (accessed October 10, 2014).

Nichol, Jim (2014) "Russian Political, Economic, and Security Issues and U.S. Interests," *Congressional Research Service Report.* March 31. https://fas.org/sgp/crs/row/RL33407.pdf (accessed June 10, 2015).

Nygren, Bertil (2011) "Russia and Georgia- From Confrontation to War," in Roger E. Kanet (Ed.) *Russian Foreign Policy in the 21st Century*. Houndmills, UK: Palgrave Macmillan.

Orban, Anita (2008) *Power, Energy, and the New Russian Imperialism*. Westport, CT: Praeger Security International.

Panin, Alexander (2014) "For Russia, Eurasian Union is About Politics, Not Economy," *The Moscow Times*. May 29. www.themoscowtimes.com/business/article/for-russia-eurasian-union-is-about-politics-not-economy/501126.html (accessed June 2, 2014).

Putin, Vladimir (2011) "A New Integration Project for Eurasia: The Future in the Making," *Izvestia*, October 3.

Remington, Thomas (2014) *Presidential Decrees in Russia: A Comparative Perspective*. New York, NY: Cambridge University Press.

Rivera, David W. and Sharon Werning Rivera (2009) "Yeltsin, Putin, and Clinton: Presidential Leadership and Russian Democratization in Comparative Perspective," *Perspective on Politics*, Vol. 7, No. 3, September.

Rose, Gideon (1998) "Neoclassical Realism and Theories of Foreign Policy," *World Politics*, Vol. 51, No. 1, pp. 144–172.

Salukvadze, Khatuna (2006) "Russia's New Doctrine of Neo Imperialism," *Analyst, The Central Asia-Caucasus Institute*, February 8.

Sakwa, Richard (2013) "Developed Putinism: Change without Development," *Russian Analytical Digest*, No. 127, May 8.

Sassounian, Harut (2009) "Azerbaijan and Turkey Protect Armenia's National Interest Inadvertently," *Keghart.com*. www.keghart.com/node/627 (accessed April 4, 2015).

Shevtsova, Lilia (2005) *Putin's Russia*. Washington, DC: Carnegie Endowment for International Peace.

Skak, Mette (2011) "Russia's New 'Monroe Doctrine'," in Roger E. Kanet (Ed.) *Russian Foreign Policy in the 21st Century*. Houndmills, UK: Palgrave Macmillan.

Starr, Frederick and Svante E. Cornell (2005) *The Baku-Tbilisi-Ceyhan Pipeline: Oil Window to the West*. Washington, DC: Central Asia-Caucasus Institute.

Sussex, Matthew, Ed. (2012) *Conflict in the Former USSR*. New York, NY: Cambridge University Press.

Tarr, David G. (2012) "The Eurasian Customs Union among Russia, Belarus and Kazakhstan: Can It Succeed Where Its Predecessor Failed?," *Centre for Economic and Financial Research at New Economic School,* No. 37, December.

Tastekin, Fehim (2013) "Turkey Extends Hand, but no Apology, to Armenia," *Almonitor*, December 12.

Tchakarova, Velina (2014) "The Eurasian Union as a Tool of Russian Geopolitics in the Era of Globalization," in Riegl Martin, Jacob Landovsky, and Irina Valko (Eds.) *Strategic Regions in 21st Century Power Politics: Zones of Consensus and Zones of Conflict*. Newcastle upon Tyne, UK: Cambridge Scholars Publishing.

Thucydides (2010) *The History of Peloponnesian War*. New York, NY: Barnes & Noble Classics.

Torbakov, Igor (2000) "Putin's Russia Defines its Foreign Policy Agenda," *EurasiaNet*. July 27. www.eurasianet.org/departments/insight/articles/eav072800.shtml (accessed June 10, 2014).

Tsygankov, Andrei (2013) "Vladimir Putin's Civilizational Turn," *Russian Analytical Digest*. No. 127, May 8.

Tsygankov, Andrei (2014) "How the West Enabled the Rise of Russian Nationalism," *The Nation*. May 12.

UN News Centre (2013) "President of Georgia, addressing UN Assembly, calls for unity in Eastern Europe." September 25. www.un.org/apps/news/story.asp?NewsID=46020#.WGMvKfkrLU (accessed October 3, 2014).

Vinokurov, Evgeny and Alexander, Libman (2012) *Eurasian Integration: Challenges of Transcontinental Regionalism*. Houndmills, UK: Palgrave Macmillan.

Wohlforth, William M. (1993) *The Elusive Balance: Power and Perceptions During the Cold War*. Ithaca, NY: Cornell University Press.

2 How do the South Caucasian cases affect the analysis of Russia's foreign policy?

Neoclassical realism stresses the primacy of the international system, and also acknowledges the importance of domestic political arrangements and the perceptions of leaders in the selection and implementation of foreign policy responses to the international environment (Lobell, Ripsman and Taliaferro 2009, p. 280). This study uses Derek Beach's definition of foreign policy, which holds that

> Foreign policy is both the broad trends of behavior and the particular actions taken by a state or other collective actor as directed towards other collective actors within the international system. Foreign policy actions can be undertaken using a variety of different instruments, ranging from adopting declarations, making speeches, negotiating treaties, giving other states economic aid, engaging in diplomatic activity as summits, and the use of military force.
>
> (Beach 2012, p. 3)

While foreign policy analysis (FPA) is an important sub-discipline of the study of IR, Beach argues that what sets FPA apart from the broader study of IR is the scope of what is to be explained. He contends that, although IR encompasses the foreign policy actions of individual states, the range of phenomena studied within IR is much broader. Thus, Beach offers to embed FPA within the broader study of IR in order to use many of the theoretical tools of IR to study foreign policy (Beach 2012, pp. 3–5). In order to avoid what Beach calls the "narrowness" of FPA, I will employ neoclassical realist theory of foreign policy to analyze Russia's foreign policy in the South Caucasus after the end of the Cold War.

It is important to note that, according to Lobell, Ripsman and Taliaferro there is no single neoclassical realist approach of foreign policy, but a diversity of neoclassical realist theories. Gideon Rose was the first one to use the term "neoclassical realism" when referring to the theories that incorporate both external and internal variables, and updating certain insights drawn from the realist school of thought (Rose 1998, p. 146). Moreover, according to Rose, neoclassical realism holds that the scope and ambitions of a state's foreign policy are driven first and foremost by its place in the international system, in general, and, in particular, by its relative material power capabilities. However, neoclassical realists argue that the impact of such power capabilities on foreign policy is indirect and complex since system pressure must be translated through intervening variables at the unit level (Rose 1998, p. 146). In other words, neoclassical realism is an approach that combines elements of system, structure, and domestic politics, of material and ideational factors, and tries to analyze international relations from a pluralist view (Kitchen 2010, p. 119).

This study, which draws upon the assumptions of neoclassical realism, focuses upon state-level factors as crucial intervening variables between systemic forces and the foreign policy goals of Russia in the South Caucasus, analyzing how and under what circumstances state-level factors matter. In this chapter, I discuss the book's research strategy and methodological approach.

Examining Moscow's international relations from a pluralist perspective

Evans contends that cases are too complicated to justify a single theory; therefore, scholars who work in this tradition are likely to draw on a variety of theoretical traditions to analyze their cases (Evans 1995, p. 4). It has been argued that the emphasis of theory-centric research is upon analyzing causal relationships between variables, using theories as explanatory tools (Beach 2012, p. 220). Beach notes that the first step in theory-centric research is to determine whether the research question has been extensively studied or not. Russia's foreign policy has received substantial attention from the IR scholars and there are numerous alternative theories that can be used as a starting point for a *deductive, theory-testing research design*. This study focuses on two such theories: neoclassical realism and regime theories, which are explored further below.

Immediately after the dissolution of the Soviet Union in 1991 Russia had difficulties in clarifying the country's new identity, and as a result defining its foreign policy choices, except the idea that due to the fall of the Iron Curtain, the West was Moscow's new political ally, and a prototype for country's economic and political development (Trenin 1996; Shevtsova 2007; Lukyanov 2013 and others). The explicit pro-Western stage in Russian foreign policy was associated with Andrei Kozyrev, Russia's first Foreign Minister, who avowed interest in strategic partnership with the West (Bogaturov 2003). Pro-Western sentiments in Kremlin policy were quickly dismissed after a couple of events that presented a classic example of unipolarity of the international system: the war in Yugoslavia; the NATO eastward expansion; a series of gas pipelines projects in the Caspian Sea region designed to bypass Russia. Consequently, Kozyrev resigned, while the new foreign minister, Evgeniy Primakov came up with the doctrine grounded in the idea of multipolarity. It is interesting to note that Primakov's foreign policy doctrine resembled pretty much "a balance of power concept," that has been developed by Vladimir Putin in the 2000s (Torbakov 2000). Russia, in Putin's first presidential term, reduced Moscow's dependence on Western economic aid thanks to the rise in oil prices, as well as identified itself as being in opposition to US hegemony. A central element in the Putin Doctrine, the state's control of the oil and gas industry, has been paramount politically to his regime as guarantors of the security and stability of the centralized Russian state that Mr. Putin created in the 2000s, when he used Rosneft to reinstate Russian oil to state control. Consequently, the government owns 69.5 percent of the company that controls about 40 percent of country's crude output. The Putin regime also re-established Russia's state-controlled natural gas-exporting company, Gazprom, thus monopolizing the key branches of the economy, which many analysts considered as a dangerous path that had already destroyed the Soviet Union with its command economy (Reznik, Bierman, and Meyer 2014).

Since the beginning of his first term, Vladimir Putin turned his country's attention to the CIS region again, aiming at deepening economic and security integration with the CIS states within the framework of existing CIS institutions and the Collective Security Treaty Organization (CSTO). The main area of cooperation between Russia and its eastern neighbors, Kazakhstan, Azerbaijan, Uzbekistan, and Turkmenistan, was energy transportation (Torbakov 2000; Nygren 2010). The "Rose Revolution" in Georgia in 2003, the Orange Revolution in Ukraine in 2004–2005, and the Tulip Revolution in Kyrgyzstan in 2005 were significant blows to Moscow's policy of tightening up its influence across the former Soviet space (Ambrosio 2009). Since then the Kremlin became very sensitive to the Western attempts to step into its backyard. The fact that extremely favorable oil and gas prices have intensified not only Russia's economic growth, but also political self-confidence, and its policies towards the near abroad, including the South Caucasus, contributed in Moscow's more assertive attitude towards the former Soviet states.

In the meantime, during his presidency in 2008–2012, Dmitry Medvedev's efforts to develop a new European security treaty that would reinforce a multipolar world, an avoidance of alliances and blocs in the sphere of security, did not bear fruit (Medvedev 2008a; 2008b; and 2008c). The European leaders criticized his proposal for the lack of substance, and argued that the treaty was just Russia's reaction to NATO's eastward expansion and USA missile defense negotiations with Central European countries. Moreover, Medvedev's critics accused him of inconsistency in developing the concept of multipolarity regarding Russia's military presence in South Ossetia and Abkhazia, when the president argued that Moscow had to act unilaterally and deployed the forces to the region in order to protect its own interests (Medvedev 2008c). Overall, the rhetoric emanating from Mr. Medvedev after the Russian–Georgian war in 2008 confirmed for the West the image of Russia as a revisionist state intent on re-establishing its role in the near abroad as well as in the international arena (Kanet 2010).

Russia's Minister of Foreign Affairs, Sergei Lavrov, explains in an exclusive interview with *Foreign Policy* magazine his state's new vision of the international system as one where Moscow is viewed as a key player, given the country's geographical size, unique geopolitical position, its centuries-old historical traditions, and national identity (Glasser 2013). Lavrov makes a couple of valid points in his interview that are relevant to this study: 1) Russia's new great-power ambition is a result of domestic changes, economic development and a higher social standard of living; 2) Russia is trying to balance NATO because of its eastward expansion; and 3) Russia is a realist state, which is trying to unite countries not to create ideological dividing lines like the European Union.

In other words, regionally, Russia promotes the creation of the Eurasian Union based on shared history, culture, traditions and values (Vinokurov and Libman 2012; Lomagin 2014; Rukavishnikov 2014). On the other hand, globally, Moscow asserts itself as a realist state that does not share ideological sentiments of the European Union and has pragmatic interests in its foreign policy choices (Glasser 2013).

This book uses theory-testing cases (both within case analysis and cross-case comparison) to examine Moscow's grand strategies in the South Caucasian states after the fall of the Iron Curtain, and the relevance for those policies in the creation of the Eurasian Union. Nicu Popescu (2014) contends that the term "Eurasian Union" refers to several entities: it indicates a Customs Union, launched in 2010, that includes Belarus, Kazakhstan and Russia, the latter transformed into a Common Economic Space of the three states. Consequently, the term is often referred to the Eurasian Economic Commission that serves as the executive for the Customs Union. Finally, it also refers to the Eurasian Economic Union that was formed in January of 2015. This study uses the term of Eurasian Union in regards to the Eurasian Economic Union, thus, these two terms will be used interchangeably throughout the book.

My choice of the case study approach is not accidental, since the essence of a case study, according to Schramm, is to illuminate a decision or set of decisions: why they were taken, how they were implemented, and with what result (Schramm 1971). Another reason for applying the case study method to my research is the fact that a "case study investigates a contemporary phenomenon within its real-life context, especially when the boundaries between phenomenon and context are not clearly evident" (Yin 2003, p. 13).

Comparative case study research design

It is important to note that Yin maintains that the use of the case study method is justified when the researcher wants to cover contextual conditions, believing that they might be relevant to his or her phenomenon of study. However, since we already recognized that phenomenon and context are not always distinguishable in real-life situations, the case study as a research strategy would include an all-encompassing method: the logic of design, data collections, and specific approaches to data analysis techniques (Yin 2003, pp. 12–15). Yin also notes that for case studies five components of a research design are especially vital: 1) a study's question; 2) its propositions; 3) its unit(s) of analysis; 4) the logic linking the data to the propositions; and 5) the criteria for interpreting the findings (Yin 2003, pp. 20–21).

George and Bennett (2005) articulate that the case study approach requires the detailed examination of an aspect of an historical episode to develop or test historical explanations that may be generalized to other events (George and Bennett 2005, p. 5). The authors define a case as an instance of a class of events, which refers to phenomena of scientific interest, such as revolution, types of government regimes, kinds of economic systems that the researcher choose to study in order to develop theory ("generic knowledge") regarding the causes of similarities or differences among cases of that class events (George and Bennett 2005, pp. 17–18). In this regard, a case study, in George and Bennett's views, is a well-defined aspect of a historical episode rather than a historical event by itself. For instance, Russia's foreign policy is a historical instance of many different classes of events: balance of power, neo-imperialism, coercive diplomacy, territorial expansion, and so on. For the purpose of this book, I decided to study one class of events—Russia's foreign policy in the South Caucasus since 1991—that I consider as a case of Kremlin's neo-imperialist policy in the near abroad, using neoclassical realism and regime theories, which determined what data from Moscow's foreign policies in Transcaucasia are relevant to my case study. As a result, this case study research includes a multiple-case design or comparative study[1] since the evidence from the three cases of Russia's foreign policy in Armenia, Azerbaijan and Georgia can be considered as more compelling and the overall study can be regarded as more robust.

Consequently, my research questions, "What explains Russia's foreign policy in the South Caucasus and the relevance for that policy of the creation of the Eurasian Union?" and "What laws, rules, norms, and beliefs guide the new economic bloc in the post-Soviet space?" are integral for selecting the cases (the three South Caucasian states) for this study as well as designing and implementing research for these cases (Figure 2.1). However, Yin warns that a multiple-case study cannot be taken lightly since every case should serve a specific purpose within the overall scope of inquiry (Yin 2003, p. 47). Likewise, the replication logic should follow a comparative case study, which is analogous to that used in multiple experiments (Hersen and Barlow 1976). For instance, Yin suggests that each case must be carefully selected so that it either predicts similar results as in the case of Russia's policies in Armenia, Azerbaijan and Georgia (a literal replication) or predicts contrasting results but for predictable reasons (a theoretical replication).

Five components of my research design

After having sorted out some of the key points relevant to the case study analysis, I now turn to the five components of my research design:

1 *A study question*:
   What explains Russia's foreign policy in the South Caucasus and the relevance for that policy of the creation of the Eurasian Union?
2 *Its propositions*:
   a Over the long term the relative amount of material power resources that Russia possesses will shape the magnitude and ambition of its foreign

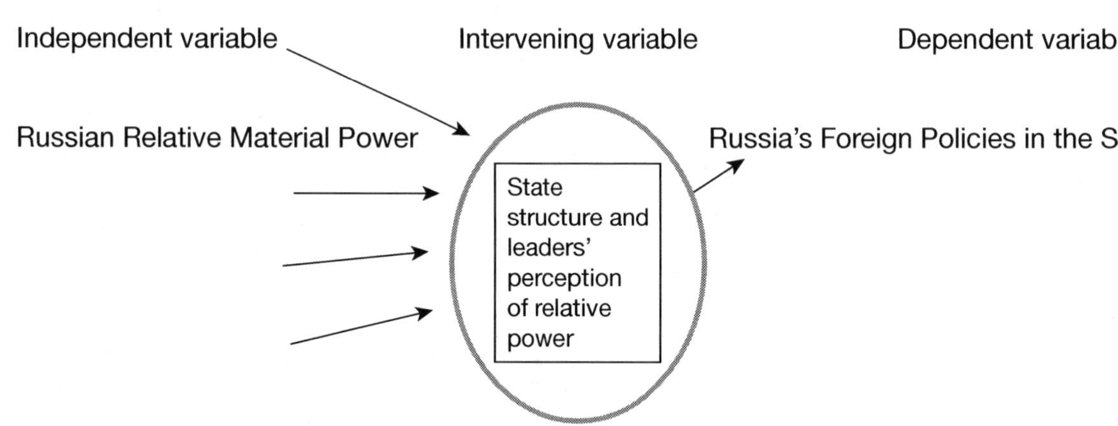

Figure 2.1 Comparative study of Russia's foreign policy in the South Caucasus

Source: Lilia A. Arakelyan

policy. The Moscow-led regional project, the Eurasian Union, helps Russia to increase its relative material power, which, in turn, makes it possible for the Kremlin to control much of its former territory, including the South Caucasus, and shape its external environment according to its own preferences.

b As soon as Moscow's relative power rises, Russia, becoming more wealthy and more powerful state once again, is able to undermine the influence of other global players in the South Caucasus—the United States, the European Union, Turkey, Iran and China.

3 *Unit(s) of analysis*:
Russia's foreign policies in Armenia, Azerbaijan and Georgia after the collapse of the Soviet Union.

4 *The logic linking the data to the propositions*:

a There is a very clear connection in the long run between Russia's economic rise and fall and its growth as an important world empire. According to Gilpin, this pattern can be explained by a more wealthy and powerful state's temptations to increase its control over the environment (Gilpin 1981, pp. 22–23; pp. 94–95).

b The new Russian foreign policy under Putin that is characterized by the growing importance of underlying economic factors, the considerations of the power game, and the defense of the traditional Russian zone of influence in the post-Soviet space (Vinokurov 2007, pp. 29–30). Thus, increased Russian capabilities help to drive policymakers' perceptions of external threats, interests and opportunities in the South Caucasus. In fact, Armenia is now an official member state of the Eurasian Union due to Russia's pressure; Azerbaijan maintains the so-called neutral stance but, nevertheless, Russia is using the Nagorno-Karabakh conflict as a bargaining chip to promote its interests in the Caspian Sea region. Finally, Tbilisi's Western choice faces challenges due to the Russia's presence in the two breakaway regions within Georgia: Abkhazia and South Ossetia.

5 *The criteria for interpreting the findings*:
When the first popularly elected leader in the country's history, Boris Yeltsin, handed the Russian presidency to unknown former KGB (Komitet Gosudarstvennoy Bezopasnosti) agent, Vladimir Putin, by resigning at the end of 1999, history was made. Mr. Putin recentralized power in a steep vertical authoritarian structure with the help of a tight-knit circle that came with him from St. Petersburg, mainly from the security services (*siloviki*), eroded the basic individual freedoms guaranteed under the 1993 Russian constitution and, thus, slowly but surely closing the political space in Russia. In fact, Putin and his team established a regime that would control privatization, restrict democracy, eliminate an independent media, and civil society (Ostrow, Satarov, and Khamada 2007).

Conventional wisdom holds that Russia has never been a democratic state, despite all attempts of Boris Yeltsin to liberalize the country's economic and political system in the 1990s (Ostrow et al. 2007). But, if Boris Yeltsin and his government made some efforts to democratize the Russian state, although those attempts did not bear fruit, Vladimir Putin made a "u-turn," taking Russia back to its historically authoritarian tendencies with no room for freedom of any kind. Mr. Putin's plans to "make Russia a great power again" benefited from favorable economic conditions resulting from global increases in oil prices and demand at the beginning of his presidency. For many Russians, Vladimir Putin became a president who brought stability to their country and stood up to the West.

Starting with the Russian–Georgian war of August 2008, Western leaders realized that Russian officials were not going to tolerate "big brother" behavior from the West, and were ready to undertake military actions to prove their right to Eurasian hegemony despite the international rules and norms. Some analysts would argue that the Putin's doctrine was born at the time, and a five-day long war against Georgia was a "dress rehearsal for Russia's invasion in Ukraine" (Whitmore 2016). After all, East–West relations had rekindled fundamental issues concerning both the globalization and fragmentation of world politics. The former drives the nations economically, socially and politically towards greater integration; the latter tears up regions, and countries to focus on their interests and concerns (Spiegel, Matthews, Taw, and Williams 2009, pp. 6–7). During the Yeltsin presidency, the Russian state's security was associated with the idea of belonging to a group of democratic nations, and Moscow's leaders considered joining NATO and the European Community as the prime national security interest rather than restoring the Soviet Union. During the Putin's presidency, the main focus in Russia's foreign policy became the protection of the near abroad and opposition to NATO and EU expansion to Eastern Europe.

It has been argued that it was Russia who gave impetus to the EaP, however, the August 2008 Russia–Georgia war, and the January 2009 Russia–Ukraine gas dispute, were a signal to Poland and Sweden to create a new EU initiative that would gradually get the countries of Eastern Europe and the South Caucasus to be involved in EU policies and programs and prepare them to integrate with the Union market (Adamczyk 2010). Consequently, if the Russian government paid little attention to the European Neighborhood Programme, that changed entirely with the foundation of the EaP in 2009. For instance, Sergei Lavrov, the Russian Foreign Minister, condemned the establishment of the EaP without Moscow's participation, and compared it to the creation of the "EU zone of interest in Eastern Europe" (Meister and May 2009). Before the Ukrainian crisis the EU officials ignored Moscow's concerns regarding the EaP initiative, and encouraged the partner states to sign the Association Agreement with the Union that would preclude them from participating in economic integration projects with Moscow. This either/or dynamic put Yerevan, Baku, Tbilisi, Minsk, Chisinau, and Kiev at a disadvantage of having to choose allegiances and reassured Kremlin that the EaP was launched to undermine Russia's interests in the region. It did not help that the underlining objective of the EaP initiative remained unclear to EU itself and was contingent on different priorities, usually determined by the dominating group interests within the Union.

The Eurasian Union: Putin's challenge to the EU

The Eastern Partnership (EaP) is an open cooperation between the EU and six countries: Armenia, Azerbaijan, Belarus, Georgia, Moldova and Ukraine with the core objectives to form a political association, establish and develop a free trade area, and remove the existing visa regime. The EaP was launched on May 7, 2009 as a tool to enhance cooperation and to support reforms in the Eastern Neighbourhood of the EU, as well as to control a south energy corridor from the Caspian region to Europe bypassing Russia (Arakelyan 2014). In its foreign policy the EU prefers bilateral relationships manifested in the accession processes where Brussels uses its economic and normative power to create a set of asymmetrical bilateral relationships between itself and the candidates where the projection of norms and values is direct (Haukkala 2010, p. 161). The EU's normative hegemony is not limited to the future member states, but has also been applied in various bilateral co-operation agreements with the FSU states. However, since membership was not formally on the table for EaP countries, the Union's asymmetric bilateral approach has been proven weak and inefficient in Eastern Europe and the South Caucasus. According to Michael Leigh, one of the architects of the ENP initiative, Brussels set high requirements for EaP states to implement EU standards of business regulation, governance, and human rights in return for too small financial and political rewards (Arakelyan 2014, p. 77). Moreover, the six EaP member states fell victim to a power game between EU vis-à-vis Russia, when Vladimir Putin announced his plans for launching the Eurasian Economic Union in January 2015, and "invited" all the former Soviet states to join his regional project. The Putin government claimed that the new economic regime would establish the general rules and norms of post-Soviet states' behavior to facilitate cooperation and promote trade in the region. However, the Eurasian Economic Union is more unattractive and less viable than it was first established by not having Ukraine, the second largest economy of any of the former Soviet states, as its member, which significantly undermined the economic and trade potential of the block. In addition, Russia's economy slipped recently into recession amid Western sanctions and the drop in oil prices, thus, the persistent weakness of the Eurasian Union's most important member state will continue to hold the union back. In fact, by the time the regional block was founded in 2015, the ruble had lost more than 20 percent of its values against the dollar (40 rubles per one U.S. dollar), and Russia's economy contracted by 3.7 percent. Moreover, over the last two years, low oil prices and Western sanctions had strained not only Russia's economy but also the economies of the Eurasian Union's member states. For instance, in 2015 growth in Kazakhstan, Armenia and Kyrgyzstan slowed to a respective 1.2, 3.0 and 3.5 percent (Stratfor 2016). Belarus GDP fell by 3.1 percent, Russia's by 3.7, while in total the Eurasian Union member states GDP fell by 3.2 percent (Stratfor 2016; Koska 2016). The first year of the Eurasian Economic Union also failed to bring

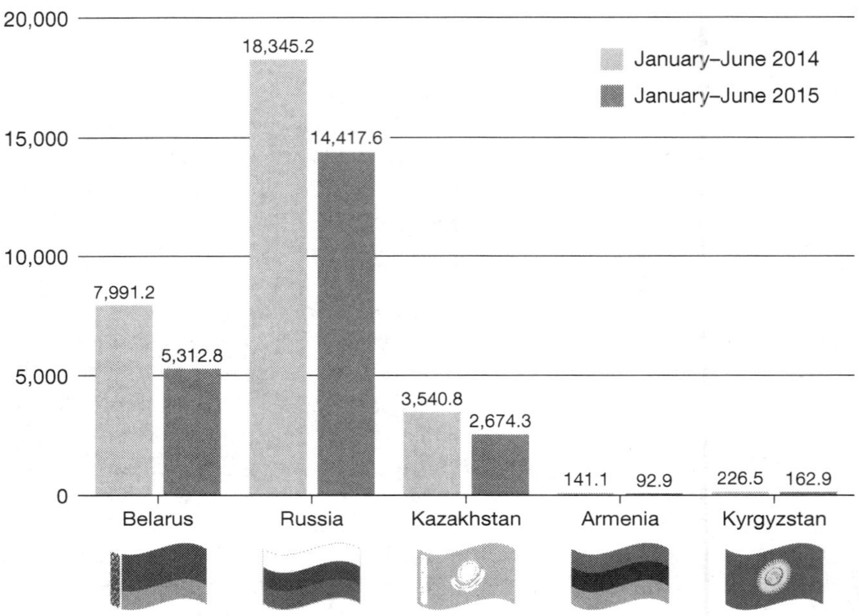

Figure 2.2 Trade within the Eurasian Economic Union (min USD)
Source: BelarusDigest.com

trade liberalization due to economic contraction in Russia. Trade inside the Eurasian Union feel by 26 percent plagued by trade disputes, sanctions regimes, and a regional economic crisis.

In addition, Russia decided to liberalize gas and oil only in 2025, which means that the member states continue paying duties to Moscow on its exports of oil products based on oil imported from Russia. Insofar, the Eurasian Union fell short even of Kremlin's expectations, Russia had been hit by a recession, Ukraine signed an Association Agreement with the EU, and its member states, Armenia and Belarus, had sought close ties with Europe and United States again. In this regard, we shall conclude that the Eurasian Union was launched mainly to implement Moscow's geo-political objectives in the near abroad, and to prevent the FSU states to seek closer ties with the West.

The influence of other key players (Turkey, Iran, the United States, the European Union and China) in Eurasia, in general, and in the South Caucasus, in particular, is also challenged by Russia's new policies in the region. Only one Transcaucasian country, Georgia, signed the Association Agreement with the EU. Moreover, Tbilisi expects a visa-free regime with the EU in 2016, which can be considered as a big victory for a country that has two breakaway regions, Abkhazia and South Ossetia, as possible accession candidates for the Eurasian Economic Union. Georgia presents the most interesting case among the three South Caucasian states, since the country is the only state in the region that is able to pursue closer ties with the EU. However, the evidence shows that Russia's influence in Georgia is growing stronger, since, despite Tbilisi's current pro-European course in foreign policy, the West is reluctant to continue its eastward expansion in order not to anger Mr. Putin. Many analysts believe that Russia uses its "soft power" in Georgia with the help of the Georgian Orthodox Church that had repeatedly denounced the "moral decadence" of the West, and advocated closer ties with Orthodox Christian Russia in order to pursue "shared spiritual and cultural values" (Rukhadze 2016). Russia also uses its TV channels and cyberspace to promote anti-Western and pro-Russian sentiments in the country. Thus, Georgia, along with Armenia and Azerbaijan, remains caught in a tug-of-war between Moscow, Washington and Brussels, and does her best not to follow the Ukrainian fate.

Azerbaijan, while making very limited progress in implementing the ENP Action Plan since it contradicts its repressive political system, serves as a key player for European energy security. In order to implement the Southern Gas corridor, the EU is ready to turn a blind eye to Baku's human rights violations and even the restriction of the operations of NGOs in the country, which are dealing with fundamental freedoms. However, the West once again used a double standard and did not impose economic sanctions against Azerbaijan, as it had in the case of human rights violations in the cases of both Russia and Belarus (EU Commission Report 2015). Moreover, Azerbaijan is making progress on WTO accession and has already joined the WTO Information Technology Agreement. In the same vein, since Azerbaijan was reclassified by the World Bank as an "upper-middle income" country in February 2014, Azerbaijan's exports to the EU were subject to the "most favored nation" trade rules (EU Commission Report 2015). However, the failure of Nabucco pipeline[2] proved once again that Moscow's carrot-and-stick-approach works, since Russia was able to pressure Azerbaijan to send its gas into the Trans Adriatic Pipeline Consortium, and, thus, Gazprom will continue be in charge of gas supplies to the markets of Central and Eastern Europe (Dempsey 2013). The EU agreed that Gazprom can use the Trans Adriatic Pipeline to move gas, if the Russian export monopoly builds the Turkish Stream pipeline and brings gas to Greece (Gotev 2015). Moscow and Ankara have put tensions over Syria behind them and signed the TurkStream agreement in October 2016, which covers the construction of two strings of a gas pipeline that will run from Russia to Turkey across the Black sea. While the first stream of the pipeline is intended for Turkish consumers, the second string will deliver gas to southern and southeastern Europe. According to Gazprom, TurkStream's offshore section will run over 900 kilometers from the Russkaya CS near Anapa across the Black Sea to the Turkish seaboard, with an onshore string for gas transit to be laid up to Turkey's border with neighboring countries. Thus, Moscow and Turkey overlooked their differences on Syria to agree closer military and intelligence cooperation, while Ankara's relations with the U.S. and the EU remained strained by what Erdogan perceived as halfhearted backing after the July 15 coup attempt in Turkey.

In addition, on July 13, 2016 Armenia, Georgia, Iran and Russia signed a roadmap to build the North–South energy corridor that is estimated to reach capacity around 1,000 MW. A power transmission line between Armenia and Iran is already built at the Iran's account, and construction of another line between Armenia and Georgia is paid from the loan extended by KfW bank, a German government-owned development bank based in Frankfurt that has been financially supporting Armenia since 1998 with low interest rates, loans, and grants totaling almost billion Euros so far (Asbarez 2016).

Nevertheless, Turkish policies in the South Caucasus are a bigger concern for Moscow than those of Iran. As a matter of fact, many Russian analysts point to a North–South axis of Russia, Armenia, and Iran that is opposed to an East–West axis of Turkey, Georgia, and Azerbaijan (Kucera 2013). Finally, Putin is building an alternative block to counter China's influence in Central Asia, where the Shanghai Cooperation Initiative turned from a regional security organization into a regional development project. In September 2013, Beijing proposed "A New Silk Road Economic Belt" that will connect the Baltic with the Pacific. This project covers three billion people and features Kazakhstan at its center. Meanwhile, Kazakhstan, a founding member of the Eurasian Union, plays a major role in the integration plans of Moscow. It seems clear that the new Eurasian economic bloc, an important tool of Russia's foreign policy in the near abroad, became a challenge to sovereign choices in the post-Soviet space.

The objectives, design, and structure of the research

There are three phases in the design and implementation of theory-oriented case studies: 1) in phase one—the objectives, design, and structure of the research are formulated; 2) in phase two—each case study is carried out in accordance with the design; and 3) in phase three—the researcher draws upon findings of the case studies and assesses their contribution to achieve the research objective of the study (George and Bennett 2005, p. 73). This chapter deals with the first phase and identifies the objectives, design, and structure of the research, while phases two and three will be discusses in the following chapters of this book.

Phase one consists of five tasks: specification of the problem and research objectives; developing of a research strategy and specification of variables; cases selection; describing the variance in variables; and formulation of data requirements and general questions (George and Bennett 2005, pp. 73–88).

Specification of the problem and research objective

George and Bennett maintain that the formation of the research objectives is the most important decision in designing research since it constrains and guides decisions that will be made regarding the other four tasks. The authors argue that the research objective must be adapted to the needs of the research program at its current stage of development (George and Bennett 2005, p. 74).

In this regard, before describing the research objective (the specification of the problem was already analyzed above), I would like to emphasize that this case study is a multiple-case design, which defies the rationale for multiple-case designs that, according to Yin, derive directly from our understanding of literal and theoretical replications (Yin 2003, p. 52). Yin asserts that the simplest multiple-case design would be the selection of two or more cases that are believed to be literal replications, for instance, set of cases with exemplary outcomes in relation to the evaluation theory. In the case of my study it is a neoclassical realism, a well-formulated theory that has specified a clear set of propositions as well as the circumstances within which the propositions are believed to be true.

This study intends to confirm and extend the neoclassical realism assumptions about the relative importance of material power and international exigencies. For example, the main argument of neoclassical realists is that the international system structures and constrains the policy choices of states. To reiterate, neoclassical realism is a theory of foreign policy, not international outcomes. For neoclassical realists, systemic and subsystemic pressures are translated through intervening variables at the unit level to explain a state's foreign policy or a specific event (Lobell et al. 2009, p. 73). Neoclassical realism tries to explain variation in the foreign policies of the same state over time, and its hypothesis[3] might explain the likely diplomatic, economic and military responses of particular states to systemic imperatives (Lobell et al. 2009, pp. 4–21). Neoclassical realists view foreign policy responses as a product of state–society coordination, while they also argue that the degree of state autonomy vis-à-vis society varies over time and across different states (for example, Yeltsin's and Putin's presidencies experienced varied degrees of state autonomy vis-à-vis society). The latter affects whether states respond to international pressures in a timely and efficient manner (Lobell et al. 2009, p. 29).

Furthermore, neoclassical realists argue that states respond to the uncertainties of international anarchy by seeking to control and shape their external environment (Rose 1998, p. 152). Rose notes that the central empirical prediction of this school of thought is that over the long term the relative amount of material power resources countries possess will shape the ambition and scope of their foreign policies: with the rise of relative power, states will seek more influence abroad, but as it declines their grand strategies will be scale back (Rose 1998, p. 152). Thus, I will treat the neoclassical realist approach as a "most likely framework for a case study," which supports the argument of this study.

The comparative case study, using an alternative theoretical framework, regime theory, will also show why the Eurasian Union cannot be considered as an economic bloc like the European Union. International regime theory may be considered as an economic theory of international norms and institutions (Gehring 1992). Gehring argues that the concept of international regimes is an effort to overcome the dichotomy between the liberal institutionalists, who believe in norms and institutions, and realists, who hold that regimes generate different benefits for states, and, thus, power is a central point of regime formation and survival (Gehring 1992, p. 15). In this regard, I shall argue that a regime theory is a weaker tool in explaining and analyzing Russia's foreign policy in the South Caucasus, identifying a clear concept of the Eurasian Union, and its contribution to establishing and maintaining cooperation among the current member states (Russia, Belarus, Kazakhstan, Armenia, and Kyrgyzstan).

Likewise, Yin contends that selecting cases for a multiple-case design requires prior knowledge of the outcomes, with the multiple-case inquiry focusing on how and why the exemplary outcomes might have occurred and hoping for direct replications of these conditions from case to case (Yin 2003, p. 52). It has been already argued that under Putin, Russia has evolved into an authoritarian state that has destroyed the hopes existed during the Gorbachev and early Yeltsin presidencies that the country would become a modern and open democracy (Van Herpen 2014, p. 146). Moreover, the greater danger, according to Van Herpen, is that there is a potential shift towards totalitarianism, since Putin's system does not tolerate alternative centers of power, even those that might be "friendly." Moreover, as Van Herpen argues, while the collapse of communism brought political instability, economic upheaval and the break-up of empire, the Putin regime revived once again imperialist dreams of a grandiose future (Van Herpen 2014, p. 82). For example, Igor Panarin, a former KGB analyst and former secretary of Roskosmos, the Russian Federal Space Agency, already in 2009 predicted the emergence of a powerful Eurasian Union led by then Russian Prime Minister, Vladimir Putin, which would have a single currency and a parliament in Saint Petersburg. According to Panarin, this union would not only revive the Soviet Union, but also the Tsarist Empire and stretch as far as the Bering Straits, with Russia playing a dominating role in Iran and in the Indian subcontinent (Van Herpen 2014, pp. 82–83).

Consequently, this study treats Russia as a great power after the collapse of the Soviet Union, and it can be argued, using Jack Snyder and Edward Mansfield's claim, that "the period of democratization by great powers has always been a moment of particular danger, in part because when states are militarily strong they may seek to use their force in pursuit of nationalist goals" (Mansfield and Snyder 2005, p. 15). In the same vein, Schweller claims that the relative power of hegemonic states in the early to mid-twentieth century may have its origins in the difficulties that even revisionist great powers face in extracting and mobilizing resources for national security. He maintains that states would not regularly pass up opportunities to expand, instead, stronger states would absorb weaker ones on a regular basis, if a state composed of elites that agree on an ambitions grand strategy; a stable and effective political regime with broad authority to pursue uncertain and risky foreign policies, and a compliant mass public that supports the state's expansionist policies and is willing to make the necessary sacrifices asked of it to implement the strategy (Schweller 2009, p. 247).

Similarly, Yin elaborates that the analytic benefits from having two or more cases may be substantial since even with two cases the researcher has the possibility of direct replication. Moreover, analytic conclusions arising from multiple cases will be more powerful because the contexts of the two cases are likely to differ to some degree. Yin believes that, if under these varied circumstances of the multiple cases, the researcher still can arrive at common conclusions from the cases, the latter will have expanded the external generalizability of the findings. Or, if the findings support the hypothesized contrast, the results show a strong beginning towards theoretical replication, thus strengthening the external validity of findings compared to those from a single case alone (Yin 2003, pp. 53–54).

Correspondingly, the idea of this project emerged in 2010, when the goal of establishing a Eurasian Economic Union was too vague and only two countries, Belarus and Russia, envisaged a full-fledged Union, while Kazakhstan had serious reservations regarding the formation of a currency union and the political nature of the bloc (Dragneva and Wolczuk 2013, pp. 28–29). Despite the fact that Armenia participated in many regional integration initiatives and organizations in post-Soviet space due to the country's dependence on Russia, Yerevan at that time was actively completing negotiations with the EU over a far reaching Association Agreement that was supposed to be initialed at the EU's summit in Vilnius in November of 2013. Azerbaijan and Georgia were also implementing the Eastern Partnership initiatives in their countries; the former even undertook a couple of energy projects with the West, bypassing Russia. Russia tried to use economic, and military leverage, as well as the frozen conflicts in the region to tighten its grip over the South Caucasus but without much success. Therefore, as I began writing this book, Armenia was not even considered as a candidate to join the Customs Union. The same can be said about Azerbaijan and Georgia. Now, the situation in the region has changed. Not only has Armenia become a full-fledged member-state of the Russian-led Eurasian Union in 2015, but Yerevan has also accepted Vladimir Putin's "Eurasian Union without Karabakh" bill, which means that a customs checkpoint would be installed on the border between Armenia and Karabakh. As a result, Armenian analysts see the Azeri hand in this deal; moreover, Russian officials continue to invite Azerbaijan to join what critics have termed the "authoritarian club." Moscow could not force Tbilisi to follow suit, but the two breakaway regions within Georgia, South Ossetia and Abkhazia, have been used by the Kremlin as a bargaining chip for quite a long time. Thus, by relating Russia's foreign policies in the South Caucasus to the creation of the Russia-centered regional integration project within the Eurasian integration, this study explains observable phenomena (or empirically verifiable) in Moscow's external politics in Armenia, Azerbaijan and Georgia. It is important to mention that the creation of the Eurasian Economic Union is treated in this study as a new instrument of Russian policy that is meant to contribute towards reestablishing Russian domination over former Soviet space. Thus, the membership (for Armenia) or non-membership (for Azerbaijan and Georgia) in the single economic space will have significant impact on Russia's policies in each country. This study will also specify how Russia's foreign policy in the South Caucasus has changed over time, starting with the collapse of the Soviet Union and Yeltsin's neglect of the region, and continuing with the Putin's return to imperialist dreams of the greater Russia in the near abroad.

There are six different kinds of theory-building research objectives: atheoretical/configurative idiographic; disciplined configurative; heuristic; theory testing; plausibility probes; and "Building Block" studies of particular types or subtypes of a phenomenon (George and Bennett 2005, p. 76). This study undertakes theory testing case study to assess the validity and scope conditions of neoclassical realism and regime theories. Consequently, I regard my test cases as most-likely for the neoclassical realist approach, and least-likely for regime theories. The scope conditions of theories (the conditions under which they are most- and least-likely to apply) are the following:

1 *Neoclassical realism*; there is a clear connection between Russia's economic rise and fall and its growth and decline as an important military power. In this respect, a shift in relative power leads to a revisionist or status-quo shift in the foreign policy of Moscow in the South Caucasus. Moreover, turning to the autonomy of leaders, when domestic constraints are weak (as in case of Putin's presidency in Russia), leaders can pursue their own conception of the national interest, whereas then they are restrictive (as was with the case of Yeltsin's presidency), the leaders are forced to accommodate the understanding of the national interest of the constraining domestic actors (Beach 2012, p. 67);
2 *Regime theories*; neoliberal insights on regimes highlight the relative gain in regime formation, whereas in the creation of the Eurasian Economic Union even the founding states, Russia, Belarus, and Kazakhstan face economic disadvantages. For instance, the Eurasian Union member states trade among themselves and are raising tariffs on imported goods from outside the group. Taking into consideration that the European Union remains the largest trading partner of Armenia, Kazakhstan and Russia, it is obvious that the states would suffer possible retaliation from joining the trading bloc and increasing tariffs on imports from the EU. Furthermore, realists regard regimes as tools that enable states to coordinate, by treating power as a key factor in establishing and maintaining treaties. But, since it was already argued that the relative power of the state may decline (for example, the Western sanctions and oil price drop have already been threatening Russia's economy) with the economic fall, Russia will be unable to coordinate the Eurasian bloc under these conditions.[4]

Specification of variables

According to George and Bennett, a research strategy requires early formulation of hypotheses and consideration of the elements (conditions, parameters, and variables) to be employed in the analysis of historical cases (George and Bennett 2005, p. 79). In this study, Russia's foreign policies in Armenia, Azerbaijan and Georgia are treated as the dependent (or outcomes) variables to be explained. Beach emphasizes that before one can proceed it is critical to define carefully the different theoretical concepts that one will be investigating. To put it differently, one should state exactly what do the variables in the study mean (Beach 2012, p. 224). In this respect, my independent variable (Russia's relative power) and dependent variable (Russia's foreign policies in the South Caucasus) are clearly defined and systematized concepts within the neoclassical realist school of thought. Neoclassical realists define the term power as "the capabilities or resources with which states can influence each other" (Wohlforth 1993, p. 4). It is important to clarify that these scholars distinguish between these power resources and a country's foreign policy goals and preferences that guide the state's external behavior (Rose 1998, p. 153). According to neoclassical realists, states are not seeking security but are responding to the uncertainties of international anarchy by seeking to control and shape their environment. Likewise, states are likely to want more rather than less external influence, and will pursue such influence to the extent that they are able to do so (Zakaria1998, p. 19). Zakaria also argues that states are influence-maximizers and their increased resources give rise to greater ambitions. Finally, my intervening variables (state structure and leaders' perception of relative power) comprise the theoretical framework for this study.

George and Bennett discuss the importance of scope conditions for theories and competitive hypothesis testing by arguing that "when theories are fairly well developed, researchers can use case studies for theory testing" (George and Bennett 2005, p. 115). Thus, one can identify whether and how the scope conditions of alternative theories should be expanded or narrowed.

Furthermore, George and Bennett argue that an explanation of a case is more convincing when the outcome could not have been predicted using the different theory explanation (George and Bennett 2005, p. 117). In regard to alternative propositions of regime theories (realist and liberal institutionalist versions), I accept Krasner's definition of international regimes "as a set of principles, norms, rules and decision making procedures around which actors expectations converge in a given area of international relations" (Krasner 1983, p. 2). Hasenclever, Mayer, and Rittberger contend that regimes are deliberately constructed, partial international orders on either a local or international level with the intentions to remove specific issues-areas of global politics from the sphere of self-help behavior (Hasenclever, Mayer, and Rittberger 2000, p. 3). Hasenclever et al. claim that by creating shared expectations about appropriate behavior and by upgrading the level of transparency in the issue-area,[5] international regimes facilitate cooperation among the states and help them to achieve join gains in security and welfare spheres. The authors argue that regimes exist in all domains of global politics, thus there are security regimes, economic regimes, environmental regimes, and human rights regimes (Hasenclever et al. 2000, p. 4). Two mainstream theories of international regimes: realism and liberalism, share the assumption that states are rational actors, operating in an anarchic system. However, liberal institutionalists see the regimes as tools to cooperate and facilitate in the world politics. For instance, Ernst Haas maintains that regime creation helps to solve challenges that can be overcome only through cooperation (Haas 1990, p. 2). This approach suggests that institutions or sets of rules and norms can have a critical impact upon state behavior, if they have mutual interests. Liberal institutionalism was developed as a critique of the original realist approach to international relations with the emphasis on how institutions can help states overcome barriers to cooperation (O'Brien and Williams 2010, p. 40).

Realists assume that regimes generate different benefits for states, and, thus, power is the focal point of regime formation and survival. They believe that all states seek to maximize their power to ensure their chances of survival, and, therefore, the states are sensitive to any decline or loss in their relative capabilities (Spiegel, Matthews, Taw and Williams, 2009, pp. 366–367). In regards to economic policy, realists treat it as a tool of power and also as the foundation of power politics, arguing that economic decisions should enhance a state's relative overall standing in the global arena, and ensure state's security and influence (Morgenthau 1948; Spiegel et al. 2009, p. 367). Finally, realists advocate for positive balances of trade, production over consumption, government interventions in the market, and protection of states' strategic resources in free trade.

Liberals, on the other hand, do not believe that trade is a zero-sum game; instead, they view it as a variable-sum game, which means that through cooperation all states can simultaneously and mutually benefit (Spiegel et al. 2009, p. 369). They offer four basic options for overcoming the problems of cheating and relative gains: reciprocity, international regimes, international law, and interdependence. This study focuses on international regimes, which, according to liberals, influence and change the costs and benefits of individual state actions. Precisely, regimes alter states' interests by reducing the attractiveness of cheating, as well as making the states willingly relinquish some degree of independent decision making in order to act in relation to established international norms (Spiegel et al. 2009, p. 371).

However, both approaches see states as rational and unitary actors, which are responsible for establishing regimes in order to promote international order. In this respect, the process-tracing procedure and congruence tests in this study will be applied to regime theories as the "least-likely" case in order to propose the alternative research questions such as:

1 Does Eurasian economic integration mean regression for the post-Soviet states into protectionism and state-regulated systems?
2 Will the creation of the new economic regime in Eurasia establish the general rules and norms of post-Soviet states' behavior to facilitate cooperation and promote trade in the region?

Case selection

George and Bennett consider the main criterion for case selection its relevance to the research objective of the study. They maintain that cases should be selected to provide the kind of control and variation required by the research problem. The latter requires the clear identification of subclass of events in order to select the cases (George and Bennett 2005, pp. 83–85). There are also important criticisms of potential flaws in case selection in studies with one or a few cases. However, George and Bennett argue that case study designs with no variance in the dependent variable do not represent a selection bias problem. Moreover, case study researchers narrow the scope of cases investigated in order to capture heterogeneous causal relations as they are careful in providing "circumscribed contingent generalizations" in order not to overgeneralize from their cases (George and Bennett 2005, p. 84). Accordingly, my decision to select the cases of Armenia, Azerbaijan, and Georgia as crucial cases in analyzing Russia's common patterns of external behavior over time is relevant to the research objective of this study.

Describing the variance in variables

George and Bennett contend that the way in which variance is described is crucial to the usefulness of case analyses in assessment of existing theories. They argue that the differentiation of types can apply to the characterization of independent as well as dependent variable (George and Bennett, pp. 84–85). In this regard, my independent variable, Russia's material power capabilities, is defined in neoclassical realist theory in terms of political, economic and technological resources and is measured in relative terms. The differentiation of the independent variable will help me to develop a more discriminating analysis of the effectiveness of Russia's material power capabilities and to identify some factors that favored or hindered the success of each variant. For instance, I expect to see that in periods where Russia's material power is very strong, Moscow's foreign policy goals will tend towards imperialism. It is also important to clarify that I use the creation of the Eurasian Economic Union to operationalize the relative power of Russia since, according to neoclassical realists, relative power is translated and operationalize into behavior of the state actors (Rose 1998, p. 164).

The dependent variable—Russia's foreign policies in the South Caucasus, varies in Armenia, Azerbaijan, and Georgia: 1) policy of neo-imperialism in Armenia; 2) soft coercion in Azerbaijan; and 3) coercive diplomacy in Georgia. Likewise, Russia's foreign policies interests and goals in the South Caucasus, I will operationalize as the degree to which they are status quo or revisionist.

The intervening variable in this study is described as state structure and leaders' perception of relative power. I identify state structure as either *weak* (decentralized) or *strong* (centralized) since, according to Zakaria, what matters in analyzing foreign policy of the state is state power, which he distinguishes from national power. "State power is that portion of national power the government can extract for its purposes and reflects the ease with which central decision makers can achieve their ends" (Zakaria 1998, p. 9). Likewise, I identify leaders' perception of relative power as either *low-level perception* or *high-level perception*. Moreover, leaders define the "national interests" and conduct foreign policies based upon their assessment of relative power and other countries intentions but this is always subject to domestic constraints, if any depending on states' structure (Lobell et al. 2009, pp. 25–26).

Formulation of data requirements and general questions

The specification of data requirements is an essential component of the method of structured, focused comparison, and will take the form of general questions to be asked of each case in this study (George and Bennett 2005, p. 86). The general questions in this study are reflecting the theoretical framework employed, thus, the collection of the data will satisfy the research objective of the study, and the type of contributions to theories that I intend to make:

1 Under what circumstances does Russia create new political and economic institutions to offset the perceived advantages of rival states?
2 Is Eurasian integration primarily a form of continental economic integration?
3 Will Russia's foreign policies towards the South Caucasian states change after the launch of the Eurasian Economic Union in 2015?

Accordingly, in order to understand Russia's foreign policies in the South Caucasus, I examined an appropriate body of material in order to illuminate the orientations of Russia's leaders towards the fundamental issues and history and politics that presumably influence their processing of information, policy preference, and final choice of foreign policy actions in the near abroad.

Notes

1 These two terms are used interchangeably in this study.
2 The idea behind the creation of Nabucco pipeline was at the heart of Europe's grand strategy to diversify its energy sources and receive gas supply from Azerbaijan bypassing Russia (Arakelyan and Kanet 2012).
3 According to neoclassical realist theory, unit-level variables (the extractive and mobilization capacity of politico–military institutions, the influence of domestic societal actors and interest groups, the degree of state autonomy from society, and the level of elite or societal cohesion) intervene between the leaders' assessment of international threats and opportunities and the actual diplomatic, military, and foreign economic policies those leader pursue (Lobell 2009, p. 4).
4 The Eurasian Union has a population of 182 million people and an aggregate gross domestic product of about $2 trillion. However, Russia accounts for the vast majority of those numbers: 143 million people and a $1.6 trillion GDP.
5 Hasenclever et al. classify international issue-areas by the dominant value being at issue (Hasenclever et al. 2000, p. 4).

Bibliography

Adamczyk, Arthur (2010) "The Role of Poland in the Creation Process of the Eastern Partnership," *Yearbook of Polish European Studies*. No. 13, pp. 195–204.

Ambrosio, Thomas (2009) *Authoritarian Backlash: Russian Resistance to Democratization in the Former Soviet Union*. Burlington, VA: Ashgate.

Arakelyan, Lilia A. and Roger E. Kanet (2012) "Russian Energy Policy in the South Caucasus," in Maria Raquel Freire and Roger E. Kanet (Eds.) *Russia and Its Near Neighbours*. Houndmills, UK: Palgrave Macmillan.

Arakelyan, Lilia A. (2014) "The Soviet Union is Dead: Long Live the Eurasian Union!," in Roger E. Kanet and Rémi Piet (Eds.) *Shifting Priorities in Russia's Foreign and Security Policy*. Aldershot, UK: Ashgate.

Asbarez (2016) "Armenia Gaining Strategic Significance in North-South Energy Corridor Construction." June 28. http://asbarez.com/152295/armenia-gaining-strategic-significance-in-north-south-energy-corridor-construction/ (accessed October 10, 2016).

Beach, Derek (2012) *Analyzing Foreign Policy*. Houndmills, UK: Palgrave Macmillan.

Bogaturov, Alexei (2003) "Mezhdunarodniy Poryadok v Nastupivshem Veke," *International Trends: Journal of Theory of International Relations and World Politics*. No.1, January–April, p. 12.

Dempsey, Judy (2013) "Victory for Russia As the EU's Nabucco Gas Project Collapses," *Carnegie Europe*. July 1.

Dragneva, Rilka and Katarina Wolczuk (2013) *Eurasian Economic Integration: Law, Policy and Politics*. Cheltenham, UK: Edward Elgar.

European Union Commission Report (2015) "Implementation of the European Neighbourhood Policy in Azerbaijan: Press in 2014, and Recommendations for Actions," March 25. http://europa.eu/rapid/press-release_MEMO-15-4688_en.htm (accessed May 18, 2015).

Evans, Peter B. (1995) *Embedded Autonomy: States and Industrial Transformation*. Princeton, NJ: Princeton University Press.

Gehring, Thomas (1992) *Dynamic International Regimes: Institutions for International Environmental Governance*. Frankfurt, Germany: Peter Lang.

George, Alexander L. and Andrew Bennett (2005) *Case Studies and Theory Development in the Social Sciences*. Cambridge, MA: MIT Press.

Gilpin, Robert (1981) *War and Change in World Politics*. Cambridge, UK: Cambridge University Press.

Glasser, Susann B. (2013) "The Law of Politics According to Sergei Lavrov. An Exclusive Interview with Russia's Top Diplomat," *Foreign Policy*. April 29. http://foreignpolicy.com/2013/04/29/the-law-of-politics-according-to-sergei-lavrov/

Gotev, Georgi (2015) "Russia Can Use Trans Adriatic Pipeline, Commission Confirms," *EurActiv.com*. March 6. www.euractiv.com/section/energy/news/russia-can-use-trans-adriatic-pipeline-commission-confirms/ (accessed October 10, 2016).

Haas, Ernst B. (1958) *The Uniting of Europe: Political, Social, and Economic Forces 1950–1957*. London, UK: Stevens.

Haas, Ernst B. (1990) *When Knowledge is Power: Three Models of Change in International Organizations*. Berkley, CA: University of California Press

Hasenclever, Andreas, Peter Mayer, and Volker Rittberger (2000) "Integrating Theories of International Regimes," *Review of International Studies*, Vol. 26, No. 1, pp. 3–33.

Haukkala, Hiski (2010) "Explaining Russian Reaction to the European Neighborhood Policy," in Richar G. Whitman and Stefan Worlff (Eds.) *The European Neighbourhood Policy in Perspective: Context, Implementation and Impact*. Houndmills, UK: Palgrave Macmillan.

Hersen, Michel and David H. Barlow (1976) *Single Case Experimental Designs: Strategies for Studying Behavior Change*. New York, NY: Pergamon Press.

Ivanov, Sergey (2006) "The New Russian Doctrine," *Wall Street Journal* (Europe), January 11.

Kanet, Roger E. (2010) "From Cooperation to Confrontation: Russia and the United States since 9/11," in Bertil Nygren, Bo Huldt, Patrik Ahlgren, Pekka Sivonen, and Susanna

Huldt (Eds.) *Russia on Our Minds: Russian Security Policy and Northern Europe*. Stockholm, Sweden: National Defense University.

Kitchen, Nicolas (2010) "Systemic Pressures and Domestic Ideas: A Neoclassical Realist Model of Grand Strategy Formation," *Review of International Studies*, Vol. 36, No. 1, pp. 117–143.

Koska, Martyna (2016) "Without Reforms Belarus's Economy Will Stagnate," *Central European Financial Observer*. March 18. www.financialobserver.eu/cse-and-cis/belarus/without-reforms-belaruss-economy-will-stagnate/ (accessed September 20, 2016).

Kucera, Joshua (2013) "Russia, Iran, Turkey, and the Caucasus," *EURASIANET.org*. March 22. www.eurasianet.org/node/66732 (accessed November 17, 2014).

Krasner, Stephen D. (1976) "State Power and the Structure of International Trade," *World Politics*, No. 28, pp. 317–347.

Krasner, Stephen D. (1983) *International Regimes*. Ithaca, NY: Cornell University Press.

Lobell, Steven E., Norrin M. Ripsman and Jeffrey W. Taliaferro (2009) *Neoclassical Realism, The State, and Foreign Policy*. Cambridge, UK: Cambridge University Press.

Lomagin, Nikita (2014) "Russia's CIS Policy and Economic and Political Transformations in Eurasia," in Roger E. Kanet and Remi Piet (Eds.) *Shifting Priorities in Russia's Foreign and Security Policy*. Aldershot, UK: Ashgate.

Lukyanov, Fyodor (2013) "Don't Expect Reset 2.0 During Obama's 2nd Term," *Russia in Global Affairs*. January 23.

Mansfield, E.D. and J. Snyder (2005) *Electing to Fight—Why Emerging Democracies Go to War*. Cambridge, MA: The MIT Press.

Medvedev, Dmitry (2008a) "Speech at Meeting with German Political, Parliamentary and Civic Leaders, Berlin." June 5. http://en.kremlin.ru/events/president/transcripts/320 (accessed June 10, 2014).

Medvedev, Dmitry (2008b) "Interview given by Dmitry Medvedev to Television Channels Channel One, Rossia, NTV." http://en.kremlin.ru/events/president/transcripts/48301 (accessed June 10, 2014).

Medvedev, Dmitry (2008c) "Dmitry Medvedev's Speech at World Policy Conference, Evian, France." October 8. http://en.kremlin.ru/events/president/transcripts/48308 (accessed June 10, 2014).

Meister, Stefan and Marie-Lena May (2009) "The EU's Eastern Partnership—A Misunderstood Offer of Cooperation," *DGAPstandpunkt*, No. 7, September.

Morgenthau, Hans J. (1948) *Politics Among Nations: The Struggle for Power and Peace*. New York, NY: Alfred A. Knopf.

Nygren, Bertil (2010) "Russia and the CIS Region: The Russian Regional Security Complex", in Maria Raquel Freire and Roger E. Kanet (Eds.) *Key Players and Regional Dynamics in Eurasia: The Return of the "Great Game"*. Houndmills, UK: Palgrave Macmillan.

O'Brien, Robert and Marc Williams (2010) *Global Political Economy: Evolution and Dynamics*. Houndmills, UK: Palgrave Macmillan.

Ostrow, Joel M., Georgiy A. Satarov, and Irina M. Khakamada (2007) *The Consolidation of Dictatorship in Russia*. Westport, CT: Praeger.

Popescu, Nicu (2014) *Eurasian Union: The Real, the Imaginary and the Likely*.Paris, France: EU Institute for Security Studies.

Reznik, Irina, Stephen Bierman, and Henry Meyer (2014) "State-Run Russian Oil Behemoth Rosneft Helps Vladimir Putin Tighten His Economic Grip," *The Washington Post*. February 7.

Rose, Gideon (1998) "Neoclassical Realism and Theories of Foreign Policy," *World Politics*, Vol. 51, No. 1, pp. 144–172.

Rukavishnikov, Vladimir (2014) "Understanding Putin's Foreign and Security Policy: Lessons from the Russian Transition," in Roger E. Kanet and Rémi Piet (Eds.) *Shifting Priorities in Russia's Foreign and Security Policy*. Aldershot, UK: Ashgate.

Rukhadze, Vasili (2016) "Russia's Soft Power in Georgia: How Does It Work?," *Eurasia Daily Monitor*, Vol. 13/34. February 19.

Schramm, Wilbur (1971) "Notes on Case Studies of Instructional Media Projects," Washington, DC: Working paper for Academy of Educational Development.

Schweller, Randall L. (2009) "Neoclassical Realism and State Mobilization: Expansionist Ideology in the Age of Mass Politics," in Steven E. Lobell, Norrin M. Ripsman and Jeffrey W. Taliaferro (Eds.) *Neoclassical Realism, The State, and Foreign Policy*. Cambridge, UK: Cambridge University Press.

Shevtsova, Lilia (2007) *Russia Lost in Transition: The Yeltsin and Putin Legacies*. Washington, DC: Carnegie Endowment for International Peace.

Spiegel, Steven, Elizabeth Matthews, Jennifer Morrison Taw and Kristen P. Williams (2009) *World Politics in a New Era*. New York, NY: Oxford University Press.

Stratfor (2016) "Why the Eurasian Union Will Never Be the EU." www.stratfor.com/analysis/why-eurasian-union-will-never-be-eu (accessed September 25, 2016).

Taliaferro, Jeffrey W. (2009) "Neoclassical Realism and Resource Extraction: State Building for Future War," in Steven E. Lobell, Norrin M. Ripsman and Jeffrey W. Taliaferro (Eds.) *Neoclassical Realism, The State, and Foreign Policy*. Cambridge, UK: Cambridge University Press.

Torbakov, Igor (2000) "Putin's Russia Defines its Foreign Policy Agenda," *EurasiaNet*. July 27. www.eurasianet.org/departments/insight/articles/eav072800.shtml (accessed June 10, 2014).

Trenin, Dmitri (1996) "Russia's Security Interests and Policies in the Caucasus Region," in Bruno Coppieters (Ed.) *Contested Borders in the Caucasus*. Brussels, Belgium: VUB University Press.

Van Herpen, Marcel H. (2014) *Putin's Wars: The Rise of Russia's New Imperialism*. Lanham, MD: Rowman & Littlefield Publishers.

Vinokurov, Evgeny (2007) "Russian Approaches to Integration in the Post-Soviet Space in the 2000s," in K. Malfliet, L. Verpoest and E. Vinokurov (Eds.) *The CIS, the EU and Russia: The Challenges of Integration*. New York, NY: Palgrave Macmillan.

Vinokurov, Evgeny and Alexander, Libman (2011) *Eurasian Integration: Challenges of Transcontinental Regionalism*. Houndmills, UK: Palgrave Macmillan.

Whitmore, Brian (2016) "The Daily Vertical: An Anniversary of a Warning (Transcript)," *Radio Free Europe Radion Liberty*. August 8. www.rferl.org/a/daily-vertical-georgia-anniversary-ukraine-puting-doctrine/27907372.html (accessed September 19, 2016).

Wohlforth, M, W. (1993) *The Elusive Balance: Power and Perceptions During the Cold War*. New York, NY: Cornell University Press.

Yin, Robert K. (2003) *Case Study Research: Design and Methods*. Thousand Oaks, CA: Sage.

Zakaria, Fareed (1998) *From Wealth to Power: The Unusual Origins of America's World Role*. Princeton, NJ: Princeton University Press.

Zakaria, Fareed (2014) "The Rise of Putinism," *The Washington Post*. July 31. www.washingtonpost.com/opinions/fareed-zakaria-the-rise-of-putinism/2014/07/31/2c9711d6-18e7-11e4-9e3b-7f2f110c6265_story.html (accessed November 17, 2014).

3 The perplexing power of Russia's relations with its neighbors

Destroy the old to build the old?

Robert Service has argued that "no Imperial power before the First World War was more reviled in Europe than the Russian Empire"[1] (Service 2005, p. 1). The last imperial power to rule Russia, the Romanov dynasty (1613–1917), was hated by generations of democrats both inside and outside Russia (Kennedy-Pipe 1998, p. 13). The early Romanovs began to limit the power of the boyars, and, in the meantime, strengthen the autocratic power of the tsar. The Romanovs' ruling also worsened the lot of a huge and oppressed class: Russian serfs. Once free peasants found themselves tied to their overlords by debt, moreover, the state eroded their rights and gave more powers to landlords. In fact, by the 1800s half of Russia's 40 million peasants were serfs, who became part of the landlord's property and whose status was hereditary (Daniels and Hyslop 2013, p. 208).

Although, this study focuses on Russia's foreign policy in the South Caucasus after the disintegration of the Soviet Union, I would like to stress here one important element of Russian foreign policy over the course of time: the continuity in behavior of governments headed by tsars, commissars, and presidents. In this regard, the call of the Bolsheviks in 1917 "to smash the old world and build a new one" never materialized in the foreign policy of the Soviet state over the seven decades and then of the Russian Federation after the collapse of the Soviet Union in 1991. Kennedy-Pipe argues that the foreign policy of the Soviet state had inherited many of its characteristics from the Tsarist Russian Empire: the tradition of autocracy, a suspicion of the West, and the tendency of the elite to view Russia's "natural" role of territorial expansion. One of the reasons for this kind of adherence to an imperial attitude in Russian foreign policy over the centuries is the fact that the different regimes may have changed the political system of the Russian government, but not its geographic position that was situated in the heart of the European continent and led to the shores of the Pacific and sought power in the east (Kennedy-Pipe 1998, p. 207). The location of Russia not only helped it to dominate the Eurasian landmass, but also made it vulnerable to outside invasion. Thus, the Bolsheviks eventually made the search for "secure borders" their primary mission. Furthermore, as some scholars have contended, the very notion of insecurity, due to geographic location, was not only a defining characteristic of both Russia and the Soviet Union but also contributed to the hostile relations between Moscow and other states.[2]

Russia has pursued balance-of-power policies throughout its history (with the exception of the 1939 Nazi–Soviet Pact or the Molotov–Ribbentrop Pact, which guaranteed that the two countries would not attack each other) like that any of great power in order to ensure its national interests and security by whatever means are available (Donaldson and Nogee 2009, p. 4). There are different means for the state to maintain the balance of power: forming or joining military alliances, military buildups, intervention in weaker countries, or the use of war (Morgenthau 1951). In this regard, Tsarist Russia was a member of the Triple Entente that also included Britain and France at the outbreak of World War I in order to counter-balance the Triple Alliance led by imperial Germany. Later, Tsarist Russia's successor state, the Soviet Union and its Eastern Bloc allies formed the Warsaw Pact in 1955 as a military counterpart to the North Atlantic Treaty Organization (Donaldson and Nogee 2009, p. 4). In the aftermath of the collapse of the Soviet Union in 1991, many scholars argue that "the balance of power has been replaced by an unbalanced unipolar order" (Dunne and Schmidt 2007). Non-realist theorists criticized what Kenneth Waltz called a "self-help system" explanation, central to structural realism, which predicts that the balance of power will be established by the states seeking to protect themselves against threats in an anarchical system (Waltz 1979, p. 118). In fact, Waltz claims that, in order to mitigate the consequences of the security dilemma, great powers will form coalitions with weaker states "to prevent anyone from winning the prize of power" (Waltz 1979, p. 126; Grieco 1988). This book adds to the existing literature on Russia's foreign policy by emphasizing the fact that the creation of the Eurasian Economic Union in 2015 should be considered as part of the Kremlin's desire for expansion and the possibility of creating a new center of power in post-Soviet space. It could also be considered as an empirical justification for the system-centric realism assumption that Russia (the major power in this case) is forming a new alliance to counterbalance the U.S., the EU, and China's rising influence in the former Soviet region.

There are prominent contributions among scholars who over the past half a dozen years have been engaged in a series of joint projects that are directly relevant to the broader aspects of the argument of this study, which examines Russian foreign and security policy after the disintegration of the Soviet Union. In this chapter I will first review their work in order to have a better understanding of Russian foreign policy in the South Caucasus and the shift in the Kremlin's external policy from its previous focus on relations with the West to its present focus on the creation of the Eurasian Union. While the main conclusion of these scholars studying Russian and post-Soviet foreign policy is that Vladimir Putin, in his third term as Russia's president, continues to pursue policies aimed at reestablishing Russia as the dominant power across Eurasia and as an influential actor in global affairs (Adomeit 2012; Fernandes 2014; Kanet 2014), others believe that at the core of Russian foreign policy is a sense of national inadequacy and a concern about honor that demands the recognition of Russia as a major world power (Tsygankov 2012).

Moreover, these political insecurities can lead to policy choices that in the West may seem counterproductive. In the same vein, Nikita Lomagin (2014) and Vladimir Rukavishnikov (2014) pointed out that the creation of the Eurasian Economic Union will help to further the regional integration in the post-Soviet space by shifting from the main trend in Russian foreign politics, geopolitics, to geo-economics with its emphasis on international economic cooperation (Rukavishnikov 2014, p. 118). Vladimir Rukavishnikov, moreover, argues that Mr. Putin's third term is associated with the domestic stability and gradual transformation in Russian foreign policy, and the open anti-Americanism in Russia is nothing else than a response to the "deep-seated cultural, economic and likely political and ideological differences between the United States and the Russian Federation" (Rukavishnikov 2014, p. 48).

This study outlines the argument of first group of scholars, who believe that president Putin's government pursues policies aimed at reestablishing Russia as a super power and playing a major role in world affairs. However, while some of these scholars have adopted a constructivist approach in their studies, this book applies the neoclassical realist approach, and argues that the scope and ambition of Russian's foreign policy is driven first and foremost by its relative material power. Consequently, this chapter will proceed to present the neoclassical realist assumptions in order to address the questions of what explains Russia's foreign policy in the South Caucasus and the relevance for that policy of the creation of the Eurasian Union. Next, this chapter will provide evidence in order to oppose the favored hypothesis that the creation of the Eurasian Union is just a logical step in furthering the regional integration process in post-Soviet space and has to do more with international economic cooperation than Russia's imperialistic tendencies. The regime theories will be introduced in order to show how various regimes have been created in the post-Soviet space, some of them within the framework of the Commonwealth of Independent States, others outside, and directed towards economic integration, but they all have demonstrated weak and ineffective institutional frameworks and lack of economic results (Dragneva and Wolczuk 2013, p. 2). Although the Eurasian Customs Union that was established in 2007 among Russia, Kazakhstan and Belarus has proved to be more credible in terms of integrative mechanism, in Dragneva and Wolczuk's views. It is also given that preexisting political and military alliances with a history of past cooperation is the main reason in attracting member states to engage in economic integration rather than seeking economically beneficial partners (Dragneva and Wolczuk 2013, p. 213). In other words, the creation of the Eurasian Union in 2015 encapsulated Moscow's imperialist ambitions in the near abroad and brought the former Soviet states back into the Kremlin's orbit. Otherwise, how can we explain the carrot-and-stick method that Russia has been using in forcing the possible candidates into the Moscow-led bloc? For instance, had Armenia chosen the Western direction instead of the Eurasian one, it would likely have shared the Ukrainian fate.

Finally, the chapter concludes by utilizing the neoclassical realist assumption that Russia will likely want more, rather than less, external influence, and will continue such influence to the extent that Moscow is able to do so. Moreover, the creation of the Eurasian Union helps Vladimir Putin to materialize his desire to reestablish Russia as a super power in world affairs. Arguably, Mr. Putin headed into 2017 on a strong note, thanks to Russia's ability to broker a cease-fire in Syria in 2016 that sidelined the Obama's administration, which also altered the dynamic of the Kremlin's involvement in other regions, especially Eastern Europe. First, Moscow's interventionism in the Middle East has enabled the Putin's government to become unavoidable in the region, and to prove to the world that Russia can protect the autocratic regimes under threat. Second, Moscow's Syrian victory had averted the world's attention from Ukraine, although the situation in the east of the country still remains unchanged. And, finally, the Kremlin's involvement in the Middle East has allowed Putin's administration to re-establish its damaged relations with Washington.[3] Thus, we shall conclude that Russia could not easily be contained in the multipolar world order, especially with the rise in the West of nationalists who hold a favorable view of Russian President, Vladimir Putin, and prefer better ties with Moscow.

The constructivist moment in Russian post-Soviet foreign policy

It is important to note that over the past half a dozen years a quite large and diverse group of scholars have been engaged in a series of joint efforts to analyze Russian foreign policy. For the purpose of this study, I will divide these scholars into two groups: the first one argues that Russia's foreign policy has undergone a major shift from its original pro-Western course taken by President Yeltsin and his first foreign minister Andrei Kozyrev in the early 1990s towards a Russia-as-a-great-power approach. The latter have been at the center of Russian policy since the late 1990s, when Vladimir Putin replaced Boris Yeltsin in the presidency (Kanet 2014, p. 2) The second group of scholars maintains that Russia's foreign policy is a so-called new civilizational discourse, which not only helps to shape Russia's domestics and international policies, but also to reestablish itself as a power capable of synthesizing the Western and Islamic influences (Tsygankov 2013a, p. 5). Moreover, Tsygankov, Rukavishnikov, Lomagin and others agree that Russian foreign policy became the reinterpretation of Russian identity with "rediscovery" of semi-Asiatic roots and Orthodox religious heritage that contradicts the individualistic and materialistic values of the Western world, and the demand that others (the West) recognize Russia as a great power, and respect its foreign policy choices as well as its interests not only in the near abroad but also across the globe (Tsygankov 2013a; Tsygankov 2013b; Rukavishnikov 2014; Lomagin 2014).

Nygren, for example, argues that, after the breakup of the USSR, all fifteen former Soviet states (FSU) adopted Western-like constitutions and hailed democracy and free-market economy as the standard model, although the former communist leaders continued to rule brand new independent countries (Nygren 2010, p. 13). Moreover, Boris Yeltsin even encouraged taking a Western orientation for the FSU, thus, Nygren considers these years as happy years for the West, which started to supply finances and technological knowledge to the post-Soviet region anticipating the final victory of democracy and free market reforms. After all, the United States already had the experience in creating the Bretton Wood system in Western Europe with the apparent triumph of the neo-liberal globalized world. However, there were quite a few obstacles to the next victory of capitalism in the East: the geographical structure of the USSR with its politically rather than ethnically-based borders; then the *nomenklatura* people of Soviet times who used free market reforms to enrich themselves; and finally, the outbreak of ethnic conflicts in many FSU states (including in Nagorno-Karabakh, Abkhazia, and South Ossetia in the South Caucasus). Gradually, the Russian economy and society deviated from the Western course into its own history to find its own place under the sun (Nygren 2010, p. 14).

On the other hand, there had been quite a few objective difficulties in the process of transformation that Russia faced in the 1990s since "no one had democratized an imperial superpower with messianic pretensions" (Shevtsova 2007, pp. 8–9). Yeltsin and his team were obliged to carry out simultaneously four revolutions: creating a free market; democratizing the political regime; liquidating an empire; and seeking a new geopolitical role for a former nuclear superpower. While the industrially developed countries had passed through the phases of nation building, developing capitalism and political democratization in sequence, Russia had to achieve all three phrases at once. It is also important to note that whereas all successful post-communist changes started with the creation of a new political regime, Russia instead started with the privatization of property before establishing independent political institutions. Shevstova maintains that Russia was out of luck, not only in terms of its history and systemic constraints, but also in regards to the leadership factor and the role of the political elite (Shevstova 2007, p. 9).

When Boris Yeltsin suddenly announced his resignation (even though his term of office had not yet expired) and introduced his chosen successor, the prime minister, and now acting president, Vladimir Putin, his announcement initially appeared enigmatic. It was only later, when Putin issued a *ukaz* (a decree) granting Yeltsin immunity from prosecution, it became clear that Yeltsin's departure was linked directly to the corruption scandal that had been developing around him and his two daughters (Holmes 2001, p. 1). Preceding Yeltsin's departure, the economic situation of Russia was difficult: Yeltsin already attracted suspicion that his administration was corrupt, including his daughter Tatyana Dyachenko, and his main financial supporter, Boris Berezovsky. Thus, the failure of government officials to deal with lawlessness and cheating, and their apparent involvement in them, created a deep distrust of politics and administration in Russian society during the transition time (Lovell 2001, p. 35). Lovell also observes that the transition from communism is never an easy task, since it does not mean the immediate end of all the problems that citizens of the communist system experienced before. Moreover, while the formal institutions of democracy have been established, the attitudes and values of political and economic elites and even citizens of themselves are trying to adapt to their requirements (Lovell 2001, p. 36). Therefore,

Lovell like other scholars mentioned above, provides a constructivist explanation of the failure of democracy not only in Russia but in many other post-Soviet states:

> The notion that cultural development lags behind structural change has long been accepted; it is even basic to the early policies of most revolutionary regimes, which try to escape quickly from the drag of the past by changing personnel and eliminating opponents. The problem in postcommunist states, therefore, is a subset of a larger question about political institutions, and what makes them work the way they do. How can the democratic institutions established in postcommunism become strong and effective? Part of the answer can undoubtedly be found in the design of the institutions themselves . . . A significant part of the answer can also be found in changing the culture within which these institutions operate.
>
> (Lovell 2001, p. 36)

As we can see, the first group of scholars provided an accurate analysis of the failure of democracy in Russia as well as in the post-Soviet states and saw the problem not only in political and economic institutions or their absence, but also in the culture of the post-Soviet countries. Nevertheless, many Western politicians and scholars assumed that there was a possibility of changing the culture, the so-called "homo sovieticus" ideology and establishing a neoliberal or Western values in the post-Soviet space. These illusions faded away almost two decades later, when President Vladimir Putin was able to shape a doctrine mobilizing the entire Russian society against a perceived Western "decadence" and to reduce Washington's influence in the FSU states. While Vladimir Putin would become an enigma to the world, the man who would be hated and feared by the West due to his zealous attempts to reestablish Russia as a resurrected great power, in the beginning of his first term, only few people within the Russian state and overseas have come to realize the influential role that the new elected president would play in shaping Russia's domestic and foreign politics.

As Politkovskaya noted, Vladimir Putin first emerged as a possible head of state rather than an unpopular director of the universally detested FSB (Federal Security Bureau), but even after becoming the president of Russia, Putin, a product of the country's intelligence service, continued to act like a KGB officer rather than a head of the country (Politkovskaya 2004, pp. 1–2).[4] However, at the time when there had been the attack by Chechen separatists in Dagestan and the bombing of apartment blocks in Moscow, Volgodonsk and Buinaksk, which resulted in the deaths of hundreds of Russian citizens, Putin became the most favored leader in Russia—an intelligence officer, who promised to "wet Chechens in the outhouse." Marvin Perry, Matthew Berg and James Krukones (2010) provide the following assessment of Putin's legacy in public office: "Vladimir Putin is one of the central figures of our times, the man who presided at the Kremlin as the broken remains of sprawling nation were restore to life, and who used his stature to reorder the Russian-speaking world's relation with the West and become the de facto spokesman of the strongmen everywhere" (Perry, Berg, and Krukones 2010, p. 469).

Shevtsova (2007) writes that Putin "was the right man, in the right place, at the right time" (Shevtsova 2007, p. 38). She describes Putin's regime as a system of government under which power is concentrated in the hands of a leader who relies on the bureaucracy, security forces, and big business, what some authors refer to as a "network state"—a system of government and private networks that control the economic and political system (Shevtsova 2007, p. 41; Kononenko and Moshes 2011). In other words, Putin undertook the recentralization of power secured by the immense support of Russian population, desperate for the new leadership after Boris Yeltsin's controversial presidency. Moreover, Putin also provided the long-anticipated stability in post-Soviet Russia thanks to high oil prices. Shevtsova believes that it was evident that at least in the beginning of his term, Vladimir Vladimirovich had a sense of mission: in 2000–2001 he introduced a package of new measures that included land reform, the introduction of a 13 percent income tax, deregulation of the economy, and administrative reform (Shevtsova 2007, p. 45). His government also started the reform of the armed forces, the pension system, Gazprom, the railway, the Unified Energy System of Russia and local governments. However, his main goal was not only to make Russia a competitive state respected by the rest of the world, but also to restore governability, which in Putin's mind meant control. But having gained control of the country, Putin began to doubt the wisdom of reforming it, since reform undermines control. Thus, an iron law of autocracy began to operate in Russia, which led to centralization of all resources (Shevtsova 2007, pp. 44–45). This is the basis for my supposition that the scope and ambition of Russia's foreign policy in the South Caucasus is driven by its place in the international system and specifically by its relative material power capabilities. In order to determine the veracity of such an assertion, I will look at the neoclassical realist argument, which maintains that relative material power constitutes the basic parameters of a country's foreign policy, allowing "the strong do what they can and the weak suffer what they must" (Thucydides 2010). The neoclassical realist approach will help me to provide a better explanation for Russia's foreign policy in Transcaucasia and the creation of the Eurasian bloc as the main instrument in reestablishing the Kremlin's position as a regional hegemon. But before that I will introduce the second group of scholars who argue that Russia is reestablishing its influence in Eurasia and around the globe and should be treated as a super power with all the respect.

"Am I a trembling creature, or do I have the right?"

Maria Raquel Freire (2010) claims that Russian foreign policy in the post-Soviet space has evolved from introspection to projection, and from ideology to pragmatism (Freire 2010, p. 56). It has been widely argued that under Boris Yeltsin's presidency, Russia "abandoned" the former Soviet republics in order to join the "civilized world" itself (Wright, Goldenberg, and Schofield 1996; Trenin 1996; Herzig 1999; Freire 2010 and others). Moreover, Trenin (1996) maintains that "1991 marked a watershed in Russia's perceptions of her own identity and interests," and that "in its desire to 'dump' the other Soviet republics, the Russian political elite consciously precipitated the collapse of the USSR" (Trenin 1996, p. 93). The "bright and secured future" for Russia was projected by its political elite within NATO and the European Community, while the Eurasian continent was torn apart by ethnic conflicts and appeared very unpleasant and dangerous at the time. As Trenin continues, the willingness to withdraw from the areas of conflict, especially in the Caucasus, was very strong among Russian political leadership (Trenin 1996, p. 93). Freire notes that from 1993 Moscow changed its strategy in an attempt to reestablish Russia's position in the former Soviet republics, and stated the former Soviet space as being of vital importance for both to the East and West in so-called a multi-vectoral formula (Freire 2010, p. 56).

Ambrosio (2005) insists that the initial foreign policy strategy of Andrei Kozyrev, the first Foreign Minister of Russia under President Boris Yeltsin, the so-called Kozyrev doctrine, sought an extremely close relationship with the West, especially the United States. But when Russia and the United States found themselves at odds over strategic international issues (the war in Bosnia, expansion of NATO and America's desire for unilateral use of force), the close partnership offered in 1992 was off the table as "the bandwagoner slid into the role of an emerging balancer" (Ambrosio 2005, p. 2). Thus, from the late 1990s to 2001, Russia began openly to discuss the need to form a coalition to balance the United States. Ambrosio relates this shift (balancing versus bandwagoning) in Russia's foreign policy to two contradictory aspects of the post-Soviet Russian state: Russian national identity that had been inherently connected to its great power status and the notion that it should play a critical role in shaping the international system, and Russia's persistent weakness relative to the United States (Ambrosio 2005, pp. 2–5). This study supports the argument that the Primakov doctrine with its emphasis on the CIS as the key to Russian security interest was furthered during the presidencies of Vladimir Putin and Dimitri Medvedev, and culminated in the idea of the creation of the Eurasian Union as the main tool not only to secure Russia's hegemonic role in the post-Soviet space but also to challenge the presence of other players in the region—the United States, EU, Turkey, Iran, and China.

However, Lomagin (2014) sees the creation of the Eurasian Union as the first truly supranational institution in the region's 20 years of post-Soviet reintegration attempts (Lomagin 2014, p. 115). He argues that after having accumulated a great amount of "soft power" in the beginning of his presidency, Putin has simulated an intensive process of economic and political reintegration in the post-Soviet space (Lomagin 2014, p. 117). It is quite contradictory to categorize Putin's power as soft,[5] while it is a widely-known fact that Russia's president used the command-and-control approach to force the former Soviet states, among them Armenia, Azerbaijan, Georgia, Moldova, and Ukraine to join the Russian-led Customs Union. While the Ukrainian opposition to Putin's "offer" turned into the annexation of Crimea and ongoing civil war in the east and south of Russian-speaking regions of the country; Azerbaijan, Georgia and Moldova were able to withstand the Moscow's pressure, and only Armenia's President, Serzh Sargisyan, rejected to initial the Association Agreement with the EU negotiated earlier, opting instead to retain and deepen country's political and economic ties with the Kremlin. As

Hamlet Khachaturian (2013) states, Vladimir Putin visited Armenia immediately after the EU Eastern Partnership summit in Vilnius that was held on November 28–29 of 2013, and since Russia's President started his visit not in Armenia's capital, Yerevan, but in Gyumri, the location of Russian military base no.102, it was a clear signal to the neighboring countries, Georgia, Turkey, Azerbaijan and Iran that Russia is not giving up its military presence in the region (Khachaturian 2013). Vladimir Putin promised to his Armenian counterpart in Yerevan during his third visit to Armenia since he took the office in 2000: "As for the South Caucasus, we never planned to leave the region. Russia's position here will be strengthened," writes *Georgia Today*'s reporter, Zaza Jgharkava (Jgharkava 2013). The latter also elaborates that, since Armenia already rejected its European opportunity by joining the Customs Union and Azerbaijan is not interested in the tax free trade relations with Europe, Georgia and its European allies are the only recipients of Putin's message.

As a side note, Joseph Nye (2013) writes in his article "What Russia and China Don't Get About Soft Power" that much of America's soft power is produced by civil societies, not from the government. Moreover, the United States is able to preserve a degree of soft power because of its critical and uncensored civil society, even when government actions (for instance, the invasion in Iraq) are undermining. Nye argues in his article that Russia and China make the mistake of thinking that government is the main instrument of soft power, and the development of soft power need not to be a zero-sum game.

In this regard, while Nikita Lomagin makes an accurate observation that Russia's economic rationale for its activism in post-Soviet space is based on the country's competitiveness in the region in opposition to developed states' markets, the author also articulates that "the Eurasian Union would be based on universal integration principles as an essential part of a Greater Europe, united by shared values of freedom, democracy, and market laws" (Lomagin 2014, p. 135). First, it is important to note that Putin has countless times emphasized the idea that Russia is not a European state, but a Eurasian one with its distinguished set of traditional values: national, cultural, religious, and even sexual that contradicts Western liberal values. In his 2013 Presidential Address to the Federal Assembly, Vladimir Putin stated:

> Today, many nations are revising their moral values and ethical norms, eroding ethnic traditions and differences between peoples and cultures. Society is now required not only to recognize everyone's right to the freedom of consciousness, political views and privacy, but also to accept without question the equality of good and evil, strange as it seems, concepts that are opposite in meaning. This destruction of traditional values from above not only leads to negative consequences for society, but is also essentially anti-democratic, since it is carried out on the basis of abstract, speculative ideas, contrary to the will of the majority, which does not accept the changes occurring or the proposed revision of values.
>
> (Putin 2013)

Consequently, Putin once again emphasized that Russia is a conservative country in comparison with the post-modern West, by incorporating the view of the Russian Orthodox Church, which criticizes the Western world for "accepting the equality of good and evil" (Rahr 2013). Moreover, while the EU criticized the Russian head of state for his alleged discrimination of sexual minorities, Putin made it clear in his 2013 Presidential speech that his country will not adopt laws that are "unacceptable for Russian society" (Putin 2013). Concomitantly, Putin indicated the main threats to Russia, when speaking about strengthening the armed forces and the defense industry: the primary cause for his concern is the American hegemony that leads, according to him, to a new arms race (Putin 2013). Rukavishnikov (2014) argues that Vladimir Putin has repeatedly stressed the fact that the weak lose in the world of today (Rukavishnikov 2014, p. 40). Thus, Rukavishnikov suggests that by the end of Putin's current term as president, the Russian leader is planning to have a small, mobile, professional and well-armed military force loyal to the President and state officials. The evolving structure of military control, according to Rukavishnikov, can indicate only one thing—Russia is moving away from a Western-style democracy (Rukavishnikov 2014, p. 40–41). Unfortunately, the author failed to clarify what is on the horizon for Russia. I suggest that Russia is on its way to become a totalitarian state. How then can we explain the abolition of all institutions in Russia except only those authorized by the ruling regime?

Nevertheless, Rukavishnikov echoes Lukyanov (2013), Tsygankov (2014), and Lomagin's (2014) arguments that Putin "had certain reasons for expressing a deep disillusionment with the West because of his failed attempts at establishing truly collaborative relations with the USA" (Rukavishnikov 2014, p. 41). For instance, Andrei Tsygankov (2014) sees the current rise of Russian nationalism as a reflective nationalist reaction to what the Kremlin considers as unjust treatment by the West. According to Tsygankov, "nationalism in Russia has been a potent force but it would not have become as influential without the Ukrainian revolution and the Western support" (Tsygankov 2014).

This is a common tactic used by some scholars and analysts in general, to blame the West in Putin's authoritarian regime, and particularly to justify his actions in Ukraine. For instance, Fyodor Lukyanov, the editor in chief of *Russia in Global Affairs*, and the Chairman of Presidium of the Council on Foreign and Defence Policy, published on February 14, 2014 that "the success of the reset between Russia and the United States was due in large part to the US decision to stop actively promoting democracy and human right in Russia." However, none of these scholars took into consideration that Russian officials made a conscious choice to stray away from democratic development. As Ambrosio (2005) states, the Kremlin went from bandwagoning the United States (1992–1993), to balancing (1995–2001), to bandwagoning again (2001–2002), and again to balancing (2002–present) in its policy (Ambrosio 2005, p. 171). Ambrosio makes a point that the Russian Federation that emerged in December 1991 is dwarfed by the United States in terms of economics, political stability, military might, and its ability to project power (Ambrosio 2005, p. 5). As Lomagin writes, the year of 2003 was a turning point in the internal and external policy of Russia, when enormous revenues of petrodollars caused Moscow to turn against the idea of a "strategic partnership" with the West (Lomagin 2014, p. 121).

Neoclassical realism

Lobell, Ripsman and Taliaferro argue that neoclassical realism identifies state as the most important actors in international politics and presents a "top-down" conception of the states. The latter means that systemic forces ultimately drive external behavior of the state, and that the states are epitomized by a national security executive, comprised of the head of government and the ministers and officials charged with making foreign security policy (Lobell, Ripsman and Taliaferro 2009, pp. 25–26). The authors continue that this executive have access to privileged information from the state's politico–military apparatus and is best equipped to perceive systemic constraints and deduce the national interest. The executive also bargains with domestic actors (such as the legislature, political parties, economic sectors, classes or the public as a whole) to ratify policy and extract resources for its policy choices (Lobell et al.2009, p. 25). Lobell and colleagues stress the fact that in contrast to liberalism and Marxism, neoclassical realism does not see states as simply mingling the demands of different societal interest groups or economic classes. The main decision makers in the neoclassical realist approach are leaders who define the "national interests" and conduct foreign policy based upon their assessment of relative power and other states' intentions (Lobell et al. 2009, p. 26).

The three different visions of Russian foreign policy emerged upon the collapse of the Soviet Union: the imperialists; the neo-Slavophiles; and the Atlanticists. The imperialists and the neo-Slavophiles disagreed with the Atlanticists over Russia's policies towards the West, since neither trusted the West and both saw westernization as alien and dangerous to Russian culture (Ambrosio 2005, p. 32). However, while they were both concerned with Russia's soul, the imperialists were more interested in geopolitical factors (desirability of Soviet reintegration, which has to be limited to Slavic republics) but not in form of isolation and Russification of the state (as Slavophiles suggested) but rather through a foreign policy of balancing. For instance, Gennady Zyuganov, Russian Communist party leader, emphasized a more defensive policy against Western hegemony and proposed to foster an increase in Russia's power through the (voluntary) reintegration of parts of the former Soviet Union (Ambrosio 2005, p. 33–34). In the same vein, Andrew Kuchins and Igor Zavelev (2012) identify three major perspectives concerning main global trends and how Russian foreign policy should be formed: 1) pro-Western liberals support major reforms of Russia's political system based on Western market democratization model and advocate for close ties with the United States and Europe; 2) the great power balancers advocate a multi-vectored Russian foreign policy that is not closely tied to Russia's economic and political development; and 3) nationalists tend to ascribe a special mission for Russia in international relations that calls for more integration (if not domination) of its former Soviet neighbors (Kuchins and Zavelev 2012, p. 148).

Dmitri Trenin (1996) writes that in 1991, during the Yeltsin presidency, Russia's security was no longer associated with global or regional balances of power but with the idea of belonging to a group of democratic countries (Trenin 1996, p. 93). Therefore, the leaders of the Russian Federation considered joining NATO and the European Community as the prime national security interest rather than restore the Soviet Union. Consequently, the willingness to cut the ties with the former Soviet states and withdraw, especially from the Caucasus, as Trenin points out, was very strong and was backed by the Russian people. However, the initially pro-democratic and pro-Western agenda was dismissed as inadequate and raw geopolitics was rediscovered in 1991, according to Trenin. The latter notes that the military doctrine, adopted in November 1993, contained more assertive attitude towards near abroad, including the Caucasus (Trenin 1996, pp. 94–95). Nicole Jackson (2003), on the other hand, argues that when it was first adopted, the 1993 military doctrine was viewed as highly aggressive since it justified future military dominance over the CIS states. However, according to Jackson, many Russian politicians and scholars (Dmitri Trenin, Andrei Zagorsky, Irina Zviagelskaya and others) have come to understand the doctrine more as a political statement rather than a concrete set of guidelines for the Russian military (Jackson 2003, p. 66).

Nevertheless, Trenin also maintains in his chapter "Russia's Security Interests and Policies in the Caucasus Region" that Arkady Volsky, the former Soviet chief administrator in Nagorno-Karabakh and leader of the Civic Union, was arguing in 1992 that the geopolitical realities in Transcaucasia have remained the same since the nineteenth century, and it would be not only impossible but also naïve for the Russians to withdraw from the Caucasus at the time of conflict (Trenin 1996, p. 94). This leads us to another focal point of neoclassical realist analysis, which holds that power analysis must also examine the strength and structure of states relative to their societies, since these factors impact the proportion of national resources that can be allocated to foreign policy. Torbakov (2000), for instance, argues that after assuming political power, the Putin administration benefited from the rise in oil prices, and Russia became stronger not only economically but also politically. As a result, in order to advance its foreign policy, Putin tried to resolve domestic challenges. First, he was able to deliver the basics of effective governance in terms of improving the health care and welfare policies, and providing the family support to prevent the demographic crisis in Russia. Second, using Russia's material power capabilities, he established Russia's position vis-à-vis the former Soviet states, including the South Caucasus.

In this regard, Randall Schweller (2009) claims that a neoclassical realist approach to foreign expansion provides critical elements that are missing in structural realism. He argues that "in the modern area, expansion requires a unified state composed of 1) elites that agree on an ambitious grand strategy; 2) a stable and effective political regime with broad authority to pursue uncertain and risky foreign policies; and 3) a compliant mass public that unreservedly supports the state's expansionist policies and its willing to make the necessary sacrifices asked of it to implement the strategy" (Schweller 2009, p. 247). From this analysis, we can presuppose that Putin's expansionist policy in near abroad is based on all three requirements that Scheweller considers as critical elements for a foreign expansion approach in the modern age: supportive elites; a stable and effective political regime that is risk-taking enough to pursue uncertain foreign policies; and mass public support that backs up the state's expansionist policies and is willing to make the necessary sacrifices to implement his strategy. Furthermore, Putin's unification project provided the ideological content that aroused the minds of average people around Eurasia. It also sought to maximize Russia's power at everyone else's expense.

International regime theories

Yin argues that there are three general analytic strategies that will help the researcher to treat the evidence fairly, produce compelling analytic conclusions, and rule out alternative explanations (Yin 2003, p. 111). While the first one is to follow the theoretical propositions (in this study a neoclassical realist interpretations of Moscow's foreign policy in the South Caucasus) that led to your case study; the second strategy is to define and test alternative explanations. Power-based (realist) and interest-based (liberal) theories of international regimes are treated in this book as alternative explanations to the case of Russia's foreign policies in Armenia, Azerbaijan, and Georgia. While I am testing the regime theories' explanations of my case studies in Chapter 5, this section challenges the existing literature on realist and neoliberal institutionalist variants of regime theories that neglect the security externalities of economic cooperation as well as the peculiarity of Eurasian integration after the end of the Cold War.

The Eurasian Economic Union agreement, which came into force on January 1, 2015, was signed by the leaders of Russia, Belarus and Kazakhstan in the Kazakh capital of Astana on May 29, 2014. According to Nikolas Gvozdev (2014) Alexander Panin (2014) and Abigail Hauslohner (2014), the assessment of many Western analysts has been predictably negative since many decried the Putin's effort to integrate the four (for now) of the former Soviet republics into the economic and political bloc as an attempt to provide Eastern counterweight to economic and political powerhouses such as the European Union and the United States. Furthermore, Panin observes that Russia's gain in entering the union that will combine the previous agreements reached between the three countries under the Customs Union (2010) and the Single Economic Space (2011) is more political rather than economic. He elaborates that Russia is still smarting from the recent failure of its attempts to draw Ukraine in the Customs Union. In the meantime, Panin also claims that Belarus and Kazakhstan are pursuing their own economic interests rather than seeking any attempt to form the super-state between Europe and Asia (Panin 2014). Furthermore, the author makes a point that Russia is likely to draw more member-states to the new bloc by transferring resources to them in the form of reduced prices for gas and oil. For instance, Armenia, which was set to enter a free-trade deal with the EU, was offered gas in 2014 at the price paid by

Belarus (about $170–$180 per 1,800 cubic meters), and changed its mind.[6] Richard Giragosian (2013) states several significant strategic concerns that Armenia will face by changing its external policy preferences, among them: a demonstration of the fundamental flaws in Armenia's closed decision-making process, given the lack of planning for such a policy shift, and the absence of analysis or assessment of its implication. I will return to Giragosian's assessment of Armenia's policy shift later by showing that indeed Yerevan and Moscow did not take into consideration the geopolitical challenges to Armenia's entry to the Eurasian Union, which only can be explained by the lack of skillful and sensitive management that in Julian Cooper's (2013) view does any integration project require.

For his part, Cooper suggests that the Kremlin should learn to behave as a more equal actor in a multilateral environment, which is already not the case given the pressure that Russia have placed on perspective member states to join the Customs Union in 2013–2014 (Cooper 2013). In the same vein, Carol Matlack (2014) notes that Moscow's motive behind the creation of the Eurasian Union appears to be more political than economic since Russia will account for more than 80 percent of the bloc's GDP and a similar share of its roughly 178 million populations. Nikolay Petrov, a scholar at the Carnegie Moscow Center, argues that the Eurasian Union is nothing else than Putin's geopolitical dream, and a demonstration that Russia is not alone in the international arena (Matlack 2014). While the motivation of the member states for joining the Eurasian Union is strong, there are serious obstacles to overcome yet. First, as Igor Shuvalov, Russian First Deputy Prime Minister, announced in Sochi on June 24, 2014, after the Eurasian Economic Union meeting, Armenia's accession to this bloc entails talks on compensation for its World Trade Organization (WTO) partners. Second, Kazakhstan president, Nursultan Nazarbaev, made it clear during the May 29 meeting of the Supreme Eurasian Economic Council that Armenia should join the Customs Union without Nagorno-Karabakh, citing a letter addressed by Azerbaijani president Ilham Aliev to all three leaders of the current Customs Union. As a result, Serzh Sargsyan has accepted Vladimir Putin's "Eurasian Union without Karabakh bill," which can be considered as a great political and diplomatic achievement for Azerbaijan, especially taking into account that Baku was able to exercise its power over the countries in question without being officially a member state of a new Eurasian bloc. Finally, Nursultan Nazarbaev also invited Turkey[7] to join the Eurasian Union, thus disregarding the thorny issues still extent between Turkey and Armenia.

Eurasian integration vs. European Union-style integration

It has been argued that the creation of the Eurasian integration theoretically followed the logic of the European economic integration, which emerged from the pressure to avoid conflicts and wars between the neighboring states (Tchakarova 2014, p. 202). Furthermore, Tchakarova (2014) suggests that we can consider the theoretical foundations of the European economic integration model as a reference point for the analytical explanation of the establishment of the Eurasian Union (Tchakarova 2014, p. 203). The architectures of the Eurasian economic integration, Vladimir Putin and Nursultan Nazarbaev, also claim that the regional integration in the post-Soviet space is based on security considerations and cross-borders risks as it was in the case of integration processes in Western Europe in the late 1940s (Eurasian Economic Commission 2014). This study shows in Chapters 4 and 5 that the foundation of the Eurasian Economic Union is not based on the economic considerations from the theoretical approach of European Economic integration despite all the claims of the leaders of Belarus, Kazakhstan and Russia, the founding members of the EEU, but rather on Russia's geopolitical concerns. Below, I am providing a brief analysis of the theoretical background of the European economic integration that took place in the second half of the twentieth century.

The history of European integration reflects the tensions between the role of supranational organizations and the power and the interests of national governments, which reflects the dichotomy of the two most prominent political theories about European integration: (neo) functionalism and intergovernmentalism (Spolaore 2013). Ernst Haas's seminal work "The Uniting of Europe" (1958) presented a starting point of an institutionalist theory of organizational evolution and change that was drawn on David Mitrany's functional approach to peace (Haas 1958; Mitrany 1966). At the time, Mitrany's functional theory focused on those areas of interstate activity that were less controversial: economy and technology. He maintained that an interdependent community of nations could be united through cooperation on economic and technical levels. Thus, according to Mitrany: "while functional neutrality is possible, political neutrality is not." Haas's neofunctionalist theory sought to explain the political regional integration process that emerged in Western Europe after World War II as well as to challenge the realist accounts of inter-state cooperation. In this regard, regional integration in Western Europe was recognized as a process where states entered *voluntarily* into arrangements with their neighbors to create new forms of engagements and new techniques to resolve conflicts between one another.

Burfisher, Robinson, and Thierfelder (2004) write that the world economy after World War II has become much more integrated with the establishment of the European Economic Community (EEC) in 1958 and its evolution into the European Union by the treaty of Maastricht in 1992 (Burfisher, Robinson, and Thierfelder 2004, p. 2). In the 1950s, the European Coal and Steal Communities united the European countries economically and politically to secure lasting peace. According to Fraser Cameron, historical reconciliation was a crucial element in developing the necessary political will for cooperation, and, ultimately, for integration. In other words, the ultimate for the success of the EU was a historical reconciliation between France and Germany that was achieved by years of sustained political effort from the both government officials (Cameron 2010).

On the contrary, there has been no such effort in Eurasia with its proclaimed ambitions of regional integration. For instance, there can be no integration without genuine reconciliation between Russia and Georgia, Armenia and Azerbaijan, Georgia and Abkhazia, Georgia and South Ossetia, Azerbaijan and Nagorno-Karabakh, and Russia and Ukraine.

Meanwhile, European intergovernmentalists believe that national governments are in charge of the decision making processes in Western Europe by using supranational institutions to purse their goals. For instance, Moravcsik (1993, 1998) is a vocal proponent of this approach, claiming that national governments have created European institutions to ensure the economic interests of their local supporters. While the political–economic theory of regional integration is well taken among the economists as well as international studies scholars, I will focus on a neofunctionalist theory in order to show the difference between the European economic integration and the Eurasian integration. Neofunctionalists advanced spill over as a driving force in furthering the integrative process in Western Europe. They shifted their attention from national leaders towards technocratic elites, politicians, and supranational interest groups. In Haas's own words: "political integration is the process whereby political actors in several distinct national settings are persuaded to shift their loyalties, expectations and political activities to a new centre, whose institutions poses or demand jurisdiction over pre-existing national states, the end result is a new political community, superimposed over the existing ones" (Haas 1958, p. 16). While I am analyzing in detail the structure of the Eurasian Union in Chapter 5, I would like to note here that all the evidence collected for this book points to the fact that Russia will not in any way give up their sovereignty or independence to the supranational body of the Eurasian Union.

Meanwhile, some observers fear that regional economic institutions—such as the European Union (EU), the North America Free Trade Agreement (NAFTA), Mercosur, and Asia–Pacific Economic Cooperation (APEC) will erode the multilateral system that has been established after the World War II, leading to protectionism and conflict (Mansfield and Milner 1999, p. 589). Mansfield and Milner point out that economic studies place little emphasize on the political conditions that shape regionalism. The authors claim that studies that focus on international politics, emphasizing how power relations and multilateral institutions affect the formation of regional institutions, the particular states composing them and their welfare implications, provide key insights into regionalism's causes and consequences (Mansfield and Milner 1999, p. 590). In this regard, Mansfield and Milner argue that the decision to form a PTA rests partly on the preferences and political power of various segments of society, the interests of state leaders, and the nature of domestic institutions. Additionally, states do not make a decision to form or enter a regional bloc in an international political vacuum; they take into consideration interstate power and security relations as well as multilateral institutions (Mansfield and Milner 1999, p. 608).

The evidence that I have collected challenges this line of argumentation. While the original purpose of the Eurasian Union was to become a dominant economic organization, the recent events in Ukraine support my proposition that Vladimir Putin attempts to shift the Eurasian Economic Union into another vehicle of Russia's neo-imperialist politics in the post-Soviet space. Andrey Suzdalzev at the Moscow Business School states that Russia cannot be a great power without its own rapidly developed integration group (Suzdalzev 2014). According to analysts, Russia adopted the idea of the Eurasian Union for three main reasons: 1) Vladimir Putin wanted to create his own economic pole that would raise Russia to the status of the major global trading powers such as the European Union, United States, and China; 2) this bloc would secure Moscow's influence over the economic developments of the former Soviet republics, particularly in Central Asia, to counterweight the Western and Chinese economic domination; and 3) the Eurasian Union would become a physical manifestation of Putin's ideology that Russia and the Eurasian region represent the anti-West, a bastion of more conservative, traditional and religious values opposed to aspects of Western culture (MacFarquhar 2014).

Another useful approach of international regime theories is Little's (2006) division of realist and liberalist schools of thought in the field. The liberal institutionalists hold that regimes can promote the common good, globalization and a liberal world order under the supervision of a benign hegemon. Whereas realists argue that regimes generate different benefits for states, and thus, power is the focal point of regime formation and survival (Little 2006, p. 370). Mansfield and Milner argue in this regard that some observers addressing the links between structural power and regionalism have placed the emphasis on the effects of hegemony. In their view, as a hegemon's power recedes, it has reason to behave in an increasingly predatory manner. Thus, to buffer the effects of such behavior, other states will form a series of preferential trade blocks. Arguably, the erosion of U.S. hegemony has stimulated a rise in the number of trading blocks and states entering them (Little 2006, pp. 608–609).

Robert Gilpin (1987) argues that this process began unfolding in the 1980s, leading to a system of loose regional economic blocks in Western Europe, the United States, and Japan that could threaten the unity of the global trade system (Gilpin 1987, pp. 88–90). Another central point to the links between international political relations and the formation of the regional blocs, according to Mansfield and Milner, are the effects of trade on states' political–military power. In general, countries are trading more freely with their political–military allies than with other states, and since PTAs liberalize trade among its members, the preferential trade agreements are most likely to be form among allies, bolstering the alliance's overall political–military capacity. Moreover, such arrangement attenuates the political risks that states benefiting less from the regional bloc might otherwise face from those benefiting more (Gilpin 1987, p. 610).

However, data that I collected for this study suggest that all the member states of the Eurasian Economic Union are actively involved in economic, humanitarian, judicial, and even political collaborations either with the European Union, the United States, China and others. Moreover, the EU continues to be Armenia's biggest export market and source of imports with 39.4 percent and 26.5 percent shares, respectively, in total Armenian exports and imports (European Commission 2015). Accordingly, the EU is also Azerbaijan's main trading partner, accounting for around 42.4 percent of the country's total trade, while 26.1 percent of Georgia's trade takes place with the EU, as well, followed by Turkey (17.2 percent), and Azerbaijan (10.3 percent) (European Commission 2015).

Dragneva and Wolczuk note that, after the dissolution of the Soviet Union, there have been several attempts of economic integration in Eurasia, some within the framework of the Commonwealth of Independent States (CIS), while others outside.[8] However, these projects featured weak and ineffective institutional frameworks and brought limited (if any) economic benefits to their participants. The authors maintain that the declarative and ultimately insubstantial initiatives resulted in skeptical attitude among observers towards all post-Soviet developments (Dragneva and Wolczuk 2013, p. 2).

The creation of the Customs Union among Russia, Kazakhstan, and Belarus in 2007 also sparked little optimism in the beginning, and only five years after this organization has proved itself as a more credible integrative mechanism. Dragneva and Wolczuk claim that "the success story" of the Customs Union renewed attention to economic integration in Eurasia. There are a couple of points that in the authors' opinion led to the successful implementation of the Customs Union: 1) there have been significant practical developments in setting up a customs union such as a common customs tariff and a common customs territory; 2) this project provides for supranational delegation, an identifiable and transparent legal basis, and binding third-party dispute resolution, which is more effective legal and institutional framework compared with previous initiatives; 3) Eurasian integration has been a fast-moving and ambitious projects; 4) the Eurasian Customs Union has been presented not in terms of past-oriented discourses about shared values and history, but offered tangible economic benefits, incorporating best international practice in the field; and 5) the ECU is seen as the nucleus for attracting other former Soviet states to the project (Dragneva and Wolczuk 2013, pp. 2–3).

In the meantime, Evgeny Vinokurov and Alexander Libman (2012) insist that Eurasian economic integration becomes more comprehensible when placed in its historical context. They describe Eurasian exchange as the mutual exchange of goods, services, people, information, ideas and technologies along established routes across the Eurasian continent (Vinokurov and Libman 2012, p. 30). They sought to show in *Eurasian Integration: Challenges of Transcontinental Regionalism* that the concept of "Eurasia" is by no means purely geographical but also economic and cultural entity. In their view, until the 1990s, Eurasia was split into competing and isolated political blocs with limited connection to the world market. After the end of the Cold War, the web of links between Europe, northern and central Eurasia and east and southeast Asia have increased. Vinokurov and Libman see the development of Eurasian integration as a network of localized and overlapping projects and communities dealing with individual challenges related to all and that these networks will establish themselves at the sub-national rather than at the national level (Vinokurov and Libman 2012, p. 228). The authors conclude that Eurasian integration is primarily a process of continental economic integration, developed from the bottom-up that could drive development by integrating energy trade, non-energy trade and transport capital and labor flows. Furthermore, open regionalism in Eurasia is an economically optimal supplement to regional integration initiatives, according to Vinokurov and Libman, and has particular significance for Russia and Central Asia. They also consider for the future research the inclusion of South Asia and the Islamic world in the greater Eurasian picture and suggest that post-Soviet regionalism should not preclude its participants' integration with the EU (Vinokurov and Libman 2012, pp. 229–230).

Yet, Dragneva and Wolczuk inquire whether or not Russia and its partners can engage in rule-based integration, given the concerns about domestic standards of the rule of law in the post-Soviet countries when Russia's interests are at stake.

> Do rules and respect of sovereignty for partner countries prevail when Russia's interests are at stake? After all, crude energy-related arm-twisting has often ended up as Russia's preferred negotiating method with the post-Soviet states. Similarly, would the new common regulation contribute to a business-friendly environment? Or would it amount to yet another mechanism for redistribution of resources between neo-patrimonial networks and oligarchs as well as the extraction of rent by corrupt state officials?
>
> (Dragneva and Wolczuk 2013, p. 5)

Another central point to the rule-based integration in Eurasia is that, because of the scale of the Russian Federation in terms of territory, population, resources and military might, any economic integration that Russia is engaged must have a highly asymmetric character (Dragneva and Wolczuk 2013, p. 81). Thus, the rival theoretical framework fails to explain the causal connection between Russia's material power capabilities and its foreign policies in the South Caucasus. Moreover, since the regime theories were mainly developed to analyze the European integration, they do not consider the peculiarities of Eurasian integration, which has geopolitical and security rationale rather than economic implication. In sum, processes in Eurasia were not fully embraced by the existence literature on regionalism and new regionalism.

Therefore, this study can be considered as timely and worthwhile since it not only explains Russia's relations with the three South Caucasian states after the dissolution of the Soviet Union by utilizing a neoclassical realist approach, but also interprets the creation of the Eurasian Union as another tool of Moscow to dominate the post-Soviet space, thus, arguing that the regime theories are not effective in explaining Eurasian regionalism since they do not take into account the perplexing nature of integration processes in the region.

Conclusion

Having reviewed the neoclassical realist approach and regime theories, I now propose the following interpretation of Russia's foreign policy in the South Caucasus and the relevance for that policy of the creation of the Eurasian Union. Russia's foreign policy in the South Caucasus shifted from abandonment in the 1990s to revanchism in the 2000s. This chapter showed that the Primakov doctrine with its emphasis on the CIS as the key to Russian security interests was furthered during the presidencies of Vladimir Putin and Dimitri Medvedev, and culminated in the idea of the creation of the Eurasian Union. The latter is used as the main tool not only to secure Russia's hegemonic position in Transcaucasia but also to challenge the presence of key players in the region—the United States, EU, Turkey, Iran, and China. A neoclassical realist approach helped me to identified that systemic forces such as the unipolar international system of the early 1990s and late 2000s, the European Union's Eastern Partnership program, NATO's expansion plans, and the American' plan to build missile defense systems in Eastern Europe facilitated Vladimir Putin's expansionist grand strategy in the near abroad. Utilizing neoclassical realist assumption, I have concluded that Russia, driven by its material power capabilities, will likely want more rather than less external influence, and will continue such influence to the extent that Moscow is able to do so. I also identified some fundamental problem with the creation of the Eurasian Union, such as the lack of skillful and sensitive management, the concerns about domestic standards of the rule of law in the post-Soviet countries, and asymmetric character of the Eurasian bloc given the scale of Russia in terms of territory, population, resources and military might. Additionally, all the governments involved in the formation of the Eurasian Union are run by authoritarian figures reluctant to share the power within their own states much less with outsiders. The latter will definitely lead to power-sharing issues in the new union. Finally, Armenia's sudden shift in the political course and its current membership in the Eurasian Union is very important for Moscow since it long sought to dominate the region military and strategically. The recent developments in the region—the proliferation of the new debates regarding the status of Nagorno-Karabakh, border issues between Yerevan and Ankara, the current economic, political and strategic problems that Armenia experiences as the fully-fledged member state of the Eurasian Union, Russia's recent arms sale to Azerbaijan, the possible re-opening of the Abkhazian section of the railroad connecting Armenia to Russia, Armenia's entry to the Eurasian Union as a junior member not the founding partner—will help Moscow to enhance its power and influence the South Caucasian region further.

Notes

1 It seems clear that the author did not take into consideration the case of the Ottoman Empire.

2 Kennedy-Pipe 1998; Petro and Rubinstein 1997; Donaldson and Nogee 2009; and others.

3 See excerpts from France 24 interview with Tatiana Jean, head of the Russia-NIS Center at IFRI that appeared in the article "2016: The year that Putin got his way."

4 On this issue see the excellent book by Karen Dawisha (2014) *Putin's Kleptocracy: Who Owns Russia.*

5 Joseph Nye (2013) argues in his article "What Russia and China Don't Get About Soft Power" that the soft power of the country rests primarily on three resources: its culture (in places where it is attractive to others); its political values (when it lives up to them at home and abroad); and its foreign policies (where they are seen as legitimate and having moral authority). But some scholars (Sergei Karaganov one of them) in the aftermath of the dispute with Georgia have noted that Russia used hard power, including military force, because it has little soft power to use, which is social, cultural, political and economic attractiveness (Nye 2013).

6 According to Michael Emerson and Hrant Kostanyan (2013), Vladimir Putin, using Russian control of gas imports to Armenia, as well as continuing selling arms and military supplies to Azerbaijan, simply pressured Armenian president, Serzh Sarkisyan to withdraw from the Deep and Comprehensive Free Trade Agreement it had negotiated with the EU.

7 Together with Turkey, Kazakhstan has played an important role in the implementation of the Cooperation Council of Turkic Speaking Countries (Turkic Council) and the Parliamentary Assembly of Turkic Speaking Countries. The trade volume between the two countries amounted to 3, 1 billion USD in 2012, while projects of Turkish firms in Kazakhstan exceed 17 billion USD. Finally, the two countries show significant cooperation in international organization such as the OSCE, CICA, the Turkic Council and the Islamic Cooperation Organization (the official website of the Ministry of Foreign Affairs of Turkey Republic).

8 In total, according to Dragneva and Wolczuk, there have been seventeen regional integration initiatives and organizations in the post-Soviet space, some of them already abandoned, others still active today. For instance, CIS (1991), GUAM Organization for Democracy and Economic Development (2006), Shanghai Cooperation Organization (2001), Collective Security Treaty Organization (2002), Free trade area (2011), and Single Economic Space (2012) (Dragneva and Wolczuk 2013, pp. 222–223).

Bibliography

Adomeit, Hannes (2012) "Putin's 'Eurasian Union': Russia's Integration Project and Policies on Post-Soviet Space," *Center for International and European Studies*. No. 4, July.

Ambrosio, Thomas (2005) *Challenging America's Global Preeminence: Russia's Quest for Multipolarity*. Aldershot, UK: Ashgate.

Aron, Leon (2013) "The Putin Doctrine: Russia's Quest to Rebuild the Soviet State," *Foreign Affairs*. Vol. 92, No. 2, March/April.

Burfisher, Mary, Sherman Robinson, and Karen Thierfelder (2004) "Regionalism: Old and New Theory and Practice," in Giovanni Anania (Ed.) *Agricultural Policy Reform and the WTO: Where are We Heading*? New York, NY: Edward Elgar Press.

Cameron, Fraser (2010) "The European Union as a Model for Regional Integration," *Council on Foreign Relations Press*. September. www.cfr.org/world/european-union-model-regional-integration/p22935 (accessed August 2, 2014).

Cooper, Julian (2013) "The Development of Eurasian Economic Integration," in Rilka Dragneva and Katarina Wolczuk (Eds.) *Eurasian Economic Integration: Law, Policy and Politics*. Cheltenham, UK: Edward Elgar.

Daniels, Patricia S. and Stephen G. Hyslop (2013) *Almanac of World History*. Washington, DC: National Geographic.

Dawisha, Karen (2014) *Putin's Kleptocracy: Who Owns Russia?* New York, NY: Simon & Schuster.

Donaldson, Robert H. and Joseph L. Nogee (2009) *The Foreign Policy of Russia: Changing Systems, Enduring Interests*. Armonk, NY: M.E. Sharpe.

Dragneva, Rilka and Katarina Wolczuk (2013) *Eurasian Economic Integration: Law, Policy and Politics*. Cheltenham, UK: Edward Elgar.

Dunne, Tim and Brian S. Schmidt (2007) "Realism," in John Baylis, Steve Smith and Patricia Owens (Eds.) *The Globalization of World Politics*. Oxford, UK: Oxford University Press.

Emerson, Michael and Hrant Kostanyan (2013) "Putin's Grand Design to Destroy the EU's Eastern Partnership and to Replace It with A Disastrous Neighbourhood Policy of His

Own," *Center for European Policy Studies.* September 17. www.ceps.eu/publications/putin%E2%80%99s-grand-design-destroy-eu%E2%80%99s-eastern-partnership-and-replace-it-disastrous (accessed April 7, 2015).

Eurasian Economic Commission (2014) "The Presidents of Belarus, Kazakhstan and Russia signed a Treaty on the Eurasian Economic Union in Astana." May 29. www.eurasiancommission.org/en/nae/news/Pages/29–05–2014–1.aspx (accessed August 20, 2014).

European Commission (2015) "Implementation of the European Neighborhood Policy in Armenia: Progress in 2014, and Recommendations for Actions," March 25. http://eeas.europa.eu/enp/pdf/2015/armenia-enp-report-2015_en.pdf (accessed May 8, 2015).

Fernandes, Sandra (2014) "Putin's Foreign Policy towards Europe: Evolving Trends of an (Un)Avoidable Relationship," in Roger E. Kanet and Remi Piet (Eds.) *Shifting Priorities in Russia's Foreign and Security Policy.* Aldershot, UK: Ashgate.

Freire, Maria Raquel (2010) "Eurasia at the Heart of Russian Politics: Dynamics of (In)Dependence in a Complex Setting," in Maria Raquel Friere and Roger E. Kanet (Eds.) *Key Players and Regional Dynamics in Eurasia: The Return of the "Great Game".* Houndmills, UK: Palgrave Macmillan.

Gilpin, Robert (1987) *The Political Economy of International Relations.* Princeton, NJ: Princeton University Press.

Giragosian, Richard (2013) "Maqsayin Miutyan Antsnele Sargsyani Amenalurj Shalne," *Gala News.* http://galatv.am/hy/news/aqsayin-miutyann-ancnely-argsyani-amenalurj-sxaln-e/ (accessed November 17, 2014).

Grieco, Joseph M. (1988) "Anarchy and the Limits of Cooperation: A Realist Critique of the Newest Liberal Institutionalism," *International Organization*, No. 42, pp. 485–507.

Gvozdev, Nikolas K. (2014) "Russia's Eurasian Union: Part of a Master Plan," *The National Interest.* May/June.

Haas, Ernst B. (1958) *The Uniting of Europe: Political, Social, and Economic Forces 1950–1957.* London, UK: Stevens.

Hauslohner, Abigail (2014) "Russia, Kazakhstan, and Belarus Form Eurasian Economic Union," *The Washington Post.* May 29. www.washingtonpost.com/world/europe/russia-kazakhstan-belarus-form-eurasian-economic-union/2014/05/29/de4a2c15-cb01-4c25-9bd6-7d5ac9e466fd_story.html?utm_term=.68778981eaad (accessed February 25, 2015).

Herzig, Edmund (1999) *The New Caucasus: Armenia, Azerbaijan and Georgia.* London, UK: The Royal Institute of International Affairs.

Holmes, Leslie (2001) "Introduction," in Vladimir Tikhomirov (Ed.) *Russia After Yeltsin.* Aldershot, UK: Ashgate.

Jackson, Nicole J. (2003) *Russian Foreign Policy and the CIS: Theories, Debates and Actions.* London, UK: Routledge.

Jgharkava, Zaza (2013) "Putin Posturing in Yerevan Sparks Georgian Concern," *Georgia Today.* December 5.

Kanet, Roger E. (2014) "Presidential Elections and 'Resets' in US-Russian Relations: Do Leaders Make a Difference?," in Roger E. Kanet and Remi Piet (Eds.) *Shifting Priorities in Russia's Foreign and Security Policy.* Aldershot, UK: Ashgate.

Kennedy-Pipe, Caroline (1998) *Russia and the World 1917–1991.* London, UK: Arnold.

Khachaturian, Haroutiun (2013) "Russia Will Not Abandon Caucasus," *The Central Asia-Caucasus Analyst*, December 11.

Kononenko, Vadim and Arkady Moshes (2011) *Russia as a Network State: What Works in Russia When State Institutions Do Not?* London, UK: Palgrave.

Kuchins, Andrew C. and Igor Zavelev (2012) "Russian Foreign Policy: Continuity in Change," *The Washington Quarterly*. Vol. 35, No. 1, pp. 147–161.

Little, Richard (2006) "International Regimes," in John Baylis and Steve Smith (Eds.) *Globalization of World Politics: An Introduction to International Relations*. Oxford, UK: Oxford University Press.

Lobell, Steven E., Norrin M. Ripsman and Jeffrey W. Taliaferro (2009) *Neoclassical Realism, The State, and Foreign Policy*. Cambridge, UK: Cambridge University Press.

Lomagin, Nikita A. (2014) "Russia's CIS Policy and Economic and Political Transformations in Eurasia," in Roger E. Kanet and Rémi Piet (Eds.) *Shifting Priorities in Russia's Foreign and Security Policy*. Aldershot, UK: Ashgate.

Lovell, David W. (2001) "Nationalism and Democratization in Post-Communist Russia," in Vladimir Tikhomirov (Ed.) *Russia After Yeltsin*. Aldershot, UK: Ashgate.

Lukyanov, Fyodor (2013) "Don't Expect Reset 2.0 During Obama's 2nd Term," *Russia in Global Affairs,* January 23.

MacFarquhar, Neil (2014) "Russia and 2 Neighbors Form Economic Union That Has a Ukraine-Size Hole," *The New York Times*. May 29. www.nytimes.com/2014/05/30/world/europe/putin-signs-economic-alliance-with-presidents-of-kazakhstan-and-belarus.html?_r=0 (accessed September 19, 2014).

Mansfield, Edward E. and Helen V. Milner (1999) "The New Wave of Regionalism," *International Organization*. Vol. 53, No. 3, Summer, pp. 589–627.

Matlack, Carol (2014) "Putin's Eurasian Union Looks Like a Bad Deal, Even for Russia," *Bloomberg Business Week*. May 29. www.bloomberg.com/news/articles/2014-05-29/putin-s-eurasian-union-looks-like-a-bad-deal-even-for-russia (accessed January 15, 2015).

Moravcsik, Andrew (1993) "Preferences and Power in the European Community: A Liberal Intergovernmentalist Approach," *Journal of Common Market Studies*. Vol. 31, No. 4, pp. 473–524.

Mitrany, David (1966) *A Working Peace System*. Chicago, IL: Quadrangle Books.

Moravcsik, Andrew (1993) "Preferences and Power in the European Community: A Liberal Intergovernmentalist Approach," *Journal of Common Market Studies*, 31 (4): 473-524.

Moravcsik, Andrew (1998) *The Choice for Europe: Social Purpose and State Power from Messina to Maastricht*. Ithaca, NY: Cornell University Press.

Morgenthau, Hans J. (1948) *Politics Among Nations: The Struggle for Power and Peace*. New York, NY: Alfred A. Knopf.

Morgenthau, Hans J. (1951) *In Defense of National Interest*. New York, NY: Alfred A. Knopf.

Nye, Joseph (2013) "What Russia and China Don't Get About Soft Power," *Foreign Policy*, April 29.

Nygren, Bertil (2010) "Conclusions: Visions of Russia's Future Foreign Policy," in Bertil Nygren, Bo Huldt, Patrik Ahlgren, Pekka Sivonen, and Susanna Huldt (Eds.) *Russia on Our Minds: Russian Security Policy and Northern Europe*. Stockholm: National Defense College.

Panin, Alexander (2014) "For Russia, Eurasian Union is About Politics, Not Economy," *The Moscow Times*. May 29. www.themoscowtimes.com/business/article/for-russia-eurasian-union-is-about-politics-not-economy/501126.html (accessed June 2, 2014).

Perry, Marvin, Matthew Paul Berg and James H. Krukones (2010) *Sources of European History: Since 1900*. Boston, MA: Wadsworth Cengage Learning.

Petro, Nikolai N. and Alvin Z. Rubinstein (1997) *Russian Foreign Policy: From Empire to Nation State*. New York, NY: Longman.

Politkovskaya, Anna (2004) *Putin's Russia: Life in a Failing Democracy*. New York, NY: Henry Holt.

Putin, Vladimir (2013) "The Annual Presidential Address to the Federal Assembly," *Official Internet Resources of the President of Russia*, The Kremlin, Moscow. December 12. http://en.kremlin.ru/events/president/news/19825 (accessed March 14, 2015).

Rahr, Alexander (2013) "Third Russia: Putin Dots His I's in the State of the National Address," *Valdai Discussion Club*. December 18. http://valdaiclub.com/a/highlights/third_russia_putin_dots_his_i_s_in_the_state_of_the_nation_address/ (accessed March 14, 2015).

Remington, Thomas (2014) *Presidential Decree in Russia: A Comparative Perspective*. New York, NY: Cambridge University Press.

Rukavishnikov, Vladimir (2014) "Understanding Putin's Foreign and Security Policy: Lessons from the Russian Transition," in Roger E. Kanet and Rémi Piet (Eds.) *Shifting Priorities in Russia's Foreign and Security Policy*. Aldershot, UK: Ashgate.

Schweller, Randall L. (2009) "Neoclassical Realism and State Mobilization: Expansionist Ideology in the Age of Mass Politics," in Steven E. Lobell, Norrin M. Ripsman and Jeffrey W. Taliaferro (Eds.) *Neoclassical Realism, The State, and Foreign Policy*. Cambridge, UK: Cambridge University Press.

Seibt, Sebastian (2016) "2016: The Year Putin Got His Way," France 24, 30 December

Service, Robert (2005) *A History of Modern Russia from Nicholas II to Vladimir Putin*. Cambridge, MA: Harvard University Press.

Shevtsova, Lilia (2007) *Russia Lost in Transition: The Yeltsin and Putin Legacies*. Washington, DC: Carnegie Endowment for International Peace.

Spolaore, Enrico (2013) "What Is European Integration Really About? A Political Guide for Economists," *The Journal of Economic Perspectives*, Vol. 27, No. 3, Summer, pp. 125–144.

Suzdalzev, Andrei (2014) "Eurasian Union: Putin's Answer to the EU," *Deutsche Welle*. May 29. www.dw.com/en/eurasian-union-putins-answer-to-the-eu/a-17669138 (accessed November 17, 2014).

Tchakarova, Velina (2014) "The Eurasian Union as a Tool of Russian Geopolitics in the Era of Globalization," in Riegl Martin, Jacob Landovsky, and Irina Valko (Eds.) *Strategic Regions in 21st Century Power Politics: Zones of Consensus and Zones of Conflict*. Newcastle upon Tyne, UK: Cambridge Scholars.

Thucydides (2010) *The History of Peloponnesian War*. New York, NY: Barnes & Noble Classics.

Torbakov, Igor (2000) "Putin's Russia Defines its Foreign Policy Agenda," *EurasiaNet*. July 27. www.eurasianet.org/departments/insight/articles/eav072800.shtml (accessed June 10, 2014).

Trenin, Dmitri (1996) "Russia's Security Interests and Policies in the Caucasus Region," in Bruno Coppieters (Ed.) *Contested Borders in the Caucasus*. Brussels, Belgium: VUB University Press.

Tsygankov, Andrei (2012) "Assessing Cultural and Regime-Based Explanations of Russia's Foreign Policy: 'Authoritarian at Heart and Expansionist by Habit?'," *Europe-Asia Studies*, Vol. 64, No. 4, June.

Tsygankov, Andrei (2013a) *Russia's Foreign Policy: Change and Continuity in National Identity*. Lanham, MD: Rowman & Littlefield.

Tsygankov, Andrei (2013b) "Vladimir Putin's Civilizational Turn," *Russian Analytical Digest*, No. 127, pp. 5–7.

Tsygankov, Andrei (2014) "How the West Enabled the Rise of Russian Nationalism," *The Nation*. May 12.

Vinokurov, Evgeny and Alexander, Libman (2012) *Eurasian Integration: Challenges of Transcontinental Regionalism*. Houndmills, UK: Palgrave Macmillan.

Waltz, Kenneth N. (1979) *Theory of International Politics*. Reading, MA: Adison-Wesley.

Wright, John F.R., Suzanne Goldenberg and Richard Schofield (Eds.) (1996) *Transcaucasian Boundaries*. New York, NY: St. Martin's Press.

Yin, Robert K. (2003) *Case Study Research: Design and Methods*. Thousand Oaks, CA: Sage.

4 Russia's foreign policy in the South Caucasus

The logic of historical explanation

This chapter transforms a rich and detailed historical explanation of Russia's foreign policy in the South Caucasus (a dependent variable in this case study) into a more abstract and selective one presented in theoretical concepts, in order to develop explanations for the outcome of each case (external policies of Moscow in Armenia, Azerbaijan and Georgia) that will reflect the theoretical framework of this study. According to Alexander George and Andrew Bennett, this is a matter of detective work and historical analysis rather than a case of utilizing a traditional quasi-experimental design (George and Bennett 2005, p. 90). This chapter also illuminates the historical context in which cases are embedded, relying on chronological narrative as an organizing device for presenting the case study materials in this book. However, in order to avoid overly long historical accounts and to provide the justifications for solving the research dilemma of this study, I will try to strike the right balance between a detailed historical description of Russia's foreign policy in Transcaucasia and development of a theoretically-focused explanation of it.

The main theoretical debates about Russia's foreign policies in the South Caucasus and the creation of the Eurasian Union

As it was previously stated, I am using case studies (Russia's foreign policies in Armenia, Azerbaijan and Georgia) for theory testing in this chapter. Hence, according to George and Bennett, the goal here is not to invalidate a theory decisively but to figure out whether and how the scope conditions of alternative theories should be expanded or limited (George and Bennett 2005, p. 115). However, George and Bennett also warn that this is a challenging process, since when a theory fails to fit the evidence in a case (or cases), it is not clear whether the theory fails to explain the specific case study or a whole class of cases, or does not explain any cases at all. Therefore, we should not be too quick to reject general theories on the ground of one or a few unorthodox cases, since these theories may still be useful for other cases. Derek Beach (2012) argues that in theory-centric research it is vital to ensure that your analysis critically studies the theory's ability to explain empirical developments across the cases. The latter can be achieved by carefully operationalizing the theory in order to clear explain what you expect to see in the empirical part if the theory is true (George and Bennett 2005, pp. 115–223).

Neoclassical realism that draws upon the theoretical insights of structural realism of Kenneth N. Waltz, Robert Gilpin, Joseph Greico and others assume that politics is a constant struggle among different states over material power and security in an anarchic world characterized by competition for scarce resources (Lobell, Ripsman and Taliaferro 2009). This chapter seeks to validate neoclassical realists' assumptions and suggests that Russia's foreign policy in the South Caucasus was and still is nothing else than the attempt to achieve centralized power within Russia and the near abroad using territorial expansion (the creation of the Eurasian Union in 2015) in order to enhance country's material power.

Derek Beach also suggests that, in order not to fall prey to confirmatory bias, one should take two alternative theoretical answers to one's research question and use them to structure one's analysis (Beach 2012, p. 223). Thus, along with applying the neoclassical realist argument to Russia's foreign policy in the South Caucasus, I am also using the regime theory argument (power-based and interest based) in order to structure my analysis. Andreas Hasenclever, Peter Mayer and Volker Rittberger (1997) classified the regime-analytical research agenda according to the explanatory variable as power-based, interest-based, and knowledge-based approaches. This study considers the two first approaches: power-based or realist that focuses on power relationships and interest-based or neoliberal, which bases its analyses on constellations of interests (Hasenclever et al. 1997, pp. 1–2). It is important to take into account that the major difference separating all three schools of thought is the degree of "institutionalism"[1] that these regime theories have embraced.

Hasenclever et al. specify that institutions, in this regard, can be vital in two cases: they may be effective and less robust or resilient. While the former involves the notion that regimes are fixed, its members abide by its norms and rules, and a regime is effective to the extent that it achieves certain objectives; resilience, on the other hand, is a dynamic measure of the significance of regimes, which refers to the "staying power" of international institutions in the face of exogenous challenges and to the extent to which previous institutional choices constrain

Table 4.1 Two schools of thought in the study of international regimes[2]

	Realism	*Neoliberalism*
Central variable	Power	Interests
"Institutionalism"	Weak	Medium
Meta-theoretical orientation	Rationalistic	Rationalistic
Behavioral model	Concerned with relative gains	Absolute gains maximizer

collective decisions and behaviour in later periods (Hasenclever et al. 1997, p. 2). To reiterate, institutions that change with every move of power among their members, or whenever the most powerful participants decide that their interests are no longer properly served by the particular regime, lack resilience. The empirical data (presented in this and following chapters) collected for the book shows that all the previous regimes created within the Soviet Union and after the end of the Cold War, lacked two important aspects of significance of institutions that Hasenclever et al., have emphasized in their study. In other words, all those institutions have neither been effective nor resilient.

As George and Bennett conclude "an explanation of a case is more convincing if it is more distinctive, or if the outcome it predicts could not have been expected from the best rival theory available" (George and Bennett 2005, p. 117). Moreover, for closely studied phenomena, such as the collapse of the Soviet Union and Russia's foreign policy in the near abroad before and after the disintegration of the Soviet Union, the finding that a case fits only one explanatory theory, in this study a neoclassical realist approach, is powerful evidence that the theory best explains the case. Another point that I would like to raise before proceeding with my case studies is that I define Russia's foreign policies in Armenia, Azerbaijan, and Georgia as crucial cases since they closely fit a neoclassical realist theory's argument that, over the long term the relative amount of material power resources Moscow possesses will shape the ambition and scope of its foreign policies: with the rise of relative power, Russia will seek more influence abroad, but as it declines, the Kremlin's grand strategies will be scaled back. To be more precise, these case studies provide the most definitive type of evidence of a neoclassical realist theory that considers not only domestic factors in a state's behavior, but also systemic forces that shape a country's external affairs. A shift in relative power leads to a shift in the foreign policy of Moscow in the South Caucasus. Moreover, in regards to the autonomy of leaders, Vladimir Putin pursues his own conception of the national interest, since domestic constraints are weak during his presidency, whereas Boris Yeltsin was forced to accommodate his understanding of the national interest to the constraining domestic actors.

Neoclassical realists contend that the scope of a state's foreign policy goals is characterized by its placement in the international system and its relative material power capabilities. As was already mentioned, relative material power establishes the basic parameters of a state's external affairs. It is important to keep in mind that foreign policy choices are made by political leaders, thus, it is their understanding of relative power that matters, not relative quantities of physical forces in being. Consequently, over the short-term to medium period of time, states' foreign policies might not closely reflect the objective material power trends (Rose 1998, p. 147). It is safe to suggest that the Ukrainian crisis became a litmus test for Putin's grand strategies in the near abroad. The latter proved that Russia's foreign policy choices in the post-Soviet space no longer matched its material power capabilities.

For instance, it has been argued that the annexation of Crimea will not magically enable Moscow to rule the region that has no overland connection to Russia and which had been dependent on its land bridge to Ukraine for trade, travel, public services, and other essential services (Hanauer 2014). Moreover, according to Russia's economic development minister, Alexei Ulyukaev, infrastructure improvements, development aid, government operations and other expenditures will cost Russia as much as $4.5 billion per year. As we can see, despite the fact that the Ukrainian crisis has already taken a toll on Russia's economy and strained budget thanks to Western sanctions and the declining price of crude oil, the Kremlin continues to follow its grand strategy.

This brings us to another point of neoclassical realism that political leaders may or may not have freedom to extract and direct national resources as they wish. Accordingly, power analysis must also examine the strength and structure of states relative to their societies since, in Rose's view, these affect the proportion of national resources that can be allocated to foreign policy (Rose 1998, p. 147). Furthermore, the national security executive, according to Lobell, Ripsman and Taliaferro, has interests that transcend any class or sector, namely *the national interest.* And since the executive receives the privileged information from state agencies, it is more aware of the national interests of the state and the requests of the international system than other local players (Lobell, Ripsman and Taliaferro 2009, p. 27). Another vital point of neoclassical realists to keep in mind is that limitations on executive autonomy in various national contexts may impair their ability to respond to shifts in the balance of power. Consequently, neoclassical realists view policy responses as a product of state-society cooperation or struggles. Lastly, the degree of state autonomy vis-à-vis society differs over time and across different countries (Lobell et al. 2009, p. 27).

On the other hand, international regimes have problematic relationships to state power, and two questions are particularly debatable, according to Keohane (1993): "1) whether international regimes must rely on the support of a single dominant power; and 2) whether the rules of the regimes have significant effects apart from the influence exerted by their supporters" (Keohane 1993, p. 778). It is also important to add that the rules of international regimes manifest not only the power of states but internationally accepted principles, such as that of sovereignty. In fact, in the long run the relative power of actors may change, while the rules remain the same, which suggests that the expected outcomes of the regimes based on the power alone frequently contrast with those discerned within the framework of international regimes (Keohane 1993, p. 778).

For instance, as was already mentioned above, Russia's relative material power resources decreased amid Western sanctions over the Ukrainian conflict and the low oil price, which has fallen by more than 40 percent since June of 2014, and it is now below $50 a barrel. Russia's recession that started in 2014 amid the Western sanctions and volatile oil prices is expected to last until 2017. Over the last few years, Moscow has been battling falling oil prices and the confrontation with Washington and Brussels over the Russia's annexation of Crimea and its military support of pro-Moscow rebels in eastern Ukraine. The price for Russia's recent assertiveness on the world stage is the country's Cold War-style standoff with the West, and the economic crisis that has hit Russia and its population hard.

Russia's GDP is expected to fall 1.5 percent in 2016 and 0.1 percent in 2017, assuming that Urals oil prices average $41 per barrel in 2016 before appreciating to $43 and $44 per barrel in the two consequent years (Sputnik, 2016).

The country's deepening economic crisis also forced the government to cut public spending and use 18 percent of its reserve fund in August to plug budget deficit that was 3.3 percent of GDP or $23.8 billion in the first seven months of 2016.[3] Russia's Finance Minister, Anton Siluanov, said that the country would run through the reserve funds generated from previously high oil prices within three years even if it is spent moderately, although, he announced that the government would not raise taxes during that time.

As values of Russian ruble tumbles (see Figure 4.2) it is taking the currencies of its neighbors (including Armenia, and Georgia) down with it (Recknagel 2014).

Moreover, as Armenian exports lose their price competitiveness in the Russian market[4] since the Russian customers can no longer afford buying some products from Armenia, especially the ones that are priced in dollars, the entire economy in Armenia has stumbled as well. For instance, Gohar Gyulumyan, the World Bank's senior economist in Yerevan, has described Armenian economic developments in recent months of 2016 as "disappointing," pointing out that after a 4.5 percent growth reported for the first quarter of the year, it has since begun to worsen dramatically since July 2016 (Arka News Agency 2017). While there is hope that Armenian economic growth in 2017 will be supported by a recovery in Russian economy and rising commodity prices,[5] there is also the balance of risks in the region that could come from falling commodity prices, financial market distraction,

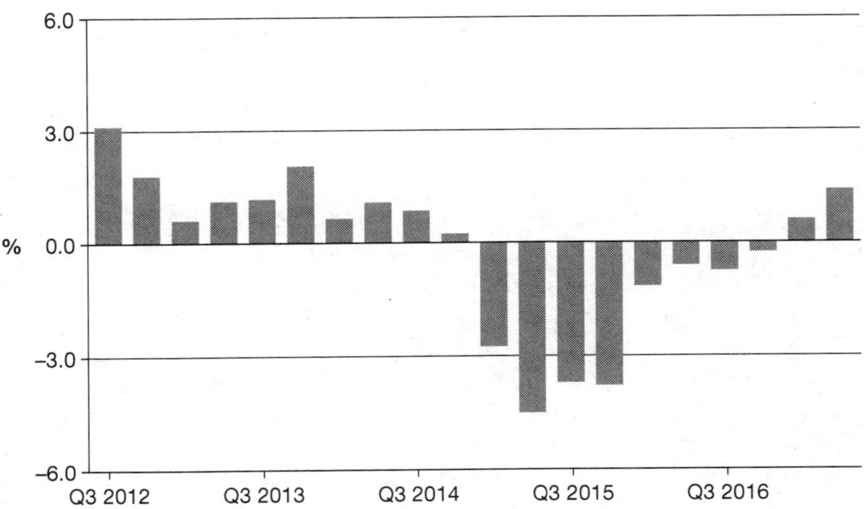

Figure 4.1 Growth of Russian GDP

Source: Federal State Statistics Service (Rosstat) and FocusEconomics Consensus Forecast

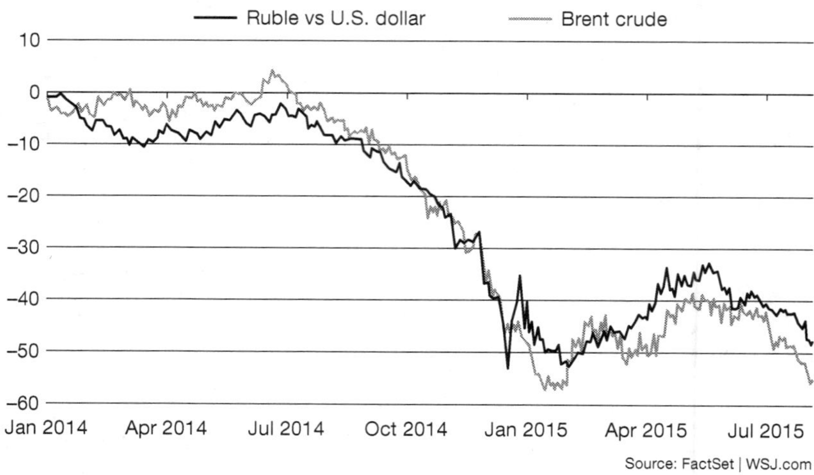

Figure 4.2 Performance of ruble exchange rate and Brent crude oil price
Source: *The Wall Street Journal*

regime uncertainty and regional instability. Accordingly, the South Caucasus during the last 30 years has mainly been associated with frozen conflicts. The region remains war-torn in Nagorno-Karabakh, Ossetia and Abkhazia. Moreover, a sharp escalation in fighting between Armenia and Azerbaijan over the disputed territory of Nagorno-Karabakh in 2014–2017 is considered to be the deadliest since the two states signed a ceasefire in 1994. Armenia provides a critical foothold for Russia in a strategic South Caucasus, hosting a large Russian military base in Gyumri, and is a member of the EEU and CSTO. But it did not stop Russia conducting an estimated $4 billion worth of deals over recent years with Azerbaijan, supplying Baku with tanks, infantry fighting vehicles, and artillery systems from Moscow. Despite its alleged commitment to resolve the frozen conflict, Moscow is playing a double game, and using the recent escalation of the conflict to its advantage. For instance, while Armenia, an official Russian ally, received discounted arms from Russia, Azerbaijan is one of the Kremlin defense industry's best customers (Kucera 2016). It has been argued that Mr. Putin offered to return the Armenian-controlled territories of Nagorno-Karabakh to Azerbaijan if Baku is willing to maintain its "friendship" with Russia. In any case, there is a possibility that Russia will enforce peacekeeping forces in Karabakh, if the situation gets out of control. Thus, Nagorno-Karabakh will follow the fate of South Ossetia and Abkhazia. The recent escalation of the conflict between Yerevan and Baku is beneficial for Moscow, since it will definitely impede the current cooperation between the West and Azerbaijan in the energy sector and will highlight Russia's role as a peacemaker and a guarantor of the stability in the South Caucasus.

On the other hand, Florian Biermann and Giorgi Tsutskiridze (2014) argue that the crisis in Ukraine will likely impact Georgia's economy in the short-run, affecting its trade and capital flows.[6] However, in the long-run, according to the authors, this crisis could improve the competitiveness of the Caucasus Transit Corridor, one of the three main routes to transport goods from Europe to the Central Asian countries, which can become the main trading route connecting the Old World and the Caspian Sea countries if transport through Ukraine and Russia will be restrained amid the conflict.[7] Meanwhile, Azerbaijan also suffers from falling oil prices since the country relies heavily on oil for most parts of its state revenue and 92 percent of export earnings. Baku experienced a decline in the share of oil revenues in Azerbaijan's GDP in recent years, dropping from 60 percent to 40 percent, with the government's expectations that it will continue to decline in 2015 (Dadashova 2014). Dadashova argues that lower oil prices in the world market have a negative impact on foreign trade turnover that will lead to a decrease in oil revenues, thus further reducing the revenues of the State Oil Fund. Samir Sharifov, Finance Minister of Azerbaijan, believes that the decline in oil demand with the slowdown in global growth can lead only to a temporary reduction in oil revenues in exporting states. The Central Bank of Azerbaijan (CBA) echoes him stating that Azerbaijan's balance of payments will have a surplus thanks to large foreign exchange reserves that will help the government to escape the current crisis for the world's oil exporters. In fact, Azerbaijan's strategic currency reserves increased by 8.3 percent or $4.2 billion, reaching $54.4 billion in the first six months of 2014. Thus, Baku enters the list of top 20 countries in the world, according to Elman Rustamov, president of CBA, thanks to the ratio of foreign currency reserves to GDP, which is 74 percent (Dadashova 2014). Azerbaijan's GDP is forecast to contract by 2.5 percent in 2016, and then grow by 1 percent in 2017 and 2.1 percent in 2018, however, the country's challenging business environment, policy uncertainty, and financial sectors vulnerabilities hinder the Caspian state's medium-term prospects.[8]

To conclude, this chapter argues that the evidence of the political and socio-economic situation in the South Caucasus (at least in regards to Georgia and Azerbaijan) disconfirms the explanatory power of regime theory (power-based and interest-based versions) since the current distribution of Russia's state power becomes too inconsistent with the rules of the Russian-led regimes in the region. Hence, according to Hasenclever et al., power-based theories of regimes emphasize relative power capabilities as a central explanatory variable and stress states' sensitivity to distributional aspects of cooperation and regimes (Hasenclever et al. 1997, p. 284). For instance, can we seriously consider Russia as a hegemon since, according to a classical example of a power-based theory of international regimes, the theory of hegemonic stability theory, the existence of effective international institutions requires a unipolar configuration of power in the issue-area in question? In the same vein, we should expect to see in the empirical material of this study that interest-based theories of regimes, which, after a realist version, consider states as self-interested, goal-seeking actors whose behavior can be explained in terms of maximization of individual utility or states, also fail to explain what caused Y (the dependent variable) to happen in most instances (Hasenclever et al. 1997, p. 23; Beach 2012, p. 224). For example, for both realists and neoliberals, foreign policies along with the international institutions are to be reconstructed as consequences of calculations of advantage made by states (Hasenclever et al. 1997, pp. 23–24). Furthermore, interest-based theories of regimes assume that actors' preferences are stable over time. Neoliberals find foreign policy officials as rational utility maximizers, emphasizing self-interest as a motive for cooperation among countries and for creation of international regimes, while realists argue that power differences shape the level of cooperation, its rules and payoffs (Harris 2013, p. 141). However, none of these schools of thought alone is capable of capturing the all-important dimensions of regimes, especially the ones created in the post-Soviet space (Boulding 1978).

With this in mind, this chapter analyzes Russia's foreign policy in the South Caucasus taking into consideration the relative material power capabilities of Russia, the state structure and leaders' perceptions of relative material power forces and their freedom to extract and direct national resources as they wish. Chapter 5 will continue with the alternative explanation, the regime theories analysis, in order to examine different regimes that were created in the South Caucasus starting with the creation of the Soviet Union in 1922 and concluding with the formation of the Eurasian Union in 2015.

Russia at the Caucasian Gate: the neoclassical realist explanation

Ronald Suny (1988) has argued that the geographic placement of Russia and its desire to expand to the south, towards the open sea (Black Sea) was the starting point for the Tsarist conquest of Transcaucasia. However, neoclassical realism assumes the impact of power capabilities on foreign policy choices as indirect, systemic pressure can limit policy choices for decision makers, but it is not enough to be a single force in a given foreign policy step of a state. One should also pay attention to internal factors to analyze why specific courses of action are taken, among others, the leaders' perception of the international context and their ability to have local support for their policies. In this regard, this chapter argues that Russia's invasion of the South Caucasus that is situated in a strategically important location between East and West resulted from various systemic and domestic factors in Tsarist Russia. At first, the Russians envisioned Transcaucasia as a trade bridge between Europe and Asia, but by the end of the 1820s, as Russia itself undertook some industrial development, Russian authorities (one of them was the Minister of Finance, Egor Kankrin) visualized the Asian continent as a source of raw materials rather than an area to be developed economically and politically (Suny 1988, p. 91). In this regard, it is safe to suggest that Russia's conquest of the Caucasus from the beginning fitted into the neoclassical realist model since the government responded to the uncertainties of international system by seeking to control and shape its external environment (see below, King and Davies' accounts of the Tsarist expansion into the region).

On the other hand, King (2004) and Davies (2007) write that the hegemony over the Black Sea steppe was crucial for Tsarist Russia, not only because it was offering rich black soil for agriculture, but also it was seen as key in determining the political fate of Moldavia and Walachia in the west and the Caucasus in the east. However, steppe colonization carried heavy protection costs since it was an apple of discord among the Crimean Khanate, the Ottoman Empire, Poland-Lithuania, and Russia. Thus, a central feature of Russian state policy from the reign of Ivan the Terrible (1533–1584) to Peter the Great (1689–1725) was an effort to control the steppe that was challenged by the Tatar Khans and the Ottomans. But what began as a defensive policy of state security transformed over the course of the eighteenth century into an expansion ideology that embraced the Russian vision of itself as a successor to Rome and the creation of the new empire that would stretch from the Black Sea to the Mediterranean (King 2004, p. 140). It is obvious that the colonization of Transcaucasia became a part of imperial ambitions of the Tsarist Russia. Trenin (1996) notes that as Russia became a multinational empire in the middle of sixteenth century, it started the expansion into Caucasus. It took three centuries to incorporate Transcaucasia fully into the mother country, following the practices of subjugation by war and the extension of protection, a policy that was driven by geopolitical and strategic concerns rather than economic or ideological significances (Trenin 1996).

The colonial attitude of the Russian government towards Transcaucasia hampered the region's economic development and transformation into the political system of the empire but, in the meantime, it helped to keep the Caucasus just as a supplier of raw materials for central Russia (Suny 1988, p. 91). This trend continued after the South Caucasian republics joined the Soviet Union and later in the 1990s, when the three republics: Armenia, Azerbaijan and Georgia gained independence with the fall of the Soviet State in 1991. For instance, in 2005, Putin described the collapse of the Soviet Union as "the greatest geopolitical catastrophe of the past century," the statement that was considered as alarming by many Western and former Soviet scholars and politicians (Kuzio 2006; Salukvadze 2006). It is not surprising that thereafter Russia's foreign policy towards its former republics has been viewed as a policy of neo-imperialism in the near abroad.

Drawing on assumptions of neoclassical realism, this chapter tends to explain why, how and under what conditions the international characteristics of a state (in this study, Russia)—the extractive and mobilization capacity of politico-military institutions, the influence of domestic societal actors and interest groups, the degree of state autonomy from society, and the level of elite or societal cohesion—intervene between the Russian leaders' assessment of international threats and opportunities and the actual diplomatic, military and foreign economic policies that those leaders pursue towards the South Caucasus from the eighteenth century up to modern day (Lobell, Ripsman and Taliaferro et al. 2009, p. 4). As Shevtsova (2007) suggests, "to this day the elite's vision of the Russian state is based on territory, military power, international prestige, and personalized power as the means of attaining them, and, finally, on identifying an enemy to justify that form of governance" (Shevtsova 2007, p. 8).

We turn now to process-tracing and historical explanation technique in order to analyze macrohistorical phenomena of Russia's foreign policy in the South Caucasus. According to George and Bennett, the process-tracing method attempts to identify the intervening causal process between an independent variable (Russia's relative power) and the outcome of the dependent variable (its foreign policy choices in Armenia, Azerbaijan, and Georgia). In other words, tracing the historical processes that may have led to the current state of external affairs of Moscow towards Yerevan, Baku and Tbilisi helps narrow the list of potential causes. However, George and Bennett warn that it may be difficult to eliminate all potential rival explanations but one (in case of human agents' involvement). Nevertheless, process-tracing makes the researcher take equifinality[9] into account and it provides the chance of mapping out one or more possible causal ways that are persistent with the outcome. Finally, process-tracing, which George and Bennett consider as an indispensable tool for theory testing, differs from methods based on covariance or comparisons across cases, since in using theories to develop explanations of cases, it requires that all the intervening steps in a case be predicted by a hypothesis or else that hypothesis must be changed to explain the case (George and Bennett 2005, p. 207). Beach notes that process-tracing techniques are in-depth, case-study tools that can be used to analyze an hypothesized causal mechanism connecting an independent variable (X) and an outcome (Y) (Beach 2012, p. 230). It is important to clarify that it is not the independent variable that creates the outcome, but the mechanism constituted of a series of parts that produces the outcome by conveying causal forces (Beach 2012, p. 232). Chapter 5 combines methods of both cross-case comparison and process-tracing in order to test whether the observed processes among variables in Russia's foreign policies in the South Caucasus match those predicted by neoclassical realist theory, that the scope and ambitions of a state's foreign policy are driven not only by its place in the international system but also by its relative material power capabilities. In addition, state-level factors serve as crucial intervening variables between systemic forces and the foreign policy goals of Moscow in Armenia, Azerbaijan, and Georgia in order to determine how and under what conditions state-level factors matter.

The Caucasus and the Russian Empire

According to Luigi Villari (1876–1959), an Italian historian, traveler and diplomat, the history of Russia has been a series of expansions to the west, the south, and the east, towards the open sea. Since Russia was not separated from her colonies by the sea, the process of absorption was much easier, as well as the line of demarcation between the mother country and her protectorates less definite, than in the case of other imperial powers, for instance Britain and France (Villari 1906, p. 15). Furthermore, since Imperial Russia was governed despotically, the question about the type of government to be adopted in the colonies was not as important as in constitutionally governed states. The main goal of the colonial regime was to assimilate the conquered nations as far as possible from Poland to the Pacific Ocean and from the Arctic sea to Mountain Ararat (Villari 1906, p. 15).

Villari claims that of all the Russia's borderlands, none exceeds in interest the Caucasus, which is a broad isthmus between the Black Sea and the Caspian extended by a great chain of mountains rising to a height of 18,000 feet. He argues that until the Russian occupation, the Caucasus had no unity, since historically it has always been split up between a number of different foreign states, and more or less independent principalities and tribes. At the time of Russian conquest, Western Transcaucasia was divided into the kingdoms of Georgia, Imeretia, and Mingrelia, the eastern provinces (Baku, Elizavetpol, and Erivan) were under Persian supremacy; Batum and Kars belonged to Turkey. Moreover, Villari finds that the political situation in the region can be explained by the racial divisions of the Caucasus. Thus, Russians, Armenians, Kurds, Persians, and Tates bracketed together as Indo-Europeans (white race); Georgians, Lezghins, and Abkhazians united among the pure Caucasian (white race as well); and Turks and Azerbaijan Tartars should be treated as a single family (Mongol or yellow race) (see Figure 2.2). In regard to a political consideration, according to Villari, Tartars and Tates should be grouped together since, although of widely different racial origin, they are both Shi'i Muslims and practically from one nationality; Russians and Armenians, also both labeled as Indo-Europeans, are widely separated by political determinations. In this case, Villari divides the Caucasian peoples according to their political considerations into the following groups: Khartvels or Georgians, Armenians, Azerbaijan Tartars, Russians, Eastern mountaineers and Western mountaineers (Villari 1906, p. 21). Yet, continues Villari, after a century of Russian rule with accentuated Russifying tendencies, Transcaucasia had not become Russian. Moreover, the Georgians, Armenians and Tartars have preserved their languages and their racial characteristics intact, and with strong nationalist feelings. He concludes that, if the Caucasus is to continue to be part of the Russian Empire, it can only be ruled on the ground of popular autonomy (Villari 1906, p. 36).

The history of Russia's foreign policy in the South Caucasus

Russian foreign policy towards the Transcaucasian republics can be traced back to the eighteenth century when Christian Georgia and Armenia, divided and passed backwards and forwards between the Persian and Ottoman empires, saw in Tsarist Russia the sole protector against the Muslim states (Light 2005). Georgia has a long and complex history with Tsarist Russia, starting with the Treaty of Georgievsk, when the Eastern Georgian kingdom of Kartli-Kakheti sought the protection of the Christian areas of Georgia against the Persian and Ottoman Muslim empires. But Russia did not offer protection against the Turkish and Persian invasion of 1785 and 1795, and in 1801 Kartli-Kakheti was annexed and declared abolished by Russian Tsar Alexander I (Mouritzen and Wivel 2011, p. 9).

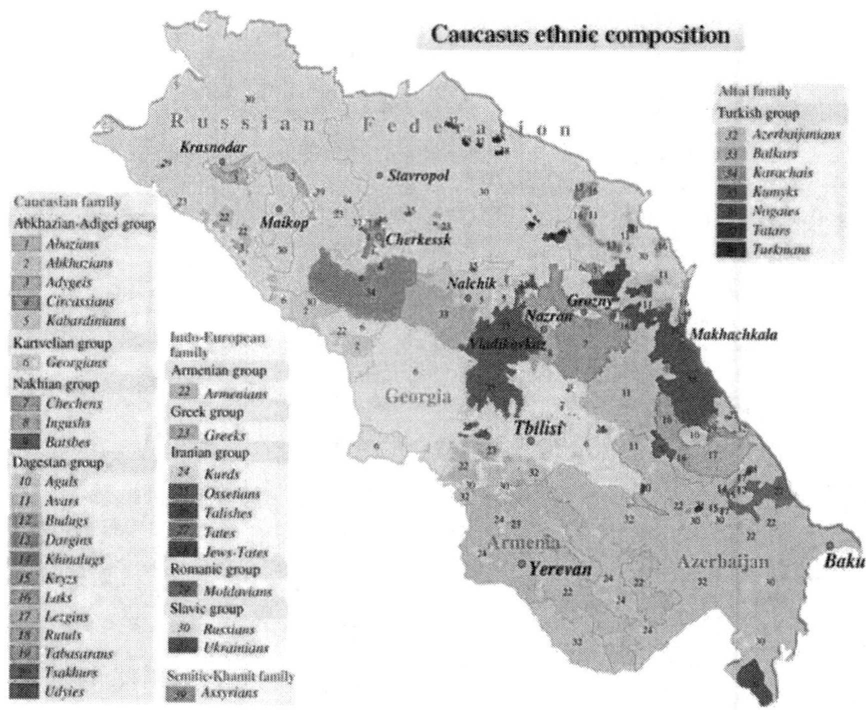

Figure 4.3 Caucasus ethnic composition

Source: Beruchashvili and Radvanie 1996, 1998

Furthermore, in 1810 Russia annexed the western Georgian kingdom of Imereti, as well as several other territories, including Abkhazia in 1864. Avalov (1901) argues that Russia, originally, did not have any imperial claims to Georgia (the Eastern Georgian kingdom of Kartli-Kakheti); on the contrary, the Georgian kings themselves sought the Russian protection, which was provided. Nevertheless, after Georgia became a part of Tsarist Russia, it was unavoidable that the law of strictly centralized and powerful Empire would override the rules of semi-feudal state (Avalov 1901, p. 6). Therefore, the legitimate wishes of Georgians had not been taken into account by the Empire's officials since they contradicted the nature of Russian nation-building and the further expansionist policies in Western Asia. Moreover, Avalov notes that Georgia's original intention to be annexed as a state and to preserve its own law (and its own tsar) was unfeasible within the authoritarian regime of Empire. In fact, Georgia was annexed as one of the Russian provinces (provinciia), and if for the former the annexation was a step forward in the political sense, for the latter it was also beneficial and set a precedent for future annexations in Western Asia (Avalov 1901, p. 7).

In the meantime, Russo–Armenian relations started as early as the tenth century, when Armenian merchants came into contact with Kievan Rus' both via the Balkans and Byzantium, the Black and Caspian Sea, as well as the Caucasus (Bournoutian 1997, p. 82). Armenian refugees moved northward after the Turkish and Mongol invasions, and by the mid-thirteenth century, Armenians established colonies in the Crimea, Ukraine, and in the fourteenth century a small Armenian trading colony settled in Moscow. There was a great expansion of Armenian trade activity in Russia and Poland in the sixteenth century as a result of the Russian conquest of Kazan (1552) and Astrakhan (1556) from the Tatars, which led to Russia's control of the Volga River and access to the Caspian Sea. According to Bournoutian, Russian forces attempted to annex Transcaucasia in the beginning of seventeenth century, responding to early appeals from a number of Georgian and Armenian leaders who sought to end the Perso–Turkish rivalry that had a devastating effect on the region. Nevertheless, Russia had to abandon its plans after several of its divisions were routed by the Muslim mountain tribes of Dagestan. It is important to note that Armenian political and religious leaders came in closer contact with Russia and began to see it as an ally of Armenians. Thus, by 1716 Armenians enjoyed the protection of Peter the Great, and the Armenian Church was granted formal recognition when Archibishop Minas Tigranian was named Prelate of all Armenians in Russia with his see in Astrakhan (Bournoutian 1997, p. 87).

Russians made a second attempt to move beyond the Caucasus in the 1720s, when a number of Russian merchants were killed in Shirvan; the Russian governor of Astrakhan urged Peter the Great to invade Persia with the promises of Armeno–Georgian support. But, as soon as the Ottomans protested to Peter, he left the region. As a result, the Turks violated the 1639 agreement and entered Transcaucasia in 1723, while Russia, fearing to antagonize the Ottomans, concentrated its efforts on the Caspian coast. Nonetheless, Russian promises of support had encouraged Armenians to armed resistance, and together with the Persians they defended Erevan and Ganja. Davit Bek[10] led the Armenian region of Karabagh-Zangezur against the Turks, and after defeating the Turkic tribal lords, he had to face the arrival of the Ottoman army in 1724. But lacking support from the Russian forces that never reached Armenia since Peter, who did not want to face another Russo–Turkish war, made a peace with the Ottomans; Transcaucasia was divided between the Russians and the Turks, with Eastern Armenia and Georgia falling into the Turkish sector (Kluchevsky 1931; Bournoutian 1997; Hovannisian 1997).

Catherine the Great and the national interest of Russia

With the death of Peter the Great in 1725, Russia abandoned Transcaucasia until Catherine the Great came to power in 1762. With Catherine's victories against the Ottoman Turks and her interest in the Christians of Transcaucasia,[11] as well as her support of Russian Armenian merchant families (the most famous among them, the Lazarev family who later founded the Lazarev Institute of Oriental Languages in Moscow), Armenians petitioned Catherine for support, offering financial and military aid in case of a Russian penetration of Transcaucasia. It is important to remember that Armenians at the time were actively emigrating to Georgia and Russia where they were involved in the diplomatic and military service as well as in the mercantile and artisan communities (Bournoutian 1997, p. 92). Catherine II seized strategic Ottoman lands in 1762–1769 along the entire northern coast of the Black Sea and therefore obliged the Sultan to recognize her empire's right to intervene on behalf of Ottoman Christian subjects (Hovannisian 1997, p. 8). It has been argued that the current Russia's President Vladimir Putin and his allies are following spiritual masters such as Empress Catherine in seeking to reestablish Russia as a great nation in the world (Winik 2007). In the same vein, Mr. Putin, like Catherine the Great, turned Moscow's gaze inward rather than westward, similarly, when it came to dealing with rebels both acted ruthlessly (Bayer 2008). Consequently, it is safe to suggest that a hypothesized causal mechanism is present in the case of Russia's foreign policies in the South Caucasus starting with the first Tsarist expansion into the Caucasus, when both systemic and subsystemic structural and unit-level forces influence behavior of the state leaders (Lobell et al. 2009, p. 64). While, in Schweller's words, dynastic states such as Prussia, Austria, Sweden and Russia never hesitated to forge alliances of convenience and to expand at the expense of weaker powers, post-Soviet Russia seemed to abandoned a great power sentiment, at least during the Yeltsin's presidency (Schweller 2009, p. 229). Thus, another hypothesized causal mechanism of neoclassical realist theory, that if a state composed of elites that agree on striving for a grand strategy along with a stable and effective political regime with broad authority, then states would undertake risky foreign affairs, is potentially present in this case. It is also important to note that the Tsarist government that ruled despotically throughout its history could pursue any uncertain or risky foreign policies without public support.

Tsarist Russia's expansion into Armenia and Georgia

In the meantime, Tsar Paul (1796–1801) violated Catherine's agreement with Iraklii II of Georgia by which Russia extended its protection over the Caucasian realm, and annexed eastern Georgia. Furthermore, Paul's successor, Alexander I (1801–1825) continued Russia's expansionist policies and seized the remaining Georgian provinces of Mingrelia, Imeretia, Guria, and Abkhazia between 1803 and 1812 and, in the Treaty of Bucharest, compelled the Ottoman Empire to abandon its claim to these lands (Hovannisian 1997, p. 8).

Afterwards, Alexander's forces moved into Persia in 1812–1813 and by the Treaty of Gulistan, restrained the Shah to renounce his pretensions to eastern Georgia and to surrender the northeastern section of the Armenian Plateau along with several khanates extending from Ganja and Karabakh to Kuba and Baku. But this settlement did not last long due to Alexander's death, the "Decembrist" unrest, and Moslem resistances in Russia's Caucasian provinces, which led to Persian Crown Prince Abbas Mirza's attempts to cede the khanates. Hovannisian maintains that only with the help of hundreds of Armenian volunteers were the

Russian armies able to expel the Persian forces (Hovannisian 1997, p. 8). Meanwhile, Tsar Nicholas' Caucasian Army[12] under command of General I.F. Paskevich in October of 1827 captured Erevan, that for decades was under Persian domination, followed by the capitulation of the Qajar dynasty of Persia and a Treaty of Turkmenchai (1828), by which the Persians recognized Russian sovereignty over the khanates of Erevan and Nakhichevan, as well as over the territory lost in 1813 (Alboyadjian 1961, p. 104). As a result of Russian military expansion in the Caucasus, the Ottoman territorial losses had serious ramifications for its domestic economic decline and military capabilities. Therefore, the Treaty of Andrianople (1829) concluded the Russo–Turkish War of 1828–1829 and granted Poti, Akhalkalak, and Akhaltsikhe to Russia, and free access for Russian merchants to Ottoman markets (Payaslian 2007, p. 112). In turn, Russians agreed to clear their forces from Kars and Ezerum, which endangered the positions of Armenians living in these vilayets. However, for the Armenians, the Treaty of Adrianople offered an option to leave their native villages within eighteen months, pass the new frontier and become the subjects of Tsar Nicholas I. As a result, by the end of 1830, precisely one hundred thousand Armenians from the plains of Erzerum and Alashkert settled in the abandoned Moslem areas of Akhalkalas, which was part of the former pashalik of Akhaltsikhe. This action contributed to an Armeno–Georgian conflict in 1918 (Hovannisian 1997, p. 9). Moreover, according

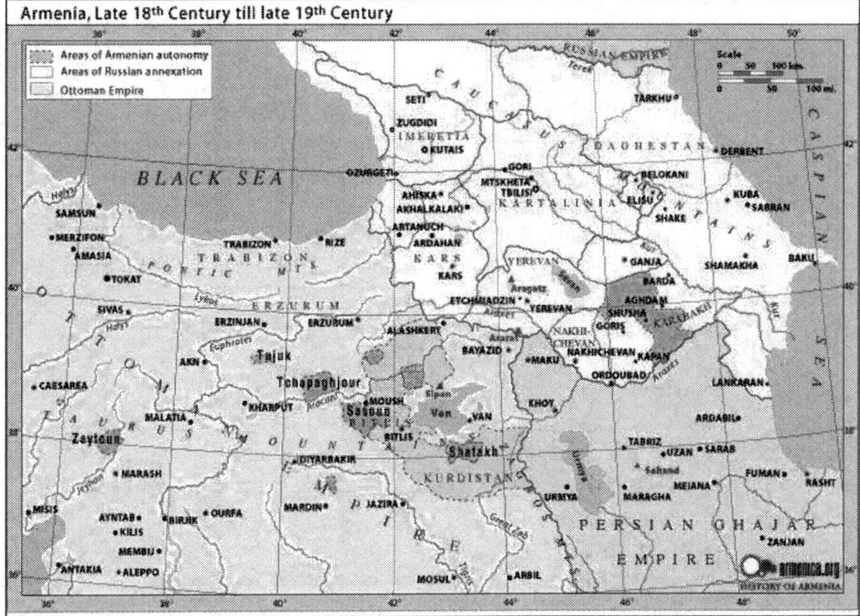

Figure 4.4 Armenia in the eighteenth–nineteenth centuries

Source: History of Armenia

Figure 4.5 The Caucasus

Source: Encyclopedia Britannica, 1998

to Payaslian, British and French diplomatic pressure forced Russia to return to Turkey the Western Armenian territories annexed during the war: Kars, Ardahan, Bayazid, Erzerum and their surrounding regions (Payaslian 2007, p. 112).

Russian Armenia, the term applied to the portion of the Plateau conquered by Tsarist Russia, emerged in the aftermath of the Romanov conquest of Transcaucasia. According to Tsar Nicholas's order, Armianskaia oblast (Armenian province) was only 8,000 square miles in area, and included the former khanates of Erevan and Nakhichevan, while several eastern districts of the Plateau, such as Akhalkalak, Lori, Kazakh, and Mountainous Karabakh were excluded from the oblast (Hovannisian 1997, p. 10). It is important to note that, when Georgia was annexed by the Russians, the urban political and economic system was controlled by the Georgian royal house. Furthermore, the majority of the urban citizens were Armenians,[13] who possessed a commercial capital in Tiflis and Gori from the sixteenth century. Therefore, with the annexation of Georgia, the Armenians lost the protectorship of the Georgian monarch, but acquired more physical security[14] behind Russian troops (Suny 1988, p. 89).

In the meantime, Azerbaijan, which, from the time of ancient Media and Achaemenid Persia, was drawn into the orbit of Iran, but later, after the conquest of the region by Arabs and the conversion to Islam in the mid-seventh century as well as the invasion of the Oghuz Turks under the Seljuk dynasty four centuries later, acquired a large proportion of Turkic inhabitants that led to the Turkification of the region (Swietochowski 1985, p. 1; Altstadt 1992). In the middle of the eighteenth century, after the end of the Safavid dynasty and the assassination of Nadir Shah in 1747, the Caucasian khanates (among them Baku, Kuba, Sheki, Shemakhi, Mountainous Karabakh, Nakhjivan, and Erevan) were ruled by Muslim khans, which led to violent clashes between the Muslim and Christian populations of the khanates (Altstadt 1992, p. 8). But, according to Muriel Atkin, "for all Catherine's professed concern over Christians living under Muslim rule, her actions in the Caucasus showed that she never allowed that issue to force her along a course that was not chosen first and foremost on the basis of Russia's best interests" (established policies that shaped Caucasia for at least two centuries) (Altstadt 1992, p. 15). Altstadt continues that the cultural gulf between Russian "invaders" and the local Azeri population was great, and Russian imperial policies (economic, political and even cultural) were different from those of the former Ottoman and Persian rulers of the Caucasus. For instance, Altstadt mentions that from the time of the Russian conquest until the 1840s, Azerbaijan was ruled directly by the Tsarist military. As stated above, the former khanates became provintsii, and each was ruled by an army officer, a commandant (Altstadt 1992, p. 18). There was a combination of local and Russian imperial law in Azerbaijan, and the latter had to be used only when the former was nonexistent or inappropriate, but Altstadt insists that the Russian commandants were unfamiliar with local customary and religious law, and as a result they applied Russian law in all the cases. Consequently, by the end of direct military rule in the 1840s, Russian law succeeded in all criminal and most civil cases. On the other hand, the jurisdiction of religious courts and their judges was confined to family law (marriage, inheritance and divorce). Altstadt also argues that the subjects of Russian empire were not equal before the law. According to her, restrictions against non-Christians affected the Azerbaijani Turks, since Tsarist censorship regulations of 1857, for instance, granted Georgian and Armenian religious authorities oversight of censorship in their own ethno–religious communities. At the same time, the local Muslim Ecclesiastical Boards did not have such authority. In fact, all Muslim religious books of any kind had to pass a censorship board in Odessa (Altstadt 1992, p. 19; "Svod Zakonov Rossiiskoi Imperii 1857–1868").

The South Caucasus on the eve of the creation of USSR

According to King (2004), already from the second half of the eighteenth century, the Russian empire extended its reach to the warm ports of Crimea, pushing back the Ottomans and unseating the Tatar khan (King 2004, p. 139). Moreover, in the west and the east, Tsarist Russia was seen first as the sole protector of eastern Christendom and later as a liberator of oppressed nations from the Turkish burden. By the end of the eighteenth century, Transcaucasia was divided between Russians and the Ottomans. Russia annexed Kars, Ardahan, and Batum as a result of the Russo–Turkish war of 1877–1878. While Armenian generals in the Tsarist service, M.T. Loris-Melikov, A.A. Ter Gukasov, and I.I. Lazarev successfully stormed the fortress of Kars and advanced into Erzrum, the rest of Russian armies entered the village of San Stefano, where the Treaty of San Stefano was signed in March of 1878. According to the treaty, the Ottomans ceded its eastern provinces of Kars, Ardahan, Batum, and Bayazit and the Plain of Alashkert, thus the Armenians felt that the remainer of the Plateau would be added to the empire as well to ensure the security of the native Christian population (Hovannisian1967, p. 12). But under the pressure of Great Britain, Tsar Alexander II accepted a revised settlement according to which Bayazit and the Plain of Alashkert were restored to the Ottomans. As a result, approximately 25,000 Ottoman Armenians followed the army of Loris-Melikov and left their native region. Hovannisian (1967) argues that the addition of the Kars and Batum oblasts to the Russian empire increased the area of Transcaucasia to over 130,000 square miles, with the estimated population of the entire region in 1886 being 4,700,000 (940,000 Armenians, 1,200,000 Georgians, and 2,220,000 Muslims). It is also important to note that the Georgians concentrated in the Kutais and Tiflis *guberniias*, had the most favorable position in Transcaucasia, while the Armenians spread throughout every province of the region had the least favorable (Hovannisian 1967, p. 13). The Armenians, unhappy with the administrative subdivisions of Transcaucasia, eagerly took the opportunity provided by the Viceroy, Count Illarion Ivanovich Vorontsov-Dashkov, who introduced the notion of *zemstvo* in 1905, an agrarian district with limited economic, cultural, and educational initiatives to the local leaders. As Hovannisian notes, previously few non-Russian areas of the empire had been granted the *zemstvo* system, which was instituted during the great liberal reforms of Alexander II. Nevertheless, the *zemstvo* system failed to be extended to Transcaucasia not only in 1905 but also in 1909, but the Armenians borrowed its mechanisms for introducing the new provincial boundaries in the region. According to their proposal, "the area of jurisdiction of each zemstvo should correspond with that of a given province, which should be as ethnically homogenous as possible" (Hovannisian 1967, p. 15).

The rise of nationalism in the South Caucasus

According to many scholars (Hovannisian 1967; Suny 1997; Payaslian 2007 and others), the Russian conquest of Transcaucasia contributed to a new national, cultural and political awareness among Armenians and Georgians. For example, Suny argues that with the integration of the South Caucasus into the Russian empire, the region underwent significant cultural and material transformations, which formed the new social groups that challenge the dominance of local nobility (Suny 1988, p. xiv). Therefore, when the Russian empire was dissolved, the local Georgian and Armenian leaders led their people to nationhood.

The emergence of modern Armenian nationalism in the nineteenth century derived from a number of factors: 1) it took place within the context of the emergence of influential elites divided along ethnic (Arab, Kurdish) lines; 2) it first appeared in the form of cultural awakening, but by the end of the nineteenth century, it had transformed into an armed revolutionary struggle in reaction to oppressive Ottoman rule; and 3) it benefited greatly from European and Russian philosophies of nationalism and socialism. As a result, Armenian cultural awakening involved the affirmation of national identity as distinct from its neighbors by incorporating European-style nationalism with its notions of liberation, nation-building, and state-formation (Payaslian 2007, p. 117). Payaslian maintains that the repressive governments under Sultan Abdul Hamid and Tsar Alexander III (1881–1894), the latter, in contrast to his predecessors, showed little tolerance for Armenian national aspirations, viewed Armenians as a threat to Russian unity, and caused significant changes in Armenian nationalism that eventually shifted from Armenian literary movements and cultural nationalism into emancipatory and revolutionary nationalism. At the time of intensified Turkish hostilities, Armenians created armed groups to defend themselves.[15]

Georgians also experienced a process of social formation in the last decades of the nineteenth century. It was different from the Armenian cultural awakening, since Georgians in Tiflis, for example, came up against Armenians and Russians, and were forced to recognize their own ethnicity. The latter, Suny claims, would have been irrelevant in the homogenous village. Thus, it was the urban Georgian elite that instigated the national revival, while the working class chose Marxist ideology, which provided a political strategy to workers in Tiflis, Batumi, and Kutaisi. Thus, by 1905, the Marxists became de facto leaders of a national liberation movement in Georgia that postulated to return Georgia to Georgians when the revolution would eliminate the dual domination of Russian bureaucracy and Armenian industrialists (Suny 1988, pp. 144–145).

The leaders of Azerbaijan's cultural and intellectual life were an educated group of writers, composers, journalists, teachers, doctors that came to their cultural and political maturity in the years before the Bolshevik revolution, led the independent republic and played a role in Soviet Azerbaijan into the 1930s (Altstadt 1992, pp. 50–51). According to Altstadt, these elites were the perpetrators of a cultural renaissance that embraces the entire Turkish world—Turkey, Crimea, the Volga-Ural region, Azerbaijan, and Turkestan in the nineteenth–twentieth centuries. It also important to add that Altstadt does not mention the weakness/absence of Azeri nationalism comparing to those of Georgian and Armenian but however notes that the debates over identity of Azerbaijani Turks were cut short by Stalin purges and were revived only after his death.

It is not surprising that Armenian and Georgian nationalism and the recognition of their ethnic identities were formed much earlier than similar developments in their immediate neighbor. For instance, Umut Ozkirimli contends that the phenomena of nationalism, can take different forms depending on historical, social and political circumstances (Ozkirimli 2010, p. 226; Kaufman 2001; after Hovannisian 1967; Suny 1988; and Payaslian 2007). Kaufman also insists that Armenians always had a strong national identity and even seventy years under the communist rule had no effect on "the Armenian question." According to him, Azerbaijani modern nationalism was formed in reaction to Armenian nationalism, and can be traced back to the "Tatar-Armenian War" of 1905–1906, when the well-organized resistance of Armenian nationalist party Dashnaksutiun led Azeris to organize their own nationalist organization "Difai" ("Defense") in 1913. After the collapse of the Russian and Ottoman Empires in 1918, the Armenian and

Azerbaijani nationalists formed their own independent states,[16] and as Kaufman (2001) claims, Dashnaks allied with the Bolsheviks in order to carry out pogroms against Muslims in Baku.[17] As a result, according to Kaufman, the Caucasian Tatars hated Armenians more than Russians, considering the former as the Russian spies, who were "competitors" for Azeri trade and "aggressors" in the "Tatar-Armenian War" (Kaufman 2001, p. 57). Hovhannisian, examining the actions of Dashnaks at the time, argues that for the Armenians of Baku, Bolshevism was equivalent to "Russianism," while Musavatism was synonymous of "Turkism"(Hovannisian 1967, p. 113). So, Eastern Armenians decided to choose the lesser of two evils in order to avoid the tragic fate of the Ottoman Armenians,[18] while Russians skillfully manipulated the complex relations among the indigenous groups in Transcaucasia.[19] The three nations of Transcaucasia will continue experiencing the ascendance of traditional bureaucratic views towards the minorities not only from the Tsarist Russia but also from the Soviets and then the government of the Russian Federation. The perplexed history of the region as well as its territorial and ethnic divisions that became even more entangled after the Tsarist authorities stepped in in Transcaucasia, was always used by the Russian government (regardless who was on the throne or in the office) as a bargaining chip to keep the three South Caucasian countries under control.

Conclusion

The Caucasus was considered to be the most turbulent region for Imperial Russia, and more recently, for the Soviet and Russian governments. The region is linked with the Northern Caucasus, which is an integral part of Russia, and Moscow regards the three Transcaucasian states as its near abroad. The security concerns of Armenia, Azerbaijan and Georgia are linked to the neighboring countries, including the North Caucasus, while for Russia, Iran and Turkey, the Caucasus constitutes an important part of their foreign policies. The Caucasus constituted a buffer zone between competing empires or an integral part of them: Greeks, Romans, Byzantines, Arabs, Mongols, Ottoman Turks, Persians and Russians. This chapter showed that the primary interests of Russia, Iran, and Turkey situated within the Caucasus region in the spheres of military, political and economic security. It has been argued that geopolitical and strategic interests, rather than trade and ideology were the main forces behind Russia's expansion into the South Caucasus, which became a buffer zone and battlefield between the predominantly Orthodox Christian empire in the north and the Muslim powers in the Middle East. Thus, the conquest of the South Caucasus coincided with the decline of the Ottoman Empire and the fading power of Persia. As a result, from the early nineteenth century, the Russians launched their hegemony in the region, which they ruled despotically, implementing the policy of "divide and rule." Since the beginning, the South Caucasian states were treated as colonies and over the centuries a pattern of client relationship was established. I conclude that Russia's conquest of the Caucasus fits the neoclassical realist model since the government responded to the uncertainties of international system by seeking to control and shape its external environment. Furthermore, since the beginning of Russia's expansion into the South Caucasus and until the collapse of the Soviet Union, I regard my cases studies (Russia's foreign policies in Armenia, Azerbaijan, and Georgia) as crucial cases since they closely fit a neoclassical realist theory's main assumption that the relative material power capabilities and the place in the international system define the scope and ambitions of a state's foreign policy. The Tsarist government had revisionist aspirations and made a bid for regional hegemony, undertaking territorial expansion at the expense of both weaker states (in this study, the South Caucasians states) and rival great powers (the Ottoman Empire, Persia, Britain). In the beginning, the territorial expansion of the Tsarist Russia was advanced through single-mindedness for conquest shared by both rulers and the South Caucasian states, the latter viewed the Tsarist officials as their emancipators.

Notes

1 By "institutionalism" the authors support the view that international institutions matter (Hasenclever et al. 1997, p. 2).
2 Adapted from Andreas Hasenclever, Peter Mayer and Volker Rittberger's (1997) *Theories of International Regimes*.
3 Russia's reserve fund fell from $38.8 billion to $32.2 billion during the course of August 2016, shrinking to over a third of pre-crisis levels, when the fund stood at $90 billion in 2014 (Kucera 2016).
4 It has been argued that one of the reasons for Armenia choosing the Eurasian Union over the European Union was the price competitiveness of Armenian exports in the Russian market.
5 See the World Bank's Global Economic Prospects: Europe and Central Asia report, which predicts that Russia is expected to grow at a 1.5 percent in the year, as the adjustment to oil low prices is completed. Strengthening activity in Russia will support other economies in the region, including Armenia, through rising trade and remittances.
6 The authors maintain that in 2013, Ukraine and Russia were the third and the fourth largest importers to Georgia, respectively (Biermann and Tsutskiridze 2014, p. 2).
7 One route goes via the Baltic ports of Klaipeda or Riga, then through Ukraine and Russia, and another route goes overland through Ukraine. The Caucasus Transit Corridor has the Georgian port city of Poti and Turkey as its Western connection locations, then goes through Georgia, Azerbaijan, and the Caspian Sea, and in the east it splits into a Kazakhstan and a Turkmenistan branch (Biermann and Tsutskiridze 2014, p. 4).
8 See the World Bank and the Asian Development Bank reports on economic prospects in Azerbaijan.
9 Equifinality is the concept of multiple paths to a common end state, conceived by Ludwig von Bertalanffy in his efforts to unify the sciences, and which is an implicit assumption of case study research that considers the alternative paths thought which the outcome could have occurred (Mills, Durepos and Wiebe 2010).
10 Davit Bek had been in the service of Vakhtang VI, king of Georgia, and in 1722 together with a number of Armenian warriors in the service of Georgia was sent to Zangeur at the request of the Armenian meliks who were being harassed by their Muslim neighbors (Bouroutian 1997, p. 88).
11 Catherine the Great, after her war with the Ottomans (1768–1774) sought to undermine the economy of Turkish Crimea, relocated the Armenian community (the major contributors to the economy) from there to a settlement along the Don River that was named Nor Nakhichevan (New Nakhichevan, now the part of Roston-on-Don). Thus,

during her reign, the Armenians, encouraged by Catherine's interest in Transcaucasia, once again sought Russian support in their struggle for autonomy (Hovannisian 1997).

12 Tsar Nicholas I of Russia (1825–1855)

13 According to Suny (1988), in Tiflis (Tblisi), Armenians made up about three-quarters of the population at the time of annexation.

14 There was hostility among many Georgian nobles towards the Armenian merchants regardless the fact that their monarch supported the Armenian dwellers (Suny 1988, p. 89).

15 Payaslian mentions that such groups included the Black Cross Society of Van (1878); the Protectors of the Fatherland in Erzerum (1881), also there were organized political parties adopting nationalist ideologies and revolutionary strategies such as the Amenakan Party in 1885 in Van, the Hnchakian Revolutionary Party in 1887 in Geneva, and the Hay Heghapokhakan Dashnaktsutiun (Armenian Revolutionary Federation, ARF) in 1890 in Tiflis (Payaslian 2007, p. 120).

16 After the disintegration of the Russian Empire in 1917, Armenia, Azerbaijan and Georgia became part of the short-lived Trans-Caucasian Democratic Federative Republic, which was dissolved in May 1918.

17 According to Hovannisian (1967), Transcaucasia was decidedly anti-Bolshevik expect the ranks of the Russian Army and part of the Baku proletariat. Moreover, there was the secret contact between Armenian Bolsheviks and Dashnaktsutiun since the leaders of both factions had been nurtured by the Russian revolutionary movement, had struggled against Tsarism, and had shared the deprivations of imprisonment and exile (Hovannisian, 1967, p. 111).

18 The Armenian Genocide was carried out by the "Young Turk" government of the Ottoman Empire in 1915–1916. As a result, one and a half million Armenians were killed out of total of two and a half million Armenians in the Ottoman Empire ("Fact Sheet: Armenian Genocide," Knights of Vartan Armenian Research Center, the University of Michigan-Dearborn, 1996).

19 When the Russian armies occupied most of the Armenian Plateau during the winter and spring of 1916, Armenians expected their support and protection for Armenian political-civic bodies. Nevertheless, Russian armies were accused in lawlessness and looting, confiscating the weapons of the Armenian peasantry and giving the Kurds freedom of action. While the Viceroy Vorontsov-Dashkov reassured the Armenians of the government's benevolence, it turned out that the representatives of the Romanov sovereign were negotiating with other members of the Entente the annexation of the eastern vilayets included no provisions for Armenian autonomy (Hovannisian 1967, p. 57).

Bibliography

Alboyadjian, Arshag (1961) *History of the Armenians in Malatia: With Topographical, Historical and Ethnographical Information.* Beirut, Lebanon: Sevan Press.

Altstadt, Audrey L. (1992) *The Azerbaijani Turks: Power and Identity under Russian Rule.* Stanford, CA: Hoover Institution Press, Stanford University.

Arka News Agency (2017) "World Bank revises downward economic growth forecast for Armenia in 2017." January 11. http://arka.am/en/news/economy/world_bank_revises_downward_economic_growth_forecast_for_armenia_in_2017/ (accessed Janaury 14, 2017).

"Armenia, Late 18th Century Until 19th Century," [map] *History of Armenia.* www.armenica.org/ (accessed January 10, 2015).

Avalov, Zurab (1901) *Prisoedinenie Gruzii k Rossii.* St. Petersburg, Russia: Tipografiia A.S. Suvorina.

Bayer, Alexey (2008) "Putting Putin into the Context of Russian History," *The Globalist*. May 5. www.theglobalist.com/putting-putin-into-the-context-of-russian-history/ (accessed June 10, 2015).

Beach, Derek (2012) *Analyzing Foreign Policy*. Houndmills, UK: Palgrave Macmillan.

Berochashvili, Nicolas and Jean Radvanie (1996, 1998) *Atlas Geopolitique du Caucase*. Paris, France: Editions Autrement.

Biermann, Florian and Giorgi Tsutskiridze (2014) "The Crisis in Ukraine and the Georgian Economy," *The Free Policy Brief Series*. Centre for Economic and Financial Researchers. March 17. http://freepolicybriefs.org/2014/03/17/the-crisis-in-ukraine-and-the-georgian-economy/ (accessed May 8, 2014).

Boulding, Kenneth (1978) *Stable Peace*. Austin, TX: University of Texas Press.

Bournoutian, George (1997) "Eastern Armenia from the Seventeenth Century to the Russian Annexation," in Richard G. Hovannisian (Ed.) *The Armenian People from Ancient to Modern Times*. New York, NY: St. Martin's Press.

Dadashova, Gulgiz (2014) "Oil Price Drop: Azerbaijan Relies on Non-Oil Sector," *Azernews*. November 28. www.azernews.az/analysis/73933.html (accessed January 5, 2015).

Davies, Brian (2007) *Warfare, State and Society on the Black Sea Steppe, 1500–1700*. London, UK: Routledge.

"Fact Sheet: Armenian Genocide," (1996) Knights of Vartan Armenian Research Center, The University of Michigan-Dearborn.

George, Alexander L. and Andrew Bennett (2005) *Case Studies and Theory Development in the Social Sciences*. Cambridge, MA: MIT Press.

Hanauer, Larry (2014) "Crimean Adventure Will Cost Russia Dearly," *The Moscow Times*. September 7. www.themoscowtimes.com/opinion/article/crimean-adventure-xwill-cost-russia-dearly/506550.htm (accessed January 6, 2015).

Harris, Paul G. (2013) *Routledge Handbook of Global Environmental Politics*. New York, NY: Routledge.

Hasenclever, Andreas, Peter Mayer and Volker Rittberger (1997) *Theories of International Regimes*. Cambridge, UK: Cambridge University Press.

Hovannisian, Richard G. (1967) *Armenia on the Road to Independence, 1918*. Oakland, CA: University of California Press.

Hovannisian, Richard G. (1992) *The Armenian Genocide: History, Politics, and Ethics*. New York, NY: St. Martin's Press.

Hovannisian, Richard G. (1997) *Armenian People from Ancient to Modern Times*. New York, NY: St. Martin's Press.

Kaufman, Stuart J. (2001) *Modern Hatreds: The Symbolic Politics of Ethnic War*. Ithaca, NY: Cornell University Press.

Keohane, Robert O. (1993) "Regime," in Joel Krieger (Ed.) *Oxford Companion to Politics of the World*. New York, NY: Oxford University Press.

King, Charles (2004) *The Black Sea: A History*. Oxford, UK: Oxford University Press.

Kluchevsky, Vasily O. (1931) *A History of Russia*, vol. 259. Translated by C.J. Hogarth. London, UK: J.M. Dent.

Kucera, Joshua (2016) "Azerbaijan Unable, or Unwilling, to Pay for Russian Weapons: Reports," *The Moscow Times*. March 6.

Kuzio, Taras (2006) "Ukraine is Not Russia: Comparing Youth Political Activism," *SAIS Review*, Vol. 26, No. 2, Summer–Fall.

Light, Margot (2005) "Russia and Transcaucasia," in John F.R. Wright and Suzanne Goldenberg (Eds.) *Transcaucasian Boundaries*. New York, NY: St. Martin's Press.

Lobell, Steven E., Norrin M. Ripsman and Jeffrey W. Taliaferro (2009) *Neoclassical Realism, The State, and Foreign Policy*. Cambridge, UK: Cambridge University Press.

Mills, Albert J., Gabrille Durepos and Elden Wiebe (2010) *Encyclopedia of Case Study Research*. Thousand Oaks, CA: SAGE Publications.

Mouritzen, Hans and Anders Wivel (2011) *Explaining Foreign Policy: International Diplomacy and the Russo-Georgian War*. Boulder, CO: Lynne Rienner Publishers.

Ozkirimli, Umut (2010) *Theories of Nationalism: A Critical Introduction*. Houndmills, UK: Palgrave Macmillan.

Payaslian, Simon (2007) *The History of Armenia: From the Origins to the Present*. New York, NY: Palgrave Macmillan.

Petro, Nikolai N. and Alvin Z. Rubinstein (1997) *Russian Foreign Policy: From Empire to Nation State*. New York, NY: Longman.

Recknagel, Charles (2014) "Money Troubles: Russia's Weak Ruble Pulls Down Neighbor's Currencies," *Radio Free Europe Radio Liberty*, December 12. www.rferl.org/a/russia-ruble-effects-neighboring-countries/26738229.html (accessed May 8, 2015).

Rose, Gideon (1998) "Neoclassical Realism and Theories of Foreign Policy," *World Politics*, Vol. 51, No. 1, pp. 144–172.

Salukvadze, Khatuna (2006) "Russia's New Doctrine of Neo Imperialism," *Analyst, The Central Asia-Caucasus Institute*, February 8.

Schweller, Randall L. (2009) "Neoclassical Realism and State Mobilisation: Expansionist ideology in the Age of Mass Politics," in Steven E. Lobell, Norrin M. Ripsman, and Jeffrey W. Taliaferro (Eds.) *Neoclassical Realism, The State, and Foreign Policy*, Cambridge, UK: Cambridge University Press.

Shevtsova, Lilia (2007) *Russia Lost in Transition: The Yeltsin and Putin Legacies*. Washington, DC: Carnegie Endowment for International Peace.

Sputnik (2016) "Russia's Recession Continues, GDP to Shrink 1.5 percent in 2016-Acra Forecast," September 12. https://sputniknews.com/business/201609121045204420-russian-recession-continues-acra/ (accessed October 10, 2016).

Suny, Ronald Grigor (1988) *The Making of the Georgian Nation*. Bloomington, IN: Indiana University Press.

Suny, Ronald (1997) *The Soviet Experiment: Russia, the USSR, and the Successor States*. New York, NY: Oxford University Press.

Suny, Ronald Grigor (2009) "The Pawn of Great Powers: The East–West Competition for Caucasia," *Journal of Eurasian Studies*, No. 1, pp. 10–25.

"Svod Zakonov Rossiiskoi Imperii" (1857–1868) Sankt-Petersburg, Rossia: Tipografiia Vtorogo Otdeleniia Sobstvennoi E.I.V. Kantseliarii.

Swietochowski, Tadeusz (1985) *Russian Azerbaijan, 1905–1920: The Shaping of a National Identity in a Muslim Community*. New York, NY: Cambridge University Press.

Trenin, Dmitri (1996) "Russia's Security Interests and Policies in the Caucasus Region," in Bruno Coppieters (Ed.) *Contested Borders in the Caucasus*. Brussels, Belgium: VUB University Press.

Villari, Luigi (1906) *Fire and Sword in the Caucasus*. London, UK: T. F. Unwin.

Winik, Jay (2007) "Vladimir the Great?," *The Washington Post*. September 2.

The World Bank Report (2017) "Global Economic Prospect: Europe and Central Asia." January 10. www.worldbank.org/en/region/eca/brief/global-economic-prospects-europe-and-central-asia (accessed January 14, 2017).

5 Testing regime theories in the post-Soviet space

Robert Yin maintains that the analysis of case study evidence is one of the least developed and most difficult aspects of doing case studies. He suggests having a general analytic strategy in the first place to treat the evidence fairly, produce compelling analytic conclusions, and rule out alternative explanations (Yin 2003, pp. 110–111). Yin proposes three strategies that will be helpful in using tools and make manipulations to produce the needed analytic result: 1) relying on theoretical propositions that led to your case study; 2) defining and testing alternative explanations; and 3) developing a descriptive framework for organizing the case study. This chapter deals with defining and testing alternative explanations using techniques such as regime theory analysis.

In this regard, the simple or direct alternative explanation of Russia's foreign policy in the South Caucasus and the creation of the Eurasian Economic Union would be that the new economic regime will establish the general rules and norms of post-Soviet states' behavior to facilitate cooperation and promote trade in the region. At the end of the day, it is reasonable to assume that the post-Soviet countries would seek economic and political reintegration, taking into account that regionalism became a major force for global change after the end of World War II. The question of whether or not Eurasian economic integration will mean regression for the post-Soviet states into protectionism and state-regulated system should also be considered (see Table 5.1). However, this chapter, after examining the regimes that have been created within the former Soviet Union (including the formation of the USSR), concludes that the Eurasian Union will follow the fate

Table 5.1 Testing alternative explanations of Russia's foreign policies in the South Caucasus

Research Question #1	*Research Question #2*
Does Eurasian economic integration mean regression for the post-Soviet states into protectionism and state-regulated systems?	Will the creation of the new economic regime in Eurasia establish the general rules and norms of post-Soviet states' behavior to facilitate cooperation and promote trade in the region?

of declarative and insubstantial initiatives directed towards economic integration in the region that failed to make much impact on post-Soviet developments (Dragneva and Wolczuk 2013, p. 2).

The realist explanation of the creation of the Union of Soviet Socialist Republics

According to Simmons, regimes often contain rules that specify their own transformation. Moreover, she emphasizes that to explain regime change per se is to explain why states agreed to alter the codified rights and rules that regulate their behavior (Simmons 1995, p. 495). This chapter maintains that from the construction of socialism within the Soviet Union to the creation of the Eurasian Union in post-Soviet space, the Soviet and Russian leaders acted not in the best interests of the nation(s) but in the best interests of the ruling class. Thus, the Tsarist "divide and rule" strategy that, in Liliana Riga's (2012) words, was often used as an integration policy, became a hallmark of the Soviet and then Russia's foreign policy in the near abroad. For example, Iosif Stalin's "Socialism in One Country" plan sought to create a unified Soviet people implementing the policy of a country with a centralized state, a centralized economy, a definite territory and a monolithic party (Stalin 1952). In order to undercut organized and effective opposition to the Soviet regime, Stalin tailored the boundaries among the Soviet states according to their loyalty to Communist principles and Moscow administration rather than the reflection of their ethno-national makeup (Janison 2014).[1] Administrative territorial divisions formed after the Bolshevik Revolution in 1917–1918 were considered as one of the most powerful tools of the Soviet government, which deliberately overlapped traditional territories and administrative boundaries in order to ensure the creation of potential "fifth columns" within the USSR to ferment the ethnic conflicts and divisions, especially in the regions (the Caucasus, Eastern Europe, Central Asia, and many others) with a history of ethnic rivalry and violence.[2]

In other words, starting with the creation of the Soviet Union, the international institutions formed within the former Soviet space lacked the fundamental principles of any given regime, which are *sets of principles*, *norms*, *rules*, and *procedures accepted by states* (Hasenclever et. al. 1997, p. 11). While promoting the spirit of camaraderie among the Soviet nations, who "fought" the Tsarist regime in order to live "happily ever after" in the "free" country, the Soviet government continued the traditions of Imperial Russia (or even surpassed it), and maintained a commanding control over the multi-ethnic country, by creating a climate of fear, distrust and mutual suspicions among its nations, with the ultimate goal to achieve the dictatorship of the Communist Party.

In Trenin's opinion, with the aim of tightening its grip on the South Caucasus, Russia tried to instigate hostility among the local players, while St. Petersburg, and later Moscow, was put in the positions of an arbiter to which all sides in any internal conflict had to appeal (Trenin 1996, p. 92). In other words, Moscow served as a lender of last resort for all the disputes among the former republics amid the absence of the rule of law within the Soviet Union and then, after the dissolution of the USSR, within Russia. Thus, Moscow acted in a flexible form to ensure the subordination of Transcaucasian nations and manifested a great pragmatism in the realm of conflict resolution in the region (Trenin 1996, pp. 92–93).

Analyzing the theory of hegemonic stability, a classical example of a power-based theory of international regimes, we should be cautious about putting this theory forward as a powerful explanation of events in the post-Soviet space (Keohane 2003, p. 114). The main problem with this theory, which assumes that strong international economic regimes depend on hegemonic power, is the fact that power is viewed in terms of tangible resources (gross domestic product, oil import dependence, and others), whereas less tangible resources (such as confidence in oneself or in a currency, or political position relative to other actors) are not considered (Keohane 2003, pp. 99–114). Taking into consideration that Russia's economy slipped recently into recession amid Western sanctions and the drop in oil prices, a power-based theory of international regimes fails to explain how Moscow continues advancing its position in the South Caucasus and Eastern Europe.

To reiterate, according to HST, hegemonic powers have the capabilities to maintain international regimes that they favor by either using coercion to enforce adherence to rules (the realist version of HST) or providing the incentives (collective goods) to those who collaborate (Keohane 2003, p. 100). In this regard, both hegemonic power and small states can benefit from such cooperation: the former gains the ability to shape and dominate its environment, while the later will receive a sufficient flow of benefits. As a result, fragmentation of power between rival countries leads to fragmentation of the international economic regime, whereas concentration of power contributes to stability (Kindleberger 1974; Gilpin 1975; and Krasner 1976). However, while HST does well at identifying the conditions for strong international economic regimes, it fails at establishing sufficient conditions for maintaining such a regime (Keohane 2003, p. 102). For instance, Robert Keohane argues that during the 1960s and early to mid-1970s, when economic power became more equally distributed among the Western European states and Japan, U.S.-created international economic regimes (such as the International Monetary Fund, the International Bank for Reconstruction and Development or the World Bank, and the General Agreement on Tariffs and Trade or GATT) have not suffered a decline. Keohane concludes that the hegemonic stability thesis is "a power-as-resource theory" that links tangible state capabilities to behavior and, thus, fails to predict accurately particular political outcomes. In order to come up with more complex theoretical framework, he suggests integrating systemic analysis with explanations at the level of foreign policy (Keohane 2003, p. 102).

Duncan Snidal identifies two strands of the theory of hegemonic stability, which vary in the way they depict the accurate character of the hegemon's policies and their distributional implications (Snidal 1985, pp. 585–590). In the so-called benevolent leadership model, according to Snidal, a hegemonic state provides the collective good (an effective international regime) all by itself. Accordingly, the other states are freed from the obligation to help to keep the regime, and can be tempted to become free-riders, when public goods are at issue. However, it does not mean that the hegemon's advantage (net gain) will be less than that of the free-riders, this model holds that the largest actor's benefits (received from the good minus costs of provision of the good) are greater than those of the smaller states (Hasenclever et.al. 1997, p. 90). In the meantime, in the case of Russia's foreign policies in Armenia, Azerbaijan and Georgia, providing public goods to the three South Caucasian states is not sufficient for Moscow to be able to reinforce its geopolitical preferences in the region, at least in case of Azerbaijan and Georgia. As was already mentioned, the European Union is still the main trading partner for the three South Caucasian states. Despite the fact that Yerevan joined the Eurasian Economic Union in 2015, Russia is the second trading partner for the country, while for Azerbaijan Russia is in third, and for Georgia in sixth place (Hautala 2015).

Moreover, even after teaming up with Russia, Kazakhstan and Belarus in the Eurasian Economic Union, Armenia is still considering signing up an Association Agreement with the EU without its free trade component. Johannes Hahn, EU commissioner for European Neighborhood Policy and Enlargement, announced that Yerevan and Brussels are currently conducting negotiations about signing up the political part of the Association Agreement, while also discussing the issues related to migration, human rights, economic reforms, and EU support to Armenia. Moreover, according to the head of the EU delegation to Armenia, Ambassador Traian Hristea, the country is one of the largest recipients of funds per capita within the framework of the EU Eastern Partnership Program.[3] Moreover, due to a lack of standardized conditions and requirements for countries seeking membership in the Eurasian Union, there is a real possibility that the creation of the Eurasian Economic Union would be far from a regression into Soviet-era stagnation and protectionism. For instance, article 42.6 of the treaty establishing the Eurasian Economic Union allows the member states to use lower import duty rate after their accession than those specified through the uniform custom tariff (Zagorski 2015, p. 7). In this regard, until 2022, Armenia will be able to apply duties that are different from the EEU tariff rates for certain agricultural products (Eurasian Economic Commission Council 2014). Overall, the Eurasian Economic Union has such a weak economic basis that an accelerated expansion of the EEU (even Turkey and Vietnam were invited to join a free trade area) could negate all the initial accomplishments (Zagorski 2015, p. 4).

It is safe to suggest that Armenia is also trying to re-strengthen ties with the West, and many observers believe that Russia's economic situation and the possibility of disintegration processes in the EEU space are the main reasons behind the back-to-the-West campaign of Yerevan (Hayrumyan 2015). In fact, Belarus and Kazakhstan are also establishing expanded ties with the European Union. On a side note, Belarus, a founding member of the Eurasian Economic Union that was launched in January of 2015, has the longest record of cooperation with the Russian Federation among the six Eastern European partner countries since the disintegration of the USSR in 1991. Belarus with its reputation as Europe's last dictatorship, has been included in the EaP from the beginning of the initiative

Table 5.2 Trade in goods with the EU-28, 2005–2015 (1) (million EUR)

	2005	*2006*	*2007*	*2008*	*2009*	*2010*	*2011*	*2012*	*2013*	*2014*	*2015*
Exports											
Armenia	355	375	409	391	222	379	437	437	383	329	397
Azerbaijan	1,950	2,905	1,251	18,712	4,738	8,216	11,584	8,974	8,669	8,707	–
Belarus	5,747	7,255	7,767	9,691	6,674	5,762	11,272	13,629	7,828	7,983	7,782
Georgia	174	179	193	227	168	221	305	275	457	470	578
Moldova	357	428	496	558	479	550	778	789	856	938	1,097
Ukraine	8,277	9,694	10,229	12,419	6,823	9,878	12,946	13,326	12,621	12,801	–
Imports											
Armenia	469	549	740	829	601	731	768	791	782	759	683
Azerbaijan	1,012	1,295	1,222	1,402	1,170	1,262	2,265	2,079	2,842	2,336	–
Belarus	2,906	4,022	4,564	5,824	4,710	5,714	6,225	7,216	7,885	9,646	5,169
Georgia	581	845	1,046	1,133	890	1,085	1,474	1,888	1,704	1,784	2,259
Moldova	837	971	1,228	1,433	1,021	1,287	1,623	1,806	1,861	1,933	1,761
Ukraine	9,814	12,923	16,250	19,659	11,057	14,445	18,540	20,414	20,365	15,852	–
Trade balance											
Armenia	–113	–174	–331	–437	–379	–353	–331	–354	–399	–430	–286
Azerbaijan	938	1,610	28	17,310	3,568	6,954	9,318	6,895	5,827	6,372	–
Belarus	2,842	3,233	3,203	3,868	1,964	48	5,047	6,412	–57	–1,663	2,613
Georgia	–408	–666	–853	–906	–722	–864	–1,169	–1,614	–1,247	–1,314	–1,681
Moldova	–480	–543	–732	–875	–542	–737	–845	–1,017	–1,005	–995	–664
Ukraine	–1,537	–3,229	–6,020	–7,240	–4,234	–4,568	–5,594	–7,088	–7,744	–3,051	–

(1) As reported by ENP–East countries

in 2009, but the country's participation with the EU has been limited due to restrained relations with Brussels over human rights, the absence of the rule of law, and many other indicators of an authoritarian regime. Within the EaP, Minsk is also excluded from bilateral cooperation with the EU but can participate in multilateral cooperation platforms (Petrov and Van Elsuwege 2016). Although Belarus always prioritized Eurasian integration over European, President Alexander Lukashenko was not overly pleased with Putin's annexation of Crimea. Lukashenko even called on the U.S. to play a central role in the Ukrainian recovery, and announced that Belarus would not become Moscow's "north-western" province (Chilcote and Kudrytski 2015). After the Ukrainian crisis Belarus found itself in a very challenging situation. On the one hand, the country does not want to get into conflicts with its closest ally, Russia. On the other, Minsk has to maintain good relations with its neighbors, war-torn Ukraine and the EU. Probably, as a token of appreciation for helping to broker a Ukrainian cease-fire deal in February 2015 by hosting the leaders of Russia, Ukraine, Germany, and France in Minsk, in February 2016 the EU ended five years of sanctions against Belarus due "to improved human rights," which again can be considered as another attempt by Brussels to maintain ties with one of its "wandering sheep."

Thus, I have found insufficient evidence to support the power-based theory of international regimes in explaining Russia's foreign policy in the South Caucasus and the creation of the Eurasian Union. Furthermore, the realist explanation of the regime theories, although emphasizing relative power capabilities as a central explanatory variable and stressing states' sensitivity to distributional aspects of cooperation and regimes, holds that states are the most important actors on the world scene, which act out of self-interest in an anarchical environment (Hasenclever et al. 1997, p. 83). Susan Strange considers such a view as a state-centric paradigm, which is "narrow-minded and limits vision of a wider reality," and ignores transnational authority (Strange 1982, pp. 479–485).

This study, following the arguments of Susan Strange (1982), maintains that, first of all, the problem with the theories of international regimes is rooted in the concept of "regime" itself. Hence, according to Strange, "regime" is one more "wooly concept that is a fertile source of discussion because people mean different things when they use it" (Strange 1982, p. 485). For instance, this concept was used by the Soviet Union as "sovereign independence socialist states" to justify its relations with East European communist states, which, in Strange's view, was nothing else than the suppression of information (Strange 1982, p. 485). Meanwhile, in the United States, scholars used "interdependence" in order to describe what was asymmetrical, uneven dependence or vulnerability. Strange concludes that the concept of "regime" is not misleading or misrepresenting, but simply confusing and disorienting. In this regard, if in Keohane and Nye's formulation, "regime" refers to explicit or implicit international arrangements ("networks of norms, rules, and procedures that regularize behavior and control its effects"), Krasner's definition of regimes as "decision-making procedures around which actors' expectations converge" is so broadened, according to Strange, that it can include any stable distribution of the power to influence outcomes (Strange 1982,

p. 485). The focal point of Strange's critique of international regime theories is that the notion of regime tends to emphasize the static quality of processes for managing the international system, which are considered to be stable and anarchic. On the contrary, Strange maintains that the international system is highly dynamic and has undergone significant changes in three important areas of regime analysis: security; money; and trade. As we have demonstrated so far, the creation of the new economic bloc in the post-Soviet space did not miraculously bring forth security, money and trade to the members of the EEU. As soon as Russia's economy fell into a recession, Armenia, Belarus and Kazakhstan started to prepare safety bags in advance. The Moscow officials, on the other hand, are behaving more like high school bullies rather as guarantors of security in the post-Soviet space. Generally speaking, the member-states of the Eurasian Economic Union are not standing shoulder to shoulder as they are supposed to be within a given regional bloc, but conducting themselves as "frenemies" in the international system, not only from economic or political point of view, but also in terms of security. The problem of security dilemma in the region is aggravated by the various ethnic conflicts, which became the cornerstone of Russian foreign policy in the near abroad. Thus, the discussion of an outbreak of the ethnic conflicts after the disintegration of the USSR is inevitable for this book since conventional wisdom holds that regional integration is one of the best solutions to the threat posed by nationalist war in the world politics. I shall return to this issue later in the chapter.

In order to avoid confirmatory bias, one should take two competing theoretical answers to one's research questions and use them to structure the analysis (Beach 2012, p. 223). In this regard, a power-based explanation of international regimes theory does not provide an answer to my research question: "What explains Russia's foreign policy in the South Caucasus and the relevance for that policy in the creation of the Eurasian Union?" First of all, this theory does not consider domestic forces; in the meantime, it holds that the presence of hegemonic power is enough to keep the international system stabilized. According to Gourevitch (1978), domestic forces help to explain changes in the international political structure, while changes in the international political structure affect domestic institutions and preferences (Gourevitch 1978, pp. 881–912). For instance, the analysis of domestic factors in the former Soviet states would help the researcher to identify a couple of obstacles that will be difficult, or even impossible, to overcome in the Eurasian Economic Union—the fear of Moscow's imperialist ambitions by the member states (Belarus, Kazakhstan, Armenia and Kyrgyzstan), and the inability of Russia to act as a unipolar configuration of power in the issue-area in question—that this study considers as mutually exclusive.[4] Another factor that power-based theories of international regimes overlook is the historical baggage of the founding member states of the Eurasian Union.

'The first pancake is always lumpy'

It has been argued that the Kremlin never treated the former Soviet republics as equal partners over the span of seven decades or even before, during the Tsarist regime. In the meantime, the economic bloc has Russia, the largest state in the region, as the main EEU donor country. As a result, since the bloc includes the smaller states whose regional influence is less important, Moscow's dominance will increase with all the consequences. As we shall see at the end of this chapter, you cannot step into the same river twice.

Caroline Kennedy-Pipe writes that, if throughout the nineteenth century Russia was seen by Western powers as a partner, albeit a little bit "troubled and troublesome one," in 1917 all that changed (Kennedy-Pipe 1998, p. 11). The creation of the Soviet Union was a radical turn in world history, when a revolutionary regime was established on the European landmass with an explicit intention to drastically change the state system and erase the class barriers. Consequently, in the beginning, the Soviet foreign policy was focused on the preservation of the revolution within the new state, which was involved in war and civil war. Violence, acts of cruelty, repressions and bloodshed became the accepted ways of life since the start of the Soviet nation (Kennedy-Pipe 1998, p. 11). Following a bloody, three-year civil war, Vladimir Ilyich Ulyanov (V.I. Lenin), the leader of the Bolshevik Revolution and the founder of Russia's Communist Party, concentrated all power in the hands of his party; reiterated the preeminence of hierarchical and bureaucratic government institutions over society; shut down the emergence of a strong judiciary or any countervailing economic, social, or cultural institutions that might limit the power of the party; and also used the secret police to suppress any opposition (Petro and Rubinstein 1997, p. 5).

One of the hallmarks of Soviet foreign policy in the period 1917–1920 was the attempt to preserve the revolution at home and to gain the recognition of the Soviet state in the international system. Moreover, another aspect of Soviet foreign policy at the time was a principle of self-determination, which many scholars (mostly from the former Soviet republics) found to be very selective. Zurab Papaskiri (2012), for example, argues that V.I. Lenin used the idea of self-determination of nations in order to destroy the Russian empire but as soon as this goal was achieved, the Bolshevik's leader attempted to bring back into the Soviet Union the former imperial territories. Ohannes Geukjian (2011) had suggested that Lenin, who initially opposed the establishment of ethno-territorial federalism, found it attractive in the aftermath of the Bolshevik's revolution as an effective tool to rebuild damaged state authority and to win political loyalty in the ethnic Russian regions (Geukjian 2011, p. 81). While in the early 1920s, Lenin promised the non-Russian people the right to self-determination, by denouncing the "Great Russian nationalism" that had dominated them during the Tsarist time, after the formation of the USSR in December 1922, Lenin[5] embarked on a Soviet policy of nation-building (Geukjian 2011, p. 81). It is important to note that Marxist–Leninists were skeptical about the creation of small states. This was a controversial topic for Lenin (1916):

> In Russia, the creation of an independent national state remains, for the time being, the privilege of the Great-Russian nation alone. We, the Great-Russian proletarians, who defend no privileges whatever, do not defend this privilege

> either. We are fighting on the ground of a definite state; we unite the workers of all nations living in this state; we cannot vouch for any particular path of national development, for we are marching to our class goal along all possible paths.

However, for Lenin and his followers the notion of self-determination was a call to fight against imperial powers, and free itself from the oppressor nation, nothing more:

> The right of nations to self-determination means only the right to independence in a political sense, the right to free, political secession from the oppressing nation.

In the meantime, Lenin was quite clear about the creation of small states:

> Consequently, this demand is by no means identical with the demand for secession, for partition, for the formation of small states. It is merely the logical expression of the struggle against national oppression in every form. The more closely the democratic system of state approximates to complete freedom of secession, the rarer and weaker will the striving for secession be in practice; for the advantages of large states, both from the point of view of economic progress and from the point of view of the interests of the masses, are beyond doubt, and these advantages increase with the growth of capitalism. The recognition of self-determination is not the same as making federation a principle. One may be a determined opponent of this principle and a partisan of democratic centralism and yet prefer federation to national inequality as the only path towards complete democratic centralism. It was precisely from this point of view that Marx, although a centralist, preferred even the federation of Ireland with England to the forcible subjection of Ireland to the English.

In sum, no matter what type of regime existed in Russia: monarchy or communist, the small nations within the empire or the Soviet Union were denied their right to self-determination. We have shown the continuation of this imperial tradition in Russia's foreign policy after the collapse of the Soviet Union in the previous chapters.

The South Caucasus was always a geopolitical battlefield between East and West since it is situated between two economically and strategically important regions, the Caspian Basin and the Black Sea. From the historical perspective, the outside powers, Turkey, Iran, Russia, Britain, and Germany, tried their best to invade the land, assimilate the locals, and exploit the natural resources of the region (de Waal 2011). After the disintegration of the Soviet Union, Russia lost more than 20 percent of the territory it controlled in the Soviet Union, almost half of the population of the USSR, and several important geostrategic regions, including resource-rich Caucasus and South Asia (Bordachev and Skriba 2015, p. 16). In this regard,

Mesbahi (2010) argues that after a short period of unipolarity in the international system and the disruption of the Russian-centric Eurasian balance of power, Moscow is on its way to create “a new version of an old and historical Russian-centric Eurasian set-up notwithstanding the US regional influence and ultimately the imposing presence of China” (Mesbahi 2010, p. 165). Thus, bringing Armenia, Azerbaijan and Georgia (along with other FSU states) back to its orbit can be considered as a focal point in the Kremlin’s policy of revanchism.

The South Caucasus indeed was always and still is an important geostrategic region for Moscow. Azerbaijan’s rise as a natural gas supplier began in 1848, and towards the end of the nineteenth century, Baku became the center of attention for the world’s capital investments (Croissant and Aras 1999, p. 102). In the 1870s and 1880s the famous Nobel brothers and the Rothschild family financed the Baku oil industry. The oil industry played not only an important role in forming the Azeri bourgeoisie class with a growing sense of national identity at the time, but also was the main reason that Russia would have no intention of freeing Azerbaijan (Croissant and Aras 1999, p. 102). After the incorporation of the country into the Soviet Union, oil revenues from Baku were seized by the central government and included in the central budget. Croissant and Aras claim that Azerbaijan received very little in an exchange for its oil, referring to the letter of Nariman Narimanov from 1923 (the leader of the Azerbaijan Soviet Socialist Republic), in which he complained that the price of kerosene was more expensive in Ganja than in Tiflis (Tiblisi). Nevertheless, in terms of oil output, the Azerbaijani oil production during the Soviet period declined from 21 million tons in 1964–1968 to 13 million tons. The authors note that on the eve of independence, Azerneft was producing nine million tons annually (Croissant and Aras 1999, p. 103).

While all three republics had centrally planned economies, the Armenian economy was considerably more advanced than those of Azerbaijan and Georgia at the end of the Soviet period (Horowitz 1985, p. 75). Armenia was one of the most industrialized countries among the former Soviet republics. Nevertheless, the economic situation of Armenia after the fall of the Soviet Union became one of the worst in the post-Soviet space as a result of several factors: a full-scale war with Azerbaijan over the Nagorno-Karabakh conflict, a massive earthquake in 1988 that killed 25,000 people and left 50,000 more homeless, and forced migration. Georgia was hit with the double crisis of the 2008 Russo–Georgian war and economic growth fell sharply to 2.3 percent during the war. The country found itself with thousands of new internally displaced people as well as those who lost their jobs and income (The World Bank 2013). Horowitz (1985) states that in terms of agricultural employment and output, as well as urbanization, Georgian economy during the Soviet Union was more advanced than Azerbaijan’s but somewhat more backward than Armenia’s (Horowitz 1985, p. 91). While the three South Caucasian countries along with the rest of the former USSR struggled significantly during the transition time from a centrally planned economy to a market economy, the main obstacles to advance their economic and political developments have been the frozen conflicts in the region—the legacy of Tsarist and Soviet foreign policies in Transcaucasia.

The ethnic war in the South Caucasus

As Thomas de Waal (2012) suggests: "there is much that makes a South Caucasus a viable region in terms of geography, culture and economic potential, but political contradictions and persistent perceptions of insecurity make for a pattern of recurring fragmentation" (de Waal 2012). The Tsars, Soviet officials, and then, Vladimir Putin, skillfully used these "political contradictions and persistent perceptions of insecurity" in order to tighten their grip on the region. The ethnic conflicts in the South Caucasus erupted in the early stages of the dissolution of the USSR, in 1987, after Mikhail Gorbachev, the former First Secretary of the Communist Party, declared "glasnost" and "perestroika". The leaders of the three Soviet republics and autonomous regions attempted to resolve the long-lasting territorial disputes in Transcaucasia. As a result, the majority of the Armenian populated region, the Nagorno-Karabakh, which was situated within the Azerbaijan Soviet Republic, proclaimed independence from Azerbaijan in 1991. In addition, the region's parliament voted to join Armenia, therefore leading to the full-scale ethnic war between Armenia and Azerbaijan, which ended in 1994. Armenian forces held Nagorno-Karabakh and declared a de facto independent state. The Georgian conflicts erupted in the autonomous regions of Soviet Ossetia and Abkhazia from 1989 onwards. Using Russian assistance, the regions defeated Georgian forces and declared independence from Georgia by establishing de facto states.

I shall emphasize that ethnicity is different from nation and nationalism, and, in the meantime, is related (Jesse and Williams 2011, p. 4). Often these two terms (ethnicity and nation) are used interchangeably ignoring the fact that the differences between ethnicity and nation matter in sense of the goals of an ethnic group versus those of a nationalist group (ibid). Anthony Smith defines an ethnic group as one that shares five key factors: a group name; a believed common descent; common historical memories; elements of shared culture such as language or religion; and attachment to a particular territory (Smith 1986, pp. 22–28). Ethnic groups are experiencing an ethnic sentiment, which can lead to ethnic solidarity. Furthermore, since ethnicity is a relational concept and an ethnic group has an in-group identity, consequently, there is an out-group or members of a different ethnic group (Jesse and Williams 2011, p. 5). In turn, nation, in Kaufman's view, is a socially mobilized group that wants political self-determination (Kaufman 2001, p. 16). Therefore, not all nations are ethnic groups (the American nation, for example, the former Soviet Union and Yugoslavia), and not all ethnic groups are nations (Kurds, Gypsies). The modern-nation state as the key political unit of sovereignty with its well-defined geographical boundaries emerged with the Treaty of Westphalia, which ended the Thirty Year's War in Europe in 1648 (Jesse and Williams 2011, p. 5). A nation, while sharing the same elements as an ethnic community, has an occupation of a historic homeland or at least the desire for occupation of a historic homeland. Therefore, a nation is more than an ethnic group since it beliefs in its right to territorial control. Accordingly, nationalism emerged from ethnic groups making claims to politically autonomous in a given territory (Kaufman 2001, Jesse and Williams 2011). Kaufman claims that nationalists may seek equality for their ethnic group but avoid being chauvinists.

The resurgence of nationalism in the 1990s proves that "the most powerful force in the world" is nationalism (Lukacs 1993). The latter, as both ideology and social movement, has been one of the formative processes of our era, but it was seen by many scholars as a rudimentary concept, a cause of wars in Europe up to 1945, the Third World colonial past but not as a rational feature of international relations (Halliday 2005, p. 522). If the Western democracies assumed that the new international order will help to promote cooperation and states would resort less to nationalism, the totalitarian regime in the former Soviet Union simply quelled ethnic passions in all fourteen republics. Communist ideology of the former USSR, which territory was divided into fifteen republics and more than one hundred autonomous regions, denied national identity of all the conquered nations, instead promoting the image of "homo Sovieticus." As a result, the extent to which many nationalities of the former Soviet empire articulated a sense of ethnic identity and nationalism depended on the historical context. Some nationalities developed a strong sense of ethnic identity that was based either on resentment against incorporation into the Russian and then Soviet empire (the Baltic States), or dissatisfaction with subordinate status within the system and desire for autonomy and independence (Armenia, Georgia, Ukraine). In the meantime, Horowitz argues that a greater articulation of national identity of Armenians was associated with higher level of economic development and a larger middle class and intellectual elite (Horowitz 1985, p. 75). However, he admits that "Armenians are historically a borderland people, repeatedly crushed, divided, partially assimilated, and exiled. Preservation of linguistic and religious identity has depended heavily on literate, entrepreneurial diaspora communities" (ibid). Examples of the weaker sense of nationalism that did not attach such significance to historical, cultural, territorial and linguistic differences, included Belorussia, Moldova, Azerbaijan, Uzbekistan, Tajikistan, Kazakhstan and Turkmenistan. Religious and cultural identities that transcended territorial boundaries of those states coexisted with patterns of economic underdevelopment.

Meanwhile, Georgian nationalism has a long-standing tradition rooted in the mid-nineteenth century, which saw Tsarist Russia as the enemy (Kernen and Sussex 2012, p. 99). While Georgian nationalism may be described as "exclusionist," Georgia always views the territories of Abkhazia and South Ossetia as part of the Georgian nation-state. Moreover, Saakashvili's provocation of Russia in South Ossetia in 2008 reflected not only serious strategic miscalculations but also a highly nationalistic and personalized notion of the Georgian nation. The latter, according to Kernen and Sussex, explains the consensus on what Georgian territorial integrity means among the country's political and social interest groups as well as the Georgian Orthodox Church (Kernen and Sussex 2012, p. 100). It is worth noting that as soon as the former Soviet Union disintegrated and with it the artificial homogeneity of the "homo Sovieticus," the quelled ethnic passions resurfaced again. It was a complex set of issues: 1) the Soviet denial of ethnic identity and political discrimination and oppression of so-called nationalist movements in the former USSR; 2) the inability of the central and regional governments of the former Soviet empire to serve its multiethnic community and to meet the needs of its minorities in terms of self-determination, equal distribution of resources and opportunities; and 3) an identity response to the vacuum left after the collapse of the communist rule (Pamir 1997). As a result, even in more liberal states (the Baltic States, Georgia) the transition to democracy has been accompanied by a force to build ethnically "pure states," where the proposals to grant citizenship were based on ethnic criteria.

In regards to Russia's foreign policy in the region, the increased militarization of the Caspian sea with the help of key players in the region (Russia considered to be the frontrunner in the militarization of the region, while the United States also has become involved in the arms race, by aiding the development of the navies of Azerbaijan, Kazakhstan, and Turkmenistan); the existence of undemocratic, corrupt and unstable governments in the region; the creation of the Russian-led Eurasian Union; the use of Caspian oil as an alternative to OPEC and AOPEC oil; the NATO expansion to the East; longstanding historical differences among local ethnic groups; three bloody and costly wars in the South Caucasus; and frozen territorial conflicts all contribute present and future threats to the security of the region.

East vs. West: which Union to join?

Meanwhile, the empirical evidence suggests that after Armenia, Azerbaijan and Georgia became the partner states of the Eastern Partnership initiative in 2009, their overall economic and political well-being (at least in case of Armenia and Georgia) significantly improved. For instance, only the Eastern Partnership Integration and Cooperation (EaPIC) program that was launched as part of Eastern Neighborhood Policy initiative in 2012–2013 has mobilized 150 million Euros for the EaP partner states (Armenia, Georgia, and Moldova) that made significant progress in deep democracy and respect for human rights.

Even more important, despite the fact that Armenian officials decided not to initial the negotiated Association Agreement with the EU in 2013, including the Deep and Comprehensive Free Trade Area, Yerevan and Brussels further continued their political and trade dialogue. In fact, the EU–Armenia visa facilitation and readmission agreements came into force in January 2014, which allow Armenia to participate in EU programmes and agencies (EU Commission Report 2015). Furthermore, Armenia is on her way to become a parliamentary state, which means that the president will be entailed with limited powers and customary rights.[6] The irony is that the EU Association Agreement that Armenia never signed included such a provision, according to which Yerevan had to reform its legislation and type of government in order to comply with the EU requirements. This brings us to the point that Armenia eschews its loyalty to Russia due to the fact that the EEU is "half dead," according to Armenian political analyst, Aghasi Yenokian. The latter suggests that Armenia is seeking to complete an updated version of the

Association Agreement with the EU since the Eurasian Union shows no sign anytime soon to fulfill its promises (Abrahamyan 2015).

Azerbaijan's foreign policy took a unique course since Baku was able to adopt a Russian-style authoritarian model of government, while portraying itself as a Western "strategic partner" on energy issues and security, using the country's energy wealth (de Waal 2014). Playing off both sides allowed Azerbaijan to preserve its oligarchic political system, simultaneously increasing country's wealth and military power, which in turn enabled the Aliev government to take a hard-core line on the protracted conflict with Armenia over the Nagorno-Karabakh region (de Waal 2014). Baku's defense spending is reported to be set at some $3.7 billion in 2013, surpassing both Armenia ($447 million) and Georgia ($400 million), thus making a Caucasian petro-state a regional leader in military strength and defense spending (Frolov 2014). Despite the fact that the EU, United States, Russia and other key players in the region expressed concerns over the latest ceasefire violations between Armenia and Azerbaijan, arms supplies are arriving into the South Caucasus, mainly from Russia, Israel, Ukraine, and Turkey, as well as from the CIS and East European countries (Frolov 2014). I shall argue that Azerbaijan is experiencing the "natural resource curse," which occurs when countries heavily dependent on revenues from oil and gas score lower on the U.N. Human Development Index, show greater corruption, devote a large chunk of government spending to military spending, and are more authoritarian because income from these resources is misused by corrupt leaders and officials instead of being directed to growth and development (Palley 2003). Not only has Azerbaijan fallen under the spell of the "natural resources curse," but the West has, as well. Starting in 1994, when Baku signed "the contract of the century"—a $7.4 billion deal with a consortium of Western oil giants, including BP, Unocal, Pennzoil, to develop and market Baku's Caspian oil reserves—Washington and Brussels made the Azeri petro dictatorship an American darling. President Clinton, for instance, declared the Caspian Sea region an area of US strategic interest, while his successors continued to coddle the Azeri dictatorship, heavily investing in energy, military and security sectors, and evoking a feeling of déjà vu since they already went through the same path with the Middle Eastern petro dictators. As soon as Baku felt strong enough to brush away the Western criticism of the Azerbaijani government, it did so. Azerbaijan joined the Non-Aligned Movement in 2011, undertook successful economic expansion in Georgia and Turkey, revived its relations with Russia (some analysts argue in order not to follow the Ukrainian example), and made it clear to the West that Baku has its own vision of the country's development, and it does not need foreign advice on economic issues[7] and the Nagorno-Karabakh dispute (Jarosiewicz 2014). Brussels, desperately trying to build bridges with the energy-rich Azerbaijan, agreed to accept Baku's own "strategic partnership agreement" that was handled by the EU diplomats at the May 2015 Riga Summit of the Eastern Partnership. This had been the first time in history, according to EU officials, when the draft of an agreement with the EU came from a partner state. It turns out that oil helped Azerbaijan to obtain freedom to choose to what extent it will participate in Brussels' offer of political association and economic integration in return for freeing some opposition journalists and activists (Gotev 2016).

As was mentioned before, Georgia continues to be the EU's poster country, although the recent "Treaty of Alliance and Strategic Partnership" between Russia and Abkhazia and the negotiations of the similar document with South Ossetia is a big concern for the EU. As a result of a fiscal stimulus package that supported household consumption and investment, in 2014 the GDP grew to 4.7 percent from 3.3 percent in 2013. One of the important trade-related developments in local economy since the implementation of the DCFTA was the increase by 7 percent in Georgia's exports towards the EU. In the meantime, Georgia was not only able to diversify its exports market, but also to secure additional financial findings from the EU (for instance, macro-financing assistance worth EUR 46 billion) to continue implementing the DCFTA regulations (Papidze 2015).

Consequently, we shall argue that Moscow promotes bilateral and regional integration to keep the former Soviet states under Russia's control and to challenge the key external players in the region. Yet, the attempts of Moscow to create the trade bloc, which is envisioned to be an EU-type organization is doomed to ultimate failure. First of all, the collapse of world oil prices in 2014, the ruble's decline in value, and the Western sanctions against Russia is already having serious consequences for Armenia, Belarus and Kazakhstan. For instance, Russia's economic issues created problems for currencies, inflation levels, remittances, and trade patterns in the Eurasian Economic Union (The Associated Press 2015).

On the other hand, the historical analysis of Russia's foreign policy in the South Caucasus lets us suggest that the Eurasian Union is another attempt by Moscow to control the Eurasian space by using threats or promises. However, we conclude that Russia cannot act either as benevolent or coercive hegemon in the given area due to the following reasons: 1) the inability to provide the collective good (an effective international regime) all by itself, while other states, in this case Armenia, Belarus, and Kazakhstan, are freed from the responsibility to help maintain the regime; and 2) the inability to force others to contribute as well, for the collective good provided under Russian leadership. The economic crises in all five member states of the Eurasian Union represent one of the main reasons that the two variants of HST cannot be applied to my case studies. Another factor that we considered is the post-Soviet states' legacy of Soviet rule. It has been argued that the Soviets did not support rights of its nations to self-determination, and that the 14 republics were never treated as equal partners, which makes the integration processes in Eurasia very problematic. Moreover, power-based theories of international regimes consider international regimes as public good and denied the ability of states to engage in collective action. The restoration of relations between Armenia, Belarus, and Kazakhstan and the EU can be considered as an independent action that includes international collective goods. It has been argued that the EU is still the main trading partner for all three states of the South Caucasus.

Thus, the empirical evidence presented above does not support an alternative proposition # 1 (see Table 5.2) since it has been argued that the Eurasian Union will follow the fate of declarative and insubstantial initiatives directed towards economic integration in the region that failed to make much impact on post-Soviet developments. In conclusion, we shall narrow the list of potential causes of Russia's foreign policy in the South Caucasus and to eliminate the power-based theories of international regimes as not a valid explanation of the South Caucasian cases studies.

Interest-based theories of international regime

Interest-based theories of international regimes, which share realists' commitment to rationalism, represent the mainstream approach in analyzing international regimes, as well as a meta-theoretical doctrine that shows states as self-interested, goal-seeking actors and maximizers of individual utility. In this regard, foreign policies and international institutions are seen as outcomes of calculations of advantage made by states (Hasenclever et.al 1997, p. 23). In the meantime, neoliberals propose to analyze regimes as strictly interest-based cases, which are created, sustained, and die according to the perspective of strategically rational but mutually indifferent actors. It is important to note that neoliberals agree with realists that cooperation is affected by power relationships; at the same time they argue that mutual interests and expectations, influenced by the presence of international institutions, are less important in this case. In order to test the second alternative proposition, which questions whether or not the creation of the new economic regime in Eurasia will establish the general rules and norms of post-Soviet states' behavior to facilitate cooperation and promote trade in the region, this section will consider the interest-based theories of international regimes. A neoliberal approach to regimes will help us to determine the probable effects (if any) of the Eurasian Economic Union on the ability of Armenia, Belarus, Kazakhstan and Russia[8] to cooperate through the new regime and to analyze the implication of different configurations of interests among the member states for the likelihood of regime maintenance as well as for the institutional form of the new bloc. In other words, I am seeking to prove that the mentioned proposition is false and the new regime in the region will not be able to establish the rules and norms of its member states in order to promote cooperation and trade in Eurasia.

This chapter examines Keohane's contractualist or functional theory of international regimes, which was labeled "neoliberal institutionalism" and asserts that international institutions play a vital role in world politics (Hasenclever et al., 1997, p. 28). According to Hodgson (2006), "institutions are the kinds of structures that matter the most in the social realm: they make up the stuff of social life" (Hodgson 2006, p. 2). Functional theory holds that institutions or sets of rules and norms can have a critical impact upon state behavior if they have mutual interests. It is worth mentioning that neoliberal institutionalism was developed as a critique of realist approaches to international relations and IPE with the emphasis on how institutions can help states overcome barriers to cooperation (O'Brien and Williams 2010, p. 40).

The disintegration of the Soviet Union in 1991 led to various attempts of Russia and the other former Soviet republics to reintegrate the Eurasian space (see Table 5.3), but without much success. For instance, the initiatives included the creation of the Union State of Russia and Belarus in the 1990s, the foundation of the Eurasian Economic Community in 2000, and GUAM that emerged in 1996 out of the Organization for Democracy and Economic Development that was launched in 1997 with Azerbaijan, Georgia, Moldova, and Ukraine as its member states. Despite the fact that such political and economic initiatives generated high volumes of international agreements and meetings they failed to make any impact on post-Soviet developments (Dragneva and Wolczuk 2013, p. 2). The main obstacle to the successful implementation of the new regimes in the post-Soviet space was their weak institutional frameworks. The only exception was the Eurasian Customs Union (ECU) launched in 2007 by Belarus, Kazakhstan and Russia, which proved to have a more credible integrative mechanism by establishing a common customs tariff in January 2010, a common customs territory in July 2010, and eliminating the internal physical border controls in January 2011.

Table 5.3 Some of the regional integration initiatives and organizations in Eurasia[9]

Initiative/ organization	*Participants*	*General status*
CIS (1991)	Armenia, Azerbaijan, Belarus, Georgia (withdrew 2008), Kazakhstan, Kyrgyzstan, Moldova, Russia, Tajikistan, Turkmenistan, Ukraine, Uzbekistan	Active
Customs Union (1992)	Belarus, Kyrgyzstan, Tajikistan, Uzbekistan	Abandoned
Economic Union (1993)	CIS members (except Ukraine)	Abandoned
Free trade area (1994)	CIS members (except Russia and Turkmenistan)	Relaunched in 1999
Customs Union (1995)	Belarus, Kazakhstan, Russia, Kyrgyzstan, Tajikistan	Transformed into EveAzES (2000)
GUAM (1997)	Azerbaijan, Georgia, Molodva, Ukraine, Uzbekistan (withdrew 2005)	Active
Free trade area (1999)	CIS members (except Russia and Turkmenistan)	Relaunched in 2011
EvrAzES (2000)	Belarus, Russia, Kazakhstan, Kyrgyzstan, Tajikistan, Uzbekistan (withdrew 2008)	Active
CSTO (2002)	Armenia, Belarus, Kazakhstan, Kyrgyzstan, Russia, Tajikistan	Active
The Eurasian Economic Union (2015)	Armenia, Belarus, Kazakhstan, Russia	Active

Furthermore, a common Customs Code of the Customs Union was adopted and replaced the consequent local legislation of Belarus, Kazakhstan and Russia. Dragneva and Wolczuk maintain that the customs union project was supported by a more effective legal and institutional framework than the previous integration initiatives in the post-Soviet space.

From the Customs Union to the Eurasian Union

The Agreement on the Commission of the Customs Union implied that this single regulatory body is responsible for the execution of decisions of the superior body of the Customs Union, the Interstate Council of EurAsEc at the level of head of states, and head of governments. The Agreement also required that the decisions made by the Commission would have binding power on the territories of the member states (MFA of Belarus 2015). Many analysts believe that the structure of the Customs Union provided for supranational delegation, a transparent legal basis and binding third-party dispute resolution. To put it differently, it was a new approach for the Eurasian integration that relied on a modern, rule-based legal and institutional framework, which also gradually transformed from a customs union to a single economic space in January 2012, and lately to a Eurasian Economic Union in January 2015 (Dragneva and Wolczuk 2013, pp. 2–3).

The Eurasian Economic Union, the third stage of economic integration preceded by the Customs Union and Common Economic space, became Mr. Putin's most ambitious initiative in the post-Soviet space. We shall agree with the popular belief in the West that this project became Putin's tug-of-war with the EU over their shared neighborhood. The second largest country in Europe, Ukraine, has been a stumbling block in Russia's relations with the EU since the launching of the Eastern Partnership initiative in 2009. Taking into account the current state of affairs in Ukraine that lost a chunk of its territory and for the last two years has been involved in civil war, Armenia's coerced entry into the bloc with Belarus, Kazakhstan and Russia, one can argue that Mr. Putin partly succeeded in his quest to gain control in the region. However, a more careful analysis of the institutional structure of the EEU would prove that disintegration processes in Eurasia are more feasible than the anticipated integration of the region.

Keohane's contractualist theory: not all regimes are created equally

Keohane's contractualist theory of regimes holds that states that are active in the issue-area concerned *must* share common interests, which they can realize only through cooperation (Keohane 1984, pp. 6–247; 1989, p. 2). However, there are a couple of contradictory points in his theory. First of all, states in many situations do have mutual interests, since international politics is not a zero-sum game for neoliberals. Yet, Keohane assumes that his theory can be applied wherever and whenever common interests exist in a relationship that has explicit security issues (Keohane 1984, pp. 6–247).

Second, the contractualist theory ignores the fact that the existence of common interests is a necessary, but not sufficient condition for cooperation (Hasenclever et al. 1997, pp. 29–30). For instance, the three South Caucasian states, Armenia, Azerbaijan, and Georgia, have common interests in opposing Russia's dominance in the region. According to Keohane, Yerevan, Baku and Tbilisi must cooperate in order to realize their common interests but in reality the three states are trying to pursue their own policies, which, in many cases, are mutually exclusive.

Another weak point of Keohane's functional theory is the failure to specify the conceptual relationship between interests, cooperation, and regime. According to Keohane, cooperation is not equivalent to harmony,[10] but instead is mutual adjustment that can be materialized as the result of a process of policy coordination (Keohane 1984, p. 52). Furthermore, he maintains that if actors' policies were not brought in line with one another, discord would follow. After bringing policies in line, states create international regimes that can help them to achieve joint gains since regimes facilitate international cooperation by altering actors' "incentives" for action (Keohane 1984, p. 26).

It is important to stress that in game-theoretic terms, regimes do not operate by changing the pay-off structure, but instead they make a different strategy more rational for the actors. The latter owing to the regime, must cooperate with others. However, Hasenclever et al. contend that a theory that regards international regimes as catalysts of international cooperation needs to distinguish conceptually the cause (regimes) and the effect (cooperation) (Hasenclever et al. 1997, p. 32). From this perspective, regimes cannot advance cooperation if the required cooperation is implicit in the regime as such. Moreover, Keohane's definition of regime, which he introduces as a kind of international agreement that provides a framework of rules, norms, principles, and procedures for negotiation, and has to be distinguished from substantive agreements, also causes ambiguity in the terminology of his functional theory (Keohane 1984, p. 153).

In Haggard and Simmons' opinion, while regimes are examples of cooperative behavior and further cooperation, the latter can take place outside of established regime (Haggard and Simmons 1987, p. 495). The authors also advised distinguishing regimes from the broader concept of institutions, pointing to the fact that regimes aid the institutionalization of portions of international life by regularizing expectations, but some institutions (for instance, the balance of power) are not tied to explicit rights and rules. Finally, Haggard and Simmons suggest to distinguish between regimes and order or stability, arguing that regimes in some cases may unintentionally contribute to instability (Haggard and Simmons 1987, p. 496).

The structure, function, and effect of the Eurasian Economic Union

Beach suggests that, when operationalizing variables and hypotheses, a key concern should be the *measurement validity* of the indicators, which he defines as whether we are actually measuring the systematized concept that we planned to measure (Beach 2012, p. 226). He identifies face validation as the most intuitive validation technique that presents common-sense arguments for why a given indicator is actually measuring the systemized concept. Thus, in an operationalization of a functional theory conceptualization of regimes that defines regimes as "sets of governing arrangements that include networks of rules, norms, and procedures that regulates behavior and control its effect," we choose "rules, norms and, procedures" of the Eurasian Economic Union as indicators to present coherent arguments for why this is not a valid measure to identify the function and effect of the mentioned regime.

This study maintains that functional theory does not provide a deep explanation for the formation of international law and institutions, in this case, the formation of the Eurasian Union. In the meantime, we agree with constructivists that the true explanation lies in the reasons states have to pursue certain outcomes and in the legitimacy of actors involved in the negotiating process (Wendt 1999).

Glazyev and Tkachuk (2015) argue that the ideological rationale behind Eurasian integration was the idea that Eurasian states share a cultural and historic environment along with an ingrained Eurasian political traditions and principles of governance. This ideological foundation was laid more than a century ago by Prince Nikolai Trubetskoi, and further elaborated by Pyotr Savitsky, Georgy Vernadsky, and Leonid Gumilev (Glazyev and Tkachuk 2015, p. 61). In this regard, Glazyev and Tkachuk consider economic integration in the post-Soviet space as a logical, historically justified, and economically viable process. On the contrary, this chapter argues that the Russian rationale behind the Eurasian integration was always political rather than economic. First, we will examine the evolution of the Eurasian integration process in order to emphasize the almost identical institutional structure of all regimes created within the post-Soviet space.

According to the Eurasian Economic Commission, the Eurasian integration follows the steps of the universal economic integration such as: stage 1—Free Trade Area; stage 2—Customs Union; stage 3—Single Economic Space; and stage 4—Economic Union. While the FTA in the Eurasian space was created under the umbrella of the Commonwealth of Independent States (CIS), a new FTA agreement that emphasized the free movement of goods was signed in October 2011. The Treaty on the establishment of the Customs Union was signed by the Presidents of Belarus, Kazakhstan and Russia in October 2007. By January 2010 the necessary legal framework for the functioning of the CU, which obligated the member states to implement a single customs tariff and commodity nomenclature on their territories, was in place (Eurasian Economic Commission 2013). The legal and regulatory framework of the CU containing more than 70 international treaties and more than 900 regulations issued by the Eurasian Economic Commission was established by the end of 2011.

It is important to mention that the Customs Union was set up as a treaty-based regime within the existing EvrAzEs. According to Dragneva and Wolczuk (2013), this origin is important to examining the legal nature and institutional boundaries of the Customs Union (Dragneva and Wolczuk 2013, p. 37). As was already mentioned, the Eurasian Economic Community (EvrAzEs) was established in 2000 by the decisions of the heads of Belarus, Kazakhstan, Kyrgyzstan, Tajikistan, and Russia with the aim to form a common economic space. Thus, the Eurasian integration project evolved from the formation of EurAsEc in 2000 to the formation of the Customs Union in 2007, the establishment of the Common Economic Space in 2012, and the emergence of the Eurasian Economic Union in 2015 (see Table 5.4).

Dragneva, while examining the legal and institutional framework of the Customs Union (which evolved into a Eurasian Economic Union), came to the conclusion that this process was fraught with fragmentation, incremental development, and often changing legal and institutional regime (Dragneva and Wolczuk 2013, p. 58). She argues that fragmentation, which derives from relying on multiple agreements and decisions, generates a complex, and potentially incoherent regime that carries critical challenges. This fragmentation puts pressure on domestic institutions, administrative and judicial bodies, which, according to Dragneva, are already challenged in regard to capacity. Furthermore, the pattern of institutional change is also the Union's Achilles heel since its institutional arrangement is characterized by periodic transformations in an organization structure of common bodies from its outset in accordance to the Moscow's political agenda instead of a comprehensive design (Dragneva and Wolczuk 2013, p. 41). Moreover, Dragneva concludes that the CU's institutional design features "hard law" characteristics, which are distinctive characteristics of the previous integration initiatives in Eurasia. For instance, the CU continued the tradition of proliferation of international agreements that was a hallmark of the CIS, the CU-95[11] as well as EvrAzEs. These agreements, lacking the binding effect, were mostly an indication of political symbolism rather than real agreements meant to impact behavior. Another issue with the organization of the Customs Union, and, consequently, the Eurasian Economic Union, is the practice of ongoing institutional reform that makes long-term planning and business initiatives fruitless or even risky (Dragneva and Wolczuk 2013, pp. 41–42).

Finally, the move to legality, Dragneva and Wolczuk suggest, will likely reaffirm Moscow's hegemonic status in the new Eurasian Union (Dragneva and Wolczuk 2013, p. 59). The structure of the Eurasian Economic Union is similar to that of the EU, except that it has a four-tiered governance system, at the lowest level of which is the executive—the Board of the Eurasian Economic Commission, consisting of 11 members, called ministers, who preside over 23 departments, and is chaired by Victor Khristenko, a former Russian deputy minister, appointed for four years (Eurasian Economic Union 2015). The Council of the Eurasian Economic Commission, which also has an annual rotating presidency, supervises the executive, and consists of five serving deputy prime ministers in the governments of Armenia, Belarus, Kazakhstan, Kyrgyzstan, and Russia. There are two more levels of decision-making bodies—the Eurasian Intergovernmental Economic Council in the format of prime ministers, and the Supreme Eurasian Economic Council in the format of four Presidents of the member states (Eurasian Economic Union 2015). The latter represents the EEU's highest body and unanimously defines the direction of cooperation. The Eurasian

Intergovernmental Commission oversees the implementation of the treaty's provisions and of the decisions of the presidents. Then, the Commission Council's espouses its decision by consensus, which is a qualified majority of two thirds of the votes. In the meantime, according to Article 30 of the EEU Commission Statute, each decision of the Commission taken by a qualified majority of votes may be vetoed by a member state and can be further considered at the prime ministerial or presidential levels. Consequently, decisions of the Supreme Eurasian Economic Council override the decisions of the Eurasian Intergovernmental Economic Council, whereas the decisions of these two highest levels outweigh the decisions of the Council of the Eurasian Economic Commission. Finally, the Court of Eurasian Economic Union resolves disputes and reinforces the parties' abidance with the adopted agreements.

There is a concern that the decision making process will take place at the presidential level of the Eurasian Economic Union (Supreme Council), which can be blocked under national legislation because of the lack of accuracy of the provisions of the EEU agreements (Popescu 2014; Jarosiewicz and Fischer 2015; Satpayev 2015 and many others). For instance, in November 2014 Russia tightened restrictions on the transit of meat products across its territory from Belarus to Kazakhstan and other countries. There have also been problems with delivering goods by Belarussian companies from the EU to Kazakhstan and Mongolia via Russia. Moscow banned food imports from the EU in response to the Western sanctions. In turn, Belarus and Kazakhstan made it clear that they are mainly interested in the economic aspect of the Eurasian Union, and are not planning to give up their sovereignty.

In other words, the Kremlin will always have the final say at the presidential level, taking into consideration the power asymmetries between Russia and the rest of the member states. The integration, in this regard, might be limited to cooperation (or Russian domination) at the highest level at the Eurasian Union, while the Commission will continue to play a technical role. On the surface, the smaller member states can block the decisions of the Supreme Council that are not favorable to them. Yet, these developments will require frequent presidential meetings, where Moscow will always pressure the weakest partners to accept the decisions suitable for the Kremlin. As Dragneva and Wolczuk point out, "a lack of legal clarity is symptomatic of the casual, 'make and mend' approach to the institutional design" (Dragneva and Wolczuk 2013, p. 49).

The functional theory falsifies Russia's foreign policy in the South Caucasus

According to Keohane, the main function of a regime is to facilitate cooperation by providing states with information or reducing their information costs (Keohane 1984, p. 97, p. 245). Hasenclever et al. argue that regimes that include monitoring arrangements (making information about others' compliance available) reduce fear of states of being double-crossed and make it easier for states to cooperate. In this case, the risks involved in cooperation are low, and the possibility of being deceived is also smaller. Moreover, greater transparency reduces the likelihood of cheating since the states fear to be "caught" (Hasenclever et al. 1997, pp. 34–35). Keohane also contends that principles, norms and rules apply to a variety of cases, when individual regimes are often a part of larger frameworks of international principles and norms. From this point of view, regimes produce "linkages" between issues, and agreements dealing with particular issues. As a result, violating a given agreement will have repercussions beyond this issue and may impact the ability of states' to achieve their goals in elsewhere (Keohane 1984, p. 89). Contractualists assume that regimes amend the conditions of application for the strategy of reciprocity through which cooperation is fixed (Keohane 1984, p. 244; Axelrod and Keohane 1986, p. 250).

We have been testing the functional theory of international regimes to determine whether or not it explains the creation of the Eurasia Economic Union as a regime that will establish the general rules and norms of post-Soviet states' behavior to facilitate cooperation and promote trade in the region. The analysis of the institutional design of the Eurasian Union, as well as its function and effect, disconfirms the explanatory power of functional theory in this case. It has been argued that the functioning of the Eurasian Union will depend primarily on Russia, as the country most interested in maintaining the new regime and having the economic means to subsidies the weakest partners.

The frequent changing structure of the EEU according to political agenda of Moscow, as well as its vague norms and rules do not facilitate cooperation in Eurasia as functionalists would predict. Moreover, none of the states involved seem committed to transparency, and the possibility of cheating is quite high. Even the weakest partners, being coerced to join the EEU, are breaking the "rule" and trying to diversify their foreign policies by continuing a partnership with the European Union, Russia's biggest adversary in this case. Yet the greatest challenge for the Eurasian Economic Union is the declining economic situation in Russia amid the Western sanctions, which also cripples the economies of member states, Armenia, Belarus, and Kazakhstan that are closely linked to Russia. In this regard, by creating economic (energy) codependency, it will be easier for Moscow to impose political

Table 5.4 Growth of Eurasian Economic Union's GDP

	GDP, USD billion	*GDP per capita USD*	*GDP per capita, PPP, USD*	*GDP per capita, PPP, % of the world*
Armenia	10.28	3,121.20	7,373.53	0.022
Belarus	76.14	8,041.75	18,161.43	0.159
Kazakhstan	212.26	12,183.51	24,019.95	0.388
Kyrgyz Republic	7.4	1,298.56	3,361.18	0.018
Russia	1,857.46	12,295.96	24,085.49	3.303
Total	2,163.5			3.89
Average		7,514	15,544	

Source: Data from the IMF

obedience in the region by using so-called economic cooperation of the states institutionalized in the EEU.

Conclusion

This chapter tested power-based and interest-based variants of international regimes theories and came to the conclusion that the predictions of both variants of regime theory in case of Russia's foreign policy in the South Caucasus proved wrong. First of all, we concluded that Eurasian economic integration is far from Soviet-era stagnation or regression since all the member states are actively involved in economic, humanitarian, judicial, and even political collaborations either with the European Union, the United States, China and others. At the same time, a lack of standardized conditions and requirements for the current or future member states makes us believe that the Eurasian Economic Union will follow the fate of previous integration initiatives within the region that failed to make much impact on post-Soviet developments. Second, the member states try to strictly limit the impact of the integration process to economic collaboration. While Moscow tries to enforce political integration under its dominance, the frequent changing institutional design of the EEU, as well as the lack of legal clarity in its norms, rules, and procedures do not facilitate cooperation in Eurasia, and make the partner states assert their national interests against Russia.

Notes

1 After a short period of independence, Armenia, Azerbaijan, and Georgia were incorporated into the single Trans-Caucasian Federated Soviet Socialist Republic in December 1922 under the jurisdiction of the Caucasian bureau of the Russian central committee. The three South Caucasian states would remain in the federation until 1936. During that time, the Kavburo, headed by Sergo Ordzhonikidze, who personally participated in overthrowing anti-communist regimes in the South Caucasus, made a couple fateful decisions that would remain a potential source of instability and ethnic violence until present times. One of them was the establishment of the Nakhichevan autonomous republic in 1923, which was allotted to Azerbaijan regardless the fact that it was separated by Armenian territory and had a small Armenian majority. The main rationale behind the Kavburo's decision was to provide Turkey with a short frontier with Azerbaijan. In addition, Nagorno-Karabakh, which was an apple of discord between Armenians and Azeris over the centuries, was granted autonomous status within Azerbaijan at Stalin's behest to ensure Armenians' cooperation with the Soviet government. At the end of the day, Armenians, despite being Russia's loyalists, had also a strong sense of nationalism that was not favored by Bolsheviks. In addition, the creation of the "fifth column" populated mainly by Armenians within the Azerbaijan territory guaranteed the obedience of Azeris.

2 For examples of this perspective on Soviet's "divide and rule" strategy see, among many others, the work of Robert Seely (2001) *The Russian-Chechen Conflict 1800–2000: A Deadly Embrace.*

3 A program of financial assistance to Armenia was recently launched in Yerevan, and about $88.6 million is intended to strengthen the borders, adapting legislation and dealing with poverty.

4 According to Hasenclever et al., a classical example of a power-based theory of international regimes is the theory of hegemonic stability, which ties the existence of effective international institutions to a unipolar configuration of power in the issue-area in question (Hasenclever et al. 1997, p. 84).
5 Even more important, Lenin was soon incapacitated and Stalin, who did not share Lenin's views on nationalities, wrote all the rules for the new Soviet state after about 1923.
6 A constitutional referendum changed the country from semi-presidential system to a parliamentary republic in 2015, which led many opposition groups to claim that Serzh Sargsyan adjusted the system to remain in power.
7 Jarosiewicz (2014) claims that Azerbaijan, thanks to Western investments, was able to position itself not as a junior partner of the West but already as a legitimate actor in the region, and the country's rejection of the Nabucco pipeline project in favor of its own project, the Trans-Atlantic gas pipeline, means that Baku will be the main architect, executor, and the largest shareholder of the planned infrastructure.
8 When I was conducting this study, the accession of Kyrgyzstan to the Eurasian Economic Union has not been yet completed.
9 Adapted from Dragneva and Wolczuk 2013, p. 222.
10 Harmony requires complete identity of interests, while cooperation can only be materialized in situations that contain a mixture of conflicting interests (Axelrod and Keohane 1986, p. 226).
11 Agreement on the Customs Union between Russia, and Belarus that was signed on January 6, 1995. Kyrgyzstan and Tajikistan joined, accordingly, in 1996 and 1997.

Bibliography

Abrahamyan, Gayane (2015) "Armenia: Yerevan Mending Fences with EU." *Eurasia Net*. https://ec.europa.eu/europeaid/sites/devco/files/eap-flyer-results.pdf (accessed August 5, 2015).

"Armenia World Bank Group Country Survey 2013," *The World Bank Group*. December 17.

The Associated Press (2015) "Russia-led Trade Bloc of 4 Nations Born in Times Troubled by Ruble's Fall, Ukraine Tensions." January 2.

Axelrod, Robert and Robert O. Keohane (1986) "Achieving Cooperation Under Anarchy: Strategies and Institutions," in Kenneth A. Oye (Ed.) *Cooperation Under Anarchy*. Princeton, NJ: Princeton University Press.

Beach, Derek (2012) *Analyzing Foreign Policy*. Houndmills, UK: Palgrave Macmillan.

Bordachev, Timofei V. and Andrei S. Skriba (2015) "Russia's Eurasian Integration Policies," *LSE IDEAS Reports*. December 7. www.lse.ac.uk/IDEAS/publications/reports/pdf/SR019/SR019-Bordachev-Skriba.pdf (accessed February 25, 2016).

Chilcote, Ryan and Aliaksandri Kudrytski (2015) "Belarus Strongman Balances Between Ukraine War, Putin, EU," *Bloomberg*. April 2. www.bloomberg.com/news/articles/2015-04-02/belarus-strongman-balances-among-war-in-ukraine-putin-eu (accessed August 2, 2016).

Croissant, Michael P. and Bulent Aras (1999) *Oil and Geopolitics in the Caspian Sea Region*. Westport, CT: Praeger.

de Waal, Thomas (2011) "Time to Shine a Light on a Hidden Conflict: Nagorno-Karabakh in 2011," *Journal of Conflict Transformation*, February 1, 2011. www.carnegieendowment.org/2011/02/01/time-to-shine-light-on-hidden-conflict-nagorno-karabakh-in-2011/2un/ (accessed December 30, 2012).

de Waal, Thomas (2012) "A Broken Region: The Persistent Failure of Integration Projects in the South Caucasus," *Europe-Asia Studies*, Vol. 64/9.

de Waal, Thomas (2014) "Azerbaijan Doesn't Want to be Western: The Rhetoric and Reality of Baku's Grand Strategy," *Foreign Affairs*. September 26.

Dragneva, Rilka and Katarina Wolczuk (2013) *Eurasian Economic Integration: Law, Policy and Politics*. Cheltenham, UK: Edward Elgar.

European Commission (2015) "Implementation of the European Neighborhood Policy in Armenia: Progress in 2014, and Recommendations for Actions." March 25. http://eeas.europa.eu/enp/pdf/2015/armenia-enp-report-2015_en.pdf (accessed May 8, 2015).

European Commission (2015) "Implementation of the European Neighborhood Policy in Azerbaijan: Progress in 2014, and Recommendations for Actions." March 25. http://eeas.europa.eu/enp/pdf/2015/azerbaijan-enp-report-2015_en.pdf (accessed May 8, 2015).

European Commission (2015) "Implementation of the European Neighborhood Policy in Georgia: Progress in 2014, and Recommendations for Actions." March 25. http://eeas.europa.eu/enp/pdf/2015/georgia-enp-report-2015_en.pdf (accessed May 8, 2015)

Eurasian Economic Commission (2013) "Eurasian Economic Integration: Facts and Figures." www.eurasiancommission.org/ru/Documents/broshura26Body_ENGL_final 2013_2.pdf (accessed April 23, 2015).

Eurasian Economic Commission Council (2014) "Reshenie No. 113 ob Utverzhdenii Perechnia Tovarov I Stavok, V Otnoshenii Kotorykh v Techenie Perekhodnogo Perioda Respublikoi Armenia Primeniaiutsia Stavki Vvoznykh Tamozhennykh Poshlin, Otlichnye ot Stavok Edinogo Tamozhennogo Tarifa Evraziiskogo Ekonomicheskogo Soiuza." December 10. www.eurasiancommission.org/ru/Lists/EECDocs/635542572696838971.pdf (accessed January 15, 2015).

Eurasian Economic Union (2015) "Governance." www.eaeunion.org/?lang=en#about-administration (accessed July 9, 2015).

Frolov, Andrei (2014) "Military Development in Transcaucasia: An arms Race?" *Russian International Affairs Council*. July 16.

"Georgia—World Bank Group Country Survey 2013," *The World Bank Group*. December 19.

Geukjian, Ohannes (2011) *Ethnicity, Nationalism and Conflict in the South Caucasus: Nagorno-Karabakh and the Legacy of Soviet Nationalities Policy*. London, UK: Ashgate.

Gilpin, Robert (1975) *U.S. Power and the Multinational Corporation: The Political Economy of Foreign Direct Investment*. New York, NY: Basic Books.

Glazyev, Sergei and Sergei Tkachuk (2015) "Eurasian Economic Union: Achievements and Prospects," in Piotr Dutkiewicz and Richard Saakwa (Eds.) *Eurasian Integration—The View from Within*. Oxford, UK: Routledge.

Gotev, Georgi (2016) "EU to launch negotiations for a new agreement with Azerbaijan," *EurActiv.com*. November 14. www.euractiv.com/section/europe-s-east/news/eu-to-launch-negotiations-for-a-new-agreement-with-azerbaijan/ (accessed November 17, 2016).

Gourevitch, Peter (1978) "The Second Image Reversed: The International Sources of Domestic Politics," *International Organization*, Vol. 32, pp. 881–912.

Haggard, Stephan, and Beth A. Simmons (1987) "Theories of International Regimes," *International Organization*, Vol. 41, pp. 491–517.

Halliday, Fred (2005) "Nationalism," in Baylis John and Smith Steve (Eds.) *The Globalization of World Politics: An Introduction to International Relations*. New York, NY: Oxford University Press.

Hasenclever, Andreas, Peter Mayer, and Volker Rittberger (1997) *Theories of International Regimes*. Cambridge, UK: Cambridge University Press.

Hautala, Heidi (2015) "When Choosing Means Losing," *Heinrich-Böll-Stiftung*. March 18. http://eu.boell.org/en/2015/03/18/when-choosing-means-losing (accessed April 8, 2015).

Hayrumyan, Naira (2015) "Armenia-EU: Brussels Opens Door to Association Agreement with Yerevan," *ArmeniaNow*. March 23. www.armenianow.com/commentary/analysis/60041/armenia_european_union_association_agreement (accessed April 13, 2015).

Hodgson, Geoffrey M. (2006) "What Are Institutions?" *Journal of Economic Issues*, Vol. 40/1.

Horowitz, Donald (1985) *Ethnic Groups in Conflict*. Berkeley, CA: University of California Press.

Janison, James (2014) "Divide and Conquer: Russian Foreign Policy Legacy Endures in Ukraine," *Brown Political Review*. September 21. www.brownpoliticalreview.org/2014/09/divide-and-conquer-russian-foreign-policy-legacy-endures-in-ukraine/ (accessed November 10, 2014).

Jarosiewicz, Aleksandra (2014) "Azerbaijan—a Growing Problem for the West," *Ośrodek Studiów Wschodnich*. September 15. www.osw.waw.pl/en/publikacje/osw-commentary/2014-09-15/azerbaijan-a-growing-problem-west (accessed January 3, 2015).

Jarosiewicz, Aleksandra and Ewa Fischer (2015) "The Eurasian Economic Union- More Political, Less Economic," *Ośrodek Studiów Wschodnich (OSW)*. January 20. www.osw.waw.pl/en/publikacje/osw-commentary/2015–01–20/eurasian-economic-union-more-political-less-economic (accessed June 10, 2015).

Jesse, Neal G., and Kristen P. Williams (2011) *Ethnic conflict: a systematic approach to cases of conflict*. Washington, DC: CQ Press.

Kaufman, Stuart J. (2001) *Modern Hatreds: The Symbolic Politics of Ethnic War*. Ithaca, NY: Cornell University Press.

Kennedy-Pipe, Caroline (1998) *Russia and the World 1917–1991*. London, UK: Arnold.

Keohane, Robert O. (1984) *After Hegemony: Cooperation and Discord in the World Political Economy*. Princeton, NJ: Princeton University Press.

Keohane, Robert O. (1986) *Neorealism and Its Critics*. New York, NY: Columbia University Press.

Keohane, Robert O. (1989) "Theory of World Politics: Structural Realism and Beyond," in *International Institutions and State Power*. Boulder, CO: Westview.

Keohane, Robert (2003) "The Theory of Hegemonic Stability and Changes in International Economic Regimes, 1967–1977," in Roe C. Goddard, Patrick Cronin and Kishore C. Dash (Eds.) *International Political Economy: State Market Relations in a Changing Global Order*. Boulder, CO: Lynne Rienner.

Keohane, Robert (2005) *After Hegemony: Cooperation and Discord in the World Political Economy*. Princeton, NJ: Princeton University Press.

Keohane, Robert O., and Joseph S. Nye, Jr. (1977) *Power and Interdependence: World Politics in Transition*. Boston, MA: Little, Brown.

Kernen, Beat and Matthew Sussex (2012) "The Russo-Georgian War: Identity, Intervention and Norm Adaptation," in Matthew Sussex (Ed.) *Conflict in the Former USSR*. Cambridge: Cambridge University Press.

Kindleberger, Charles P. (1974) *The Formation of Financial Centers: A Study in Comparative Economic History*. Princeton, NJ: Princeton University Press.

Krasner, Stephen D. (1976) "State Power and the Structure of International Trade," *World Politics*, Vol. 28, pp. 317–347.

Lenin, Vladimir I. (1916) "The Social Revolution and the Right of Nations to Self-Determination," *Sbornik Sotsial-Demokrata*, No. 1, October.

Lukacs, John (1993) *The End of the Twentieth Century and the End of the Modern Age*. New York, NY: Ticknor and Fields.

Mesbahi, Mohiaddin (2010) "Eurasia between Russia, Turkey, and Iran," in Roger E. Kanet and Maria R. Freire (Eds.) *Key Players and Regional Dynamics in Eurasia: The Return of the "Great Game."* New York, NY: Palgrave Macmillan.

Ministry of Foreign Affairs of the Republic of Belarus (2015) "Eurasian Economic Union." http://mfa.gov.by/en/organizations/membership/list/aa16658947a49c28.html (accessed October 2, 2015).

O'Brien, Robert and Marc Williams (2010) *Global Political Economy: Evolution and Dynamics*. Houndmills, UK: Palgrave Macmillan.

Palley, Thomas (2003) "Lifting the Natural Resource Curse," *Foreign Service Journal*, No. 80, December, pp. 54–61.

Pamir, Peri (1997) "Nationalism, Ethnicity and Democracy: Contemporary Manifestations," *The International Journal of Peace Studies*, Vol. 2, No. 2, July.

Papaskiri, Zurab (2012) "Another Look at One of the False Historical Postulates of the Abkhazian Separatist Ideology: On the Question of Abkhazia's Political-State Status in 1921–1931," *The Caucasus and Globalization*, Vol. 6, No. 2.

Papidze, Mary (2015) "EU Delegation to Georgia: Diversify Export Markets and Improve Productivity," *European Dialogue*, January 30. http://eurodialogue.eu/EU%20Delegation%20to%20Georgia%3A%20Diversify%20export%20markets%20and%20improve%20productivity%20 (accessed June 26, 2015).

Petro, Nikolai N. and Alvin Z. Rubinstein (1997) *Russian Foreign Policy: From Empire to Nation State*. New York, NY: Longman.

Petrov, Roman and Peter Van Elsuwege (2016) *Legislative Approximation and Application of EU Law in the Eastern Neighborhood of the European Union: Towards a Common Regulatory Space?* London, UK: Routledge.

Popescu, Nicu (2014) "Eurasian Union: The Real, the Imaginary and the Likely." Paris, France: EU Institute for Security Studies.

Riga, Liliana (2012) *The Bolsheviks and the Russian Empire*. New York, NY: Cambridge University Press.

Satpayev, Dosym (2015) "Kazakhstan: Economic Integration Without Relinquishing Sovereignty," in Felix Hett and Susanne Szkola (Eds.) *The Eurasian Economic Union: Analyses and Perspectives from Belarus, Kazakhstan, and Russia*. Berlin, Germany: Friedrich-Ebert.

Seely, Robert (2001) *The Russian-Chechen Conflict 1800–2000: A Deadly Embrace*. London, UK: Frank Cass.

Simmons, Beth A. (1995) "International Economics and Domestic Politics: Notes on the Twenties," in Charles H. Feinstein (Ed.) *Banking, Currency and Finance in Europe Between the Wars*. Oxford, UK: Oxford University Press.

Smith, Anthony (1986) *The Ethnic Origins of Nations*. Oxford, UK: Basil Blackwell.

Snidal, Duncan (1985) "The Limits of Hegemonic Stability Theory," *International Organization*, Vol. 39, pp. 585–590.

Stalin, Iosif (1952) *Works*. 13 vols. The Basic Collection of Stalin's Writings. Moscow, Russia.

Strange, Suzanne (1982) "Cave! Hic Dragones: A Critique of Regime Analysis," *International Organization*, Vol. 36, pp. 479–496.

Trenin, Dmitri (1996) "Russia's Security Interests and Policies in the Caucasus Region," in Bruno Coppieters (Ed.) *Contested Borders in the Caucasus*. Brussels, Belgium: VUB University Press.

Wendt, Alexander (1999) *Social Theory of International Politics*. Cambridge, UK: Cambridge University Press.

Yin, Robert K. (2003) *Case Study Research: Design and Methods*. Thousand Oaks, CA: Sage.

Zagorski, Andrey (2015) "Caught between the Economy and Geopolitics," in Felix Hett and Susanne Szkola (Eds.) *The Eurasian Economic Union: Analyses and Perspectives from Belarus, Kazakhstan, and Russia*. Berlin, Germany: Friedrich-Ebert.

Conclusion

Did Russia restore its hegemony in Eurasia?

How did Russia become so strong and powerful over the course of 15 years that it was able to challenge the United States and the European Union when they had tried to step into her backyard? What gave the Kremlin the ability to bring Armenia back into its orbit, when the country was on its way to initial the Association Agreement with the European Union in 2013? Why did Azerbaijan and Georgia, for their parts, try to avoid antagonizing Russia, regardless of the fact that Baku had adopted a foreign policy of neutrality towards Moscow, while Tbilisi took a big step towards closer ties with Brussels as the country signed the Association Agreement with the EU in 2014? Finally, can we conclude that Russia did restore its sphere of influence in Eurasia?

These are some of the questions that this book has examined as they pertain to Russia's foreign policy in the South Caucasus. The study set out to explore Russia's external affairs with Armenia, Azerbaijan and Georgia and the relevance for those affairs of the creation of the Eurasian Economic Union. It was not an easy task taking into consideration the evolving nature of Russia's relations, not only with the former Soviet states, but also with the rest of the world. When I started conducting this study, many in the West and in the East took Mr. Putin's Eurasian integration agenda with a grain of salt. After all, Moscow's credibility to be a normative power in the post-Soviet space was treated with skepticism even in the common neighborhood due to the failure of almost all the economic integration projects launched after the disintegration of the USSR in 1991.

Russia at the time was a disorganized and broken state, which desperately tried to establish friendly relations with the United States and create a free market economy under the Yeltsin presidency. In other words, Russia tried to join the civilized world on equal footing with the rest of major powers, mainly the United States and the European Union. Unfortunately, the Western countries were not as enthusiastic as Russia about the idea of a new international order based on mutual confidence, cooperation, and binding agreements between the East and West. Although the United States and its allies decided that American national interests would be best served if Washington will support the neo-liberal market reforms in the Russian Federation, in the meantime, the Western powers preferred not to have Moscow in the front ranks in the international status order. Otherwise, the reshaping of the Cold War bipolar world into a more complex system would disrupt the liberal international order that was built in the second half of the twentieth century.

Therefore, since the 1990s Russian interests were downplayed by Washington and Brussels, while the United States undertook a couple of policy actions that simply ignored Moscow's interests: the NATO eastward expansion, military intervention in former Yugoslavia, the 2003 invasion of Iraq, the emplacement of a missile defense system in Central Europe, a series of gas pipelines projects in the Caspian Sea region designed to bypass Russia (Kanet 2010, pp. 61–62). As a result, the so-called Kozyrev doctrine in Moscow's foreign policy, adopted in April 1993, which asserted interest in strategic rapprochement and partnership with the West, had been replaced with the Primakov doctrine that offered a more pragmatic approach and pushed Russia towards a more aloof position with the Western powers. Moreover, the Russian policymakers started to identify themselves more with the state interests in the near abroad, as a new (or well-forgotten old) goal of Russian foreign policy. At the time, Primakov's appointment in 1996 as foreign minister indicated a critical break with the early Yeltsin's attempts to integrate with the West towards a restoration of Russia as a major power in its former sphere of interests and in the international arena.

Accordingly, the South Caucasus with its rich natural resources and the geopolitical importance had become once again a source of conflicting interests between Washington, Brussels and Moscow. When Vladimir Putin came to power in 2000, he furthered Primakov's "balance of power" concept, by reducing Moscow's dependence on Western economic aid due to the rise in oil prices, and identifying country's opposition to US hegemony. Since the beginning of his presidential term, Mr. Putin turned Russia's attention to the former Soviet Union states, seeking to deepen economic and security integration with the CIS states.

This study, using theory-testing cases, argued that Moscow's foreign policy in Transcaucasia was and still is driven by its place in the international arena and specifically by its relative material power capabilities. I considered Russia's external relations with the South Caucasian states as a case of the Kremlin's neo-imperialist policy in the near abroad. Thus, defining the creation of the Eurasian Economic Union as a neo-imperialist concept is my main contribution to a neoclassical realism theory. Putin's regime used the new economic bloc for its expansionist plans in the near abroad, in order to avoid the creation of a free trade area encompassing the countries in the region (Armenia, Azerbaijan, Georgia, Belarus, Moldova, and Ukraine) and the European Union.

I concluded that the Kremlin responded to the systemic pressure by trying to control the former Soviet Union space, including the strategically important region, the South Caucasus, thus, shaping its external environment according to its wishes. In other words, Mr. Putin sought to restore the authority of the Russian state within Russia and in the near abroad. It was the increased Russian capabilities in the beginning of Putin's presidency that helped to drive policymakers' perceptions of external threats, interests and opportunities in the South Caucasus. As a result, Armenia was coerced to join the Eurasian Union in 2015 along with Russia, Belarus, Kazakhstan, and, eventually, Kyrgyzstan. Azerbaijan, on the other hand, had to revive its relations with Russia in order to avoid the Ukrainian scenario and to have its say in the Nagorno-Karabakh conflict. Finally, there is a possibility that Georgia's two breakaway regions, South Ossetia and Abkhazia, will be also incorporated into the Eurasian Economic Union, thus, Russian troops on Georgian soil will definitely impede Tbilisi's quest to join NATO and the European Union.

In this regard, this study showed a clear connection in the long run between Russia's economic rise and fall and its growth as an important world empire. This pattern was explained by a tendency of a more wealthy and powerful state's temptations to increase its control over its environment. In fact, this work concluded that the establishment of the Eurasian Union also creates the normative challenges to the interests of global players in the South Caucasus—Turkey, Iran, the United States, the European Union, and China. Below I reflect on this study's main findings, employing neoclassical realist theory of foreign policy and rejecting regime theories analysis for my case studies.

Russian foreign policy in the South Caucasus explained

This comparative case study, which was conducted as a multiple-case design, used three cases of Russian foreign policy in Azerbaijan, Georgia, and Armenia in order to test neoclassical realism and international regime theories. It is important to note the South Caucasian states had been incorporated into the Russian empire long ago, and, after the October Revolution in 1917, became the Soviet Socialist Republics within the USSR. After the fall of the Iron Curtain, the countries participated, to some extent or another, in various regional projects that took place in the post-Soviet region, including the Eastern Partnership Initiative, which was established in 2009. Thus, it was inevitable for me to discuss in this book the domestic and foreign policies of other FSU states, for instance, Belarus, Kazakhstan, Ukraine, Kyrgyzstan, and others, which were not selected for my research design. Nevertheless, these countries are key players in various post-Soviet regional initiatives, and presented some empirical evidence on peculiarity of Russian foreign policy in Eurasia and the integration processes in the area. Yet, my research questions—What explains Russia's foreign policy in the South Caucasus and the relevance for that policy of the creation of the Eurasian Union? What laws, rules, norms, and beliefs guide the new economic bloc in the post-Soviet space? Under what circumstances does Russia create new political and economic institutions to offset the perceived advantages of rival states? Is Eurasian integration primarily a form of continental economic integration? Will Russia's foreign policies towards the South Caucasian states change after the launch of the Eurasian Economic Union in 2015?—were paramount in selecting the three South Caucasian cases for this study.

Considering the cases of Armenia, Azerbaijan, and Georgia as crucial ones, I established historical explanations of Russia's common patterns of external behavior towards the South Caucasus over time in order to confirm and extend the neoclassical realism assumptions about relative material power and international exigencies. The historical analysis indicated that the geographic placement of Russia and its desire to expand to the west, the south, and the east was the focal point for the Tsarist conquest of the region. However, the evidence suggested that the impact of power capabilities on foreign policy choices was indirect, and systemic pressure could limit policy choices for the Tsars; it was not a single force in Imperial Russia's quest to annex Transcaucasia. The invasion of the South Caucasus resulted from various systemic and domestic factors in Tsarist Russia. In the beginning, the Russians envisioned the region as a trade bridge between Europe and Asia, but, by the end of the 1820s, the colonization of Transcaucasia became a part of a broader expansionist policy of Tsarist Russia that envisioned itself as a successor to Rome. In this regard, the historical analysis suggested that Russia's conquest of the Caucasus from the beginning fitted into the neoclassical realist model since the government responded to the uncertainties of international system by seeking to control and shape its external environment.

The control over the Black Sea steppe was crucial for Tsarist Russia because it offered not only rich black soil for agriculture, but also determined the political fate of Moldavia and Walachia in the west and the Caucasus in the southeast. The historical analysis revealed that what began as a defensive policy of state security (a central feature of Russian state policy from the reign of Ivan Terrible to Peter the Great was an effort to control the steppe that was challenged by the Tatar khans and the Ottomans), later transformed into an expansion ideology aimed at creating the empire that would stretch from the Black Sea to the Mediterranean. The tsars, having revisionist aspirations, undertook territorial expansion at the expense of both weaker states, the South Caucasian states, and rival great powers, the Ottoman Empire, Persia and Britain.

The evidence suggested that the South Caucasus was incorporated into the Russian empire over the course of three centuries by using the practices of subjugation by war and the extension of protection. This policy was driven by geopolitical and strategic concerns rather than by economic or ideological considerations. The Russians launched their hegemony in the region implementing the policy of "divide and rule." The evidence indicated that since the beginning the three South Caucasian states were treated as colonies and over the centuries a pattern of client relationship was established. Moreover, the territorial expansion of Imperial Russia was advanced through a single-mindedness for conquest shared by both the rulers and the South Caucasian nations, which considered the Tsarist officials as their emancipators from Islamic domination.[1]

Finally, the study came to the conclusion that one of the important elements of Russian foreign policy over the course of time was the continuity in behavior of governments headed by tsars, commissars, and presidents. Russian foreign policy in Armenia, Azerbaijan, and Georgia after the dissolution of the Soviet Union was treated as the dependent (or the outcomes) variables, while Russia's relative power was treated as an independent variable. Using these clearly defined and systematized concepts within the neoclassical realist theory helped me to assess the validity and scope conditions of a given theory. I concluded that the success of Russia's hegemonic tendencies and expansionist agendas in the South Caucasus varied across the three nations and time periods. However, a neoclassical realist approach did not provide a clear explanation of why Russia's foreign policies varied across the three states or time periods. The shortcomings of a neoclassical realist theory will be addressed later in the conclusion.

Russian policy towards Armenia

This work provided a systematic analysis of Russian foreign policy in Armenia (a crucial case), and showed that in the long run the relative amount of material power resources Moscow possesses shaped the ambition and scope of its foreign policy choices towards Yerevan. First, the process-tracing evidence indicated that, with the rise of relative power in the 2000s, during Putin's presidency, Russia sought more influence abroad, while in the 1990s, when it was in decline during the Yeltsin's presidency, the Kremlin's grand strategies in its near abroad were nonexistent. Second, the evidence demonstrated that Moscow's foreign policy in Yerevan is the most definitive type of evidence of a neoclassical realist theory, which considers not only domestic factors in a state's behavior but also systemic forces that shape a country's foreign affairs. The findings analyzed in Chapter 4 confirmed that a shift in relative power of Russia in the 2000s led to a shift in its external relations with Armenia after Vladimir Putin came to power. Since the beginning of his presidency, Mr. Putin placed a high priority on Moscow's muscle-flexing in the South Caucasus through military-strategic, economic and political leverage. Fifteen years later Vladimir Putin saw in the creation of the Eurasian Union the fruits of his labor, when the European-oriented Armenia joined the Moscow-led project and took a pro-Russian course in its external and internal affairs, while Azerbaijan and Georgia did their best not to fend off Russia by their foreign and domestic choices. However, a neoclassical realist approach failed to show why Armenia was so easily drawn into Russia's orbit, while Georgia and Azerbaijan were able to keep a significant independence in their relations with a big brother.

Why Armenia joined the Eurasian Union

However, the evidence in this study suggests that there are quite a few explanations behind Armenia's accession to the Eurasian Economic Union. First of all, the Kremlin challenged the enlargement of the Euro–Atlantic institutions—NATO and the EU—into post-Soviet space after the end of the Cold War. Armenia is one of the six partner countries of the Eastern Partnership Initiative (EaP) that was launched in the spring of 2009 as the EU's attempts to control a south energy corridor from the Caspian region to Europe avoiding Russia. The fiasco at an EU Eastern Partnership summit in Vilnius, when only two partner countries, Georgia and Moldova, initialled the Association Agreement with the EU, has been mainly blamed on Russia's pressure. After all, Armenia had been very acceptant of EaP initiatives and was one of the first partner countries to adopt a number of EU policy and institutional models over the period of five years. The EU officials considered Armenia an "easy" country with which to negotiate in contrast to Ukraine and

Georgia; in fact, Yerevan and Brussels concluded all negotiations by July 2013 (Delcour and Wolczuk 2015). Nevertheless, Armenia's political regime, dominated mainly by oligarchic groups, was reluctant to undertake the political changes that it would be required to adopt in case of initialling the Association Agreement with the EU. In the meantime, with the EU's growing involvement in the eastern neighbourhood, the Kremlin also intensified its pressure on the partner countries, using all the means, political, economic, and military. As a result, Armenia not only accessed to the Eurasian Union in January 2015, but has also accepted Vladimir Putin's "Eurasian Union without Karabakh bill."

A second factor that explains Armenia's decision to opt for membership in the Eurasian Union results from the degree of Armenia's dependence on Russia represented by the predominance of Russian capital in strategic sectors of the country's economy (the energy, transport and telecommunication sectors), as well as the country's traditional reliance on the political and military alliance with the Kremlin. Third, the Armenian officials opted for maintaining a well-known corrupt and authoritarian post-Soviet system of governance rather than trying to create a free market democracy.

Then, systemic forces (the growing Western influence in the region) also shaped Moscow's external policy towards Yerevan. As the evidence showed, Putin's message to Armenian President, Serzh Sargsyan in September of 2013 was clear: "my way—Armenian membership in the Eurasian Union; or highway —without the Russian economic (energy) and military support to Yerevan." However, despite Yerevan's outsized dependence on Russia and the membership in the Eurasian Union, Armenia remains interested in further engagement with the EU. The latter will show to what extent Russia is ready to tolerate the independent foreign policies of the Eurasian Union's member states.

Russian policy towards Azerbaijan

This study related Russia's foreign policies in the South Caucasus to the creation of the Moscow-led Eurasian Union in order to explain Moscow's external choices in Armenia, Azerbaijan and Georgia empirically. In this regard, the non-membership of Azerbaijan in the single economic space had a significant impact on Russia's policies in the country. First of all, Baku was able to continue its favorable foreign policy by adopting a Russian-style authoritarian model of government, while portraying itself as a Western "strategic partner" on energy issues and security, using the country's energy wealth (de Waal 2014). Playing off both sides against each other allowed Azerbaijan to preserve its oligarchic political system, simultaneously increasing the country's wealth and military power, which in turn enabled the Aliev government to take a hard line on the protracted conflict with Armenia over the Nagorno-Karabakh region. However, the empirical evidence indicated that Russia used the Nagorno-Karabakh conflict in order to bring Azerbaijan back into its orbit. As a matter of fact, this study showed that there is already a shift in Baku's foreign policy towards Moscow, which will make Russia less inclined to defend Armenia in case of a new war against Azerbaijan.[2] Then the Aliev regime in Azerbaijan is also willing to team up with the friendly authoritarian Putin regime, while a closer relationship with Washington and Brussels would require unwanted democratic changes in the political system. Baku was lately criticized by the United States and the EU for the human rights violations, and many analysts consider the geopolitical shift towards Russia as Baku's payback for the Western intervention in its domestic issues. Hence, Washington, in pursuit of punishing Russia economically, is still interested in using Azerbaijani natural gas as an important alternative to Russian gas for Europe. Thus, Brussels and Washington continue pouring billions of dollars into Baku's energy sector.

In the meantime, the empirical evidence suggests that the failure of the Nabucco pipeline proved once again that Baku prefers not to upset Russia as a pipeline competitor despite Western pressure. Moscow in return delivered up to $1 billion worth of military equipment to Baku, and promised to return some part of Karabakh to Azerbaijan if the country joins the Eurasian Union. As in the case study of Armenia, the empirical evidence supports the assumption that the recent escalation of the conflict between Yerevan and Baku is beneficial for Moscow, since it will definitely impede the current cooperation between the West and Azerbaijan in the energy sector and will highlight Russia's role as a peacemaker and a guarantor of the stability in the South Caucasus. Thus, once again, we linked Russia's quest to bring Azerbaijan back into its orbit to Moscow's capabilities (power) in terms of economic, military, and political leverages. The Kremlin wishes to enlarge the Eurasian Economic Union (India, Pakistan, Iran and Turkey also have been invited to join the bloc), and there is also a possibility that the union will establish a free trade zone with China and Israel in the near future. Baku has close economic and political relations with many of the Eurasian Union member states (except Armenia), while Turkey and Israel are considered to be Azerbaijan's strategic partners. Thus, Moscow will have even more bargaining power with Baku in the case of a possible EEU's enlargement.

Russian policy towards Georgia

After Armenia and Azerbaijan, the Georgian case study was also shown to be the crucial case for neoclassical realist theory in analyzing Russia's common patterns of external behavior since the end of the Cold War. The empirical evidence shows that Georgia was the only country among the three South Caucasian states that initialized the Association Agreement with the EU in Vilnius, in November 2013. Moreover, Georgia expected a visa-free regime with the EU in 2016, which can be considered as a big victory for a country that has two breakaway regions, Abkhazia and South Ossetia, as possible accession candidates for the Eurasian Economic Union. Georgia presented the most interesting case study among the three South Caucasian states, since the country was the only state in the region that was able to pursue closer ties with the EU. However, the evidence showed that Russia's influence in Georgia is growing stronger.

The process-tracing methods helped to identify the domestic political processes in Russia as the crucial intervening variables between systemic pressure and the foreign policy of the Russian state from the eighteenth century up to modern day in order to suggest that the Russian officials' vision of the state was, and still is, based on territory, military power, international prestige, and personalized power. These tools were first obtained by the elites and then used in order to identify an enemy for justification the authoritative form of government. The empirical evidence indicated that Russia, originally, did not have any imperial claims to Georgia (the Eastern Georgian kingdom of Kartli-Kakheti). On the contrary, the Georgian kings themselves sought the Russian protection, which was provided. After Georgia became a part of Tsarist Russia, it was unavoidable that the law of the strictly centralized and powerful Empire would override the rules of a semi-feudal state. Therefore, Georgia's original intention to be annexed as a state and to preserve its own law (and its own tsar) was unfeasible within the authoritarian regime of the Russian Empire. In fact, Georgia was annexed as one of the Russian provinces, and if, for the former, the annexation was a step forward in the political sense, for the latter it was also beneficial and set a precedent for future annexations in Western Asia.

Thus, this study concludes that these historical processes had led to the current state of external affairs of Moscow towards Tbilisi (as well as Yerevan and Baku), which was identified in the study as a neo-imperialist policy. It has been argued that Vladimir Putin and his allies are following spiritual masters such as Empress Catherine in seeking to reestablish Russia as a great nation in the international arena. Putin, like Catherine the Great, turned the Kremlin's gaze inward rather than westward. Similarly, when it came to dealing with rebels both acted ruthlessly. For instance, the Russo–Georgian war that broke out on August 8, 2008, can be considered as an instructive example, when the Russian military overwhelmed Georgian forces, gained control of South Ossetia, and Abkhazia.

Consequently, the empirical evidence suggests that a hypothesized causal mechanism is present in the case of Russia's foreign policy in the South Caucasus starting with the first Tsarist expansion into the Caucasus, when both systemic and sub-systemic structural and unit-level forces influenced behavior of the state leaders. The current Russia's pressure on Georgia can also be considered as successful, since, despite Tbilisi's current pro-European course in foreign policy, the West is reluctant to continue its eastward expansion in order not to anger Putin. Thus, Georgia, along with Armenia and Azerbaijan, remains caught in tug-of-war between Moscow, Washington and Brussels, and does her best not to follow the Ukrainian fate.

Explaining variables

Russia's material power capabilities, which were defined as the political, economic and technological resources with which states can influence each other, was treated as an independent variable and measured in relative terms in this study. It was argued that these power resources guided Moscow's foreign policies (dependent variables in this book) in all three South Caucasian states. In the meantime, the differentiation of the independent variable helped me to develop a more discriminating analysis of the effectiveness of Russia's material power capabilities and to identify specific factors that favoured or hindered the success of each variant. I used the creation of the Eurasian Union to operationalize the relative power of Russia, since the bloc was created using Moscow's increased political, economic and military resources.

The dependent variables—Russia's foreign policies in the South Caucasus, varied in Armenia, Azerbaijan and Georgia: 1) neo-imperialism in Armenia; 2) soft coercion in Azerbaijan; and 3) coercive diplomacy in Georgia. I operationalized Russia's foreign policies interests and goals in the South Caucasus as the degree to which they are status quo (during the Yeltsin presidency) or revisionist (under Putin's rule).

My intervening variables, state structure and leaders' perception of relative power comprised the theoretical framework of this study. The historical analysis suggested that while Tsarist Russia never hesitated to forge alliances of convenience and to expand at the expense of weaker powers, post-Soviet Russia seemed to abandon a great power sentiment, at least during the Yeltsin's presidency. Thus, another hypothesized causal mechanism of neoclassical realist theory that if a state composed of elites that agree on implementing grand strategy along with a stable and effective political regime with broad authority, then states would undertake risky foreign affairs, was potentially present in this case. It was also determined that the Tsarist government or Putin's administration that ruled despotically throughout its history could pursue any uncertain or risky foreign policies without public support.

In regard to the autonomy of leaders, Vladimir Putin, one of the most authoritarian leaders of modern Russia, followed his own conception of the national interest of the state since domestic constraints were extremely weak during his presidency, while Boris Yeltsin was stipulated to accommodate his vision of the national interest to the constraining domestic actors, mainly oligarchs. The evidence derived from the Armenia case study suggest that Putin had freedom to extract and direct national resources of Russia to pressure Armenia into joining the Eurasian Union and undertaking a pro-Russian direction in its foreign policy. Chapter 4 showed that Putin's understanding of the relative power of Russia was what mattered, not the relative quantities of physical force in being. In other words, Moscow's imperial ambitions in the post-Soviet space did not match Russia's material power capabilities since the Ukrainian crisis and the Western sanctions had significantly damaged Russia's economy. In addition, foreign policy responses of the Putin administration in the South Caucasus were a product of state–society coordination, which meant that the Russian state had more autonomy vis-à-vis society during Putin's presidency than during Yeltsin's presidency. Thus, the Kremlin responded to growing Western engagement in the South Caucasus in a timely and efficient manner.

In this regard, I concluded that that the unipolar international system of the 1990s and early 2000s, as well as the distribution of revisionist and status quo interests among Russia, the United States and the European Union, facilitated Vladimir Putin's adoption of authoritarian and centralized domestic institutions that led to an aggressive foreign policy in Armenia, Azerbaijan and Georgia, including revisionist claims. Russia was considered as an influence-maximizer and its increased resources during the Putin's presidency gave rise to greater ambitions in its external behavior in the Near Abroad.

Alternative theory: international regime theories rejected

As I have noted, both variants of regime theory posit a particular causal mechanism as an explanation of Russian foreign policy in Transcaucasia (Eurasian economic integration and the typical behavior of a regional hegemon), but have proved to be demonstratively absent or inconsistent in Moscow's relations towards its southern neighbors. As a result, regime theory proved to be weak as an explanation for this multiple-case design, although I am not excluding that there is still a possibility of omitted variables or measurement error.

Chapter 5 tested power-based and interest-based variants of international regime theory and came to the conclusion that the predictions of both variants of regime theory in the case of Russia's foreign policy in the South Caucasus proved wrong. I concluded that Russia would not (or not be willing to) act either as a benevolent or coercive hegemon since the creation of the Eurasian Economic Union did not follow the typical regime formation path that was assumed by both variants of regime theories. First of all, the benevolent leadership model of hegemonic stability theory that was analyzed in this book requires a hegemon that provides the collective good (an effective international regime) all by itself, whereas the smaller states are freed from the responsibility to help maintain the regime. The study showed that the smaller actors in the Eurasian Economic Union (Azerbaijan and Georgia were not taken into consideration in this scenario due to their non-membership in the bloc) cannot be considered as free riders in the Moscow-led regime. According to the benevolent leadership model, Russia would put up with its "exploitation" by Armenia, Belarus, Kazakhstan, which is clearly not the case in the Eurasian Union. The coercive model of the hegemonic stability theory is also a weak theoretical framework for my case studies since the main assumption of this approach "for the world economy to be stabilized, there has to be a stabilizer, one stabilizer" is not consistent with the empirical evidence of this work (Kindleberger 1974, p. 305). The presence of Russia is not sufficient condition for the provision for an international public good in the region. Moreover, the leadership in the Eurasian Economic Union is provided by more than one state. For instance, Kazakhstan, as Azerbaijan's close ally, was successfully opposing Armenia's accession to the Eurasian Union and was behind the acceptance of the "Eurasian Union without Karabakh" bill.

In the meantime, Keohane's contractualist theory has also failed to explain the Eurasian integration developments over the last 24 years. This theory focuses on the external structural conditions under which governments make foreign policy choices, while neglecting the domestic factors that influence the choices of actors.

Moreover, the contractualist theory operates under a specific precondition: the states that are active in the issue-area concerned must share common interests, which they can realize only through cooperation (Hasenclever et al. 1997, pp. 29–32). The empirical evidence showed that the states with common interests (Armenia, Azerbaijan, and Georgia) do not always cooperate, thus the existence of such interests is not sufficient condition for cooperation. On the other hand, this theory regards the international regimes per se as catalysts of cooperation, whereas the Eurasian Economic Union cannot be considered as a regime that furthers cooperation, if all the cooperation that is involved in the situation is implicit in the regime as such. Finally, the constantly changing institutional structure of the Eurasian Union along with its vague norms and rules will not promote cooperation in the region. In the meantime, its member states are not committed to transparency, thus, the possibility of cheating is also quite high. Furthermore, the smaller states (Armenia is among them) in the bloc are already challenging the "rules" of the regime and trying to retain the so-called multivector pluralism in their foreign policies by seeking for renewed cooperation with the EU.

Limitations and recommendations for further research

It is important to note the methodological limitations of the three South Caucasian case studies analyzed in this book. First of all, the most likely theoretical framework for these cases, a neoclassical realist approach, has been accused of lacking the parsimony and precision in predictive power that allow the falsification of propositions. For instance, while this study focused on Russia's foreign policy in the South Caucasus from 1991 until 2015, the distribution of power among the three states, Armenia, Azerbaijan, and Georgia that had significantly been changed over the course of 26 years, has not been taken into account in this study. In the meantime, Azerbaijan has quickly transformed itself into an upper middle-income country, thanks to rich natural gas and oil resources, while Armenia and Georgia are remaining lower middle-income economies. As a result, the distribution of power among the three South Caucasian affected the aforementioned differentiation in Russia's foreign policy towards Armenia, Azerbaijan, and Georgia. Moreover, it also affected the Western economic and political support (in the cases of Azerbaijan and Georgia) or non-support (in the case of Armenia) for these states, which, in turn, directly related to country's ability to withstand Russia's pressure in joining or not the Eurasian Economic Union.

Another important limitation of this study is the reliance on neoclassical realism in explaining Moscow's actions in Transcaucasia after the end of the Cold War. Beside the material capabilities' power and the systemic pressure, Russia's more assertive position in the near abroad had partially defensive explanation.

The present study did not examine the effect of U.S.–Iranian relations on Russia's foreign policy in the South Caucasus. Meanwhile, the political and economic isolation of Iran by the Western countries significantly increased Russia's role as a mediator and guarantor of stability in the Middle East. The U.S.–Iranian relations also affected the foreign policy choices of Azerbaijan.

Future research may consider the variation in Russia's foreign policies in the South Caucasus as a promising area for a new study.

The future of the South Caucasus

In 1989 Francis Fukuyama famously announced the end of history and the victory of liberal capitalist democracy over communism. At the end of the day, even in their sweetest dreams, the Western capitalist states did not anticipate the bloodless end of the Cold War and the collapse of the Soviet Union. Despite the fact that the United States was also caught off guard by the demise of the "Evil Empire," it did not take long for Washington to figure out that now it could take under its liberal umbrella the former Soviet states, including Russia, in the same fashionable way as it did with the Western European states and Japan after the World War II. It turned out to be a bad idea, and, in the case of Ukraine, a dangerous idea, doomed to failure from the start. What Fukuyama forgot to consider, and with him the rest of the Western world, is that history tends to follow a well-known cycle: states rise, they peak, they decline, they collapse . . . and sometimes they rise again, especially with the help of a strong leader. Despite the current Western sanctions against Moscow that have inflicted an increasing toll on the Russian economy, Putin's regional integration plans and his grand strategies in the near abroad, including the South Caucasus, can be considered as successful. Russian president Vladimir Putin was not only able to create the Eurasian Union, bully the European-oriented Armenia into the bloc, contain Azerbaijan and Georgia, but he also made the EU and the United States take into consideration Russia's interests while dealing with the former Soviet states. It is hard to predict what will happen in the near future in the South Caucasus, which considered to be a region of special geopolitical and economic interests for Russia. There is a possibility of an outbreak of a new war between Armenia and Azerbaijan over Nagorno-Karabakh, as well as more Russian "land grab" in Georgia. But one thing is clear—Russia is back in the Great Game and will not be ignored anymore.

Notes

1 This is the case of Armenians and Georgians, two old Christian nations, who shared numerous traditions, including related erstwhile dynastic families. See Richard G. Hovannisian (1971) *The Republic of Armenia: The First Year 1918–1919*. Berkeley and Los Angeles, CA: University of California Press.

2 This book was written before the outbreak of the four-day war in Nagorno-Karabakh between Armenia and Azerbaijan in April, 2016. While both sides accused each other in launching the attack, it was clear that Baku took the initiative this time since Armenians are controlling the territory for more than 22 years, and were satisfied with the current status quo in the region. In addition, Ilham Aliev declared on Twitter that he will return Karabakh back to Azerbaijan in order to boost his falling popularity among his people. The four-day war proved my main point that Russia is using the Nagorno-Karabakh conflict in order to keep two states under its radar, but is not interested in solving the frozen conflict or standing up for one of the Eurasian Union's member states. Thus, we cannot consider the Eurasian Economic Union as a new bloc

that promotes economic integration and regional cooperation among its participants. This book identifies the rationale behind the creation of a new union as to advance Russia's interests in the Near Abroad using all necessary means. Moscow did not provide actual military assistance to its only ally in the South Caucasus, Armenia, on the contrary, it sold large quantities of arms to Baku. Dmitry Medvedev suggested to Armenians to view the latter as a business transaction rather than an act of betrayal. Meanwhile, Russia strengthened its position in the South Caucasus as de facto guarantor of the ceasefire, which led some analysts to speculate that the recent outbreak of conflict was part of a broader Kremlin's plan to change the situation around Karabakh to its favor by introducing Russian troops into the region as peacekeepers. For more detailed analysis on this issue see Aleksandra Jarosiewicz and Maciej Falkowski (2016) "The Four Day War in Nagorno Karabakh," *Ośrodek Studiów Wschodnich*, April 6.

Bibliography

de Waal, Thomas (2014) "Azerbaijan Doesn't Want to be Western: The Rhetoric and Reality of Baku's Grand Strategy," *Foreign Affairs*, September 26.

Delcour, Laure and Kataryna Wolczuk (2015) "The EU's Unexpected 'Ideal Neighbour?' The Perplexing Case of Armenia's Europeanisation," *Journal of European Integration*, Vol. 37, No. 4, pp. 491–507.

Freire, Maria Raquel and Roger E. Kanet (Eds.) *Key Players and Regional Dynamics in Eurasia: The Return of the "Great Game"*. Houndmills, UK: Palgrave Macmillan.

Fukuyama, Francis (1989) "The End of History?" *The National Interest*. Summer, pp. 3–18.

Hasenclever, Andreas, Peter Mayer, and Volker Rittberger (1997) *Theories of International Regimes*. Cambridge, UK: Cambridge University Press.

Jarosiewicz, Aleksandra and Maciej Falkowski (2016) "The Four Day War in Nagorno Karabakh," Osrodek Studiow Wschodnich, April 6.

Kanet, Roger E. (2010) "From Cooperation to Confrontation: Russia and the United States since 9/11," in Bertil Nygren, Bo Huldt, Patrik Ahlgren, Pekka Sivonen, and Susanna Huldt (Eds.) *Russia on Our Minds: Russian Security Policy and Northern Europe*. Stockholm: National Defense University.

Kindleberger, Charles P. (1974) *The Formation of Financial Centers: A Study in Comparative Economic History*. Princeton, NJ: Princeton University Press.

Index